RIDDY ANN
OVERCOMING THE ODDS

By: Dr. Eurydice Moore

McClure Publishing, Inc.

Riddy Ann Overcoming the ODDs - Copyright © 2016

All rights reserved. Printed and bound in the United States of America. According to the 1976 United States Copyright Act, no part of this book may be reproduced or utilized in any form or by any means, electronic or mechanical, including photocopying, recording, or by any information storage or retrieval system, except by a reviewer who may quote brief passages in a review to be printed in a magazine or newspaper, without permission in writing from the Publisher: Inquiries should be addressed to McClure Publishing, Inc. Permissions Department, 398 West Army Trail Road, #124, Bloomingdale, Illinois 60108. Publication date: December 25, 2016.

The author and publisher have made every effort to ensure the accuracy and completeness of information contained in this book. We assume no responsibility for errors, inaccuracies, omissions, or any inconsistencies therein.

Any slights of people, places, belief systems or organizations are unintentional. Any resemblance to anyone living, dead or somewhere in between is truly coincidental.

ISBN 13: 978-0-9915335-5-8

Cover Design Images by: David Dickerson

Interior Layout by Kathy McClure
http://www.mcclurepublishing.com

Order additional copies, please contact
books@mcclurepublishing.com
800-659-4908

If you overcome the ODDS in your personal life,
you will overcome odds in your business life as well. Everything begins
with the personal.

This book project is dedicated to Aunt Dorothy Martin
a/k/a Big Dot who passed on November 29, 2016
during this project production.

ACKNOWLEDGEMENTS

Madea Norwood
Maternal Grandmother

Riddy was in the kitchen talking to Annie Norwood a/k/a Madea. Madea had her back turned to Riddy cooking breakfast and stirring a pot of her delicious lump free grits, she suddenly stopped and walked around the kitchen table with her eyes sternly looking into Riddy's and said, "Childe you need to write a book." This was 41 years ago, so I dedicate this book to Madea my Maternal Grandmother with love and fond memories. Signed Eurydice Ann a/k/a Riddy Ann.

Benjamin Polk

I salute and thank you for a jump start in the revision of the book that my maternal grandmother told me to write. I thank you for the writing classes that you conducted with such a zest for life. You made writing simple, and fun filled. I also dedicate this book in appreciation of your service to mankind and in the development of writers. You are awesome.

Steve Sondheimer

Thank you for believing in me and confirming that I would do well and that I would be successful.

Last but certainly not least - **God**

Last but not least the love of my life. The melody in my heart. The joy in my soul. My Healer. My Deliverer. You have carried me through valleys and storms. You have held me in your loving arms and have kept me. YOU ARE MY EVERYTHING and it's because of you that I live, and move and have my being. I love you. My God.

This book project was made possible
through the partnership of
The Chicago Housing Authority (CHA)
& Housing Urban Development (HUD)'s
Section 3 Business Concern
Competitive Grant

Table of Contents

Prologue

Chapter One	11
Chapter Two	19
Chapter Three	25
Chapter Four	31
Chapter Five	37
Chapter Six	45
Chapter Seven	53
Chapter Eight	59
Chapter Nine	69
Chapter Ten	77
Chapter Eleven	85
Chapter Twelve	89
Chapter Thirteen	101
Chapter Fourteen	113
Chapter Fifteen	121
Chapter Sixteen	129
Chapter Seventeen	141
Chapter Eighteen	147
Chapter Nineteen	155
Chapter Twenty	165
Chapter Twenty-One	171
Chapter Twenty-Two	177
Chapter Twenty-Three	183

Chapter Twenty-Four 187
Chapter Twenty-Five 195
Chapter Twenty-Six 203
Chapter Twenty-Seven.. 209
Chapter Twenty-Eight 221
Chapter Twenty-Nine.. 235
Chapter Thirty... 241

From the Author's Desk - Epilogue

Dr. Eurydice Moore, Business Consultant

PROLOGUE

Riddy Ann awoke to find herself, looking in the mirror and seeing someone who had to make a decision. She was going to either stop right there and come apart, or she was going to find ways to break every wall around her that had been built to stop her from progressing and advancing. It seemed as if a dark shadow was following her most of her life. This dark shadow was crippling.

Having a mother that did not want to have a relationship with her, left Riddy Ann feeling abandon and left out in the cold, something was missing. Riddy Ann's mother Kat felt that Riddy was going to be in the way of what she really wanted to do in life, so her mother decided to treat Riddy as if she did not exist. Even when her mother came to visit when Riddy was a little girl, she never acknowledged that Riddy was in the room.

This led to heartbreak and illnesses that caused Riddy not do well in school. She became illiterate to the educational system. Riddy grew up getting attention from all the wrong sources. It became difficult to bear and there was no way out.

As you read through the pages of this book, you will find the depth of Riddy's pain that caused her to break out of the mundane life that was taking her on a vicious cycle to keep repeating what was not working. Her life became monotonous; lacking in liveliness which was overpowering that it became repetitious of one awful experience after another.

Eventually, Riddy made up her mind and took control of her life and decided NO MORE. There comes a time in life where you can only take so much and then the breaking of a new day arises.

Chapter One

December 1956 early winter, the temperature was cold but not enough to snow. Several brown project buildings surround and engulf the deserted playground since winter has set. Searching for somewhere to place the baby, Kat's focus zooms in on a set of empty swings. She rushes over.

In the third swing lay a bundled-up sleepy baby, three-months-old. She was carefully cushioned in her pink and yellow baby blankets. Pushing the swing forward then backwards, while the rusted chains squeak loudly, finally coming to a place to desert the baby, Kat gives one final glance then quickly runs away. A dark shadow appears behind the swing.

After a little while, the swing comes to a halt, and the baby is gone, thankfully, just before it begins to rain.

Kat met her lover at his place a well finished apartment on the other side of town. She felt no guilt whatsoever that this was a friend of her husband's. Although it was a cheap affair and they could not be seen in public together, it still brought her solace.

After the great time she had, Kat heads home only to find Ed, Riddy's father, there waiting on her and the baby to come home.

* * *

As soon as Kat walks in the door, Ed screams at the top of his lungs, "Where is she?" as he gives Kat a backhand slap. "Where is she?" Ed screams again as he kicks and punches Kat's tiny frame. Ed then grabs Kat by the collar and pushes her out the door in search of their child.

The couple splits up and goes in separate directions searching for the baby. Nightfall slowly approaches. Kat rushes to the third swing looking for a bundled-up sleepy baby. When she saw the baby was gone, she fell to the ground on her knees in agony weeping covering her eyes with her hands. Thinking to herself, *Where could she be? Why would someone take her?*

Neighbors spy out their windows shaking their heads. Viola, a paid babysitter in the neighborhood, tells Jennifer, Viola's friend, that she wants no parts in aiding and abetting Kat in an adulterous affair anymore as they look out the window.

"I'm so, so sorry. I should have watched the child," Viola tells Jen in a guilty whisper.

Jennifer puts her arms around Viola to comfort her saying, "You had no idea that Kat would go to such extreme. This is all her fault, not yours."

Viola cries, "Where is she? I don't understand. Where is the baby?"

Kat was free spirited and she cared less about how others felt when she made a decision to do whatever she wanted.

* * *

Years earlier, Kat comes switching into the house fresh from the skating rink with her roller skates tied together and slung over her shoulder. She was on cloud nine.

Kat says, "Mother dear, I am going to marry this man. He is everything that I ever dreamed of, and he is the guy for me."

Madea asked, "Kat aren't you tired of going from one man to another?"

"Mom, I am not listening to what you are saying."

"I am really tired of the way you are looking for love everywhere. You are finding these men from where I do not know."

At that time, Kat stood five feet, even and weighed in at ninety-five pounds with a tiny frame wearing a size five. Kat had brunette hair, mulatto colored skin with strong facial features. She had Chinese cut bangs and the remaining part of her hair in a ponytail tied with a green scarf. Kat has on a white scoop neck pulled over blouse with several buttons down the front of a green sweater. She has a belted waist with a bounce poodle skirt. She is determined to marry.

She was stood up for prom, but she will not be stood up in life and be denied the privilege of romance, marriage or children just like the movie stars.

Kat's favorite movie stars were Elizabeth Taylor, Hedy Lamarr, and Susan Haywood all of Hollywood tempests and divas.

Henry, Kat's prom date, just did not know what he was missing out on. When Kat set her mind on something she is like a steamroller. She TOLD Henry that he was taking her to the prom. Henry must have been nervous because he left Kat sitting on the couch in her blue chiffon wide skirt dress ALL NIGHT in hopes that he would appear.

It was when the clock struck midnight that Kat realized that she was not going anywhere. Her Cinderella story was just the opposite. Kat felt a pain in the pit of her stomach and jumped from the couch and ran to the bathroom to purge with tears streaming down her face.

Two weeks passed before Henry would return to school. Kat knew for sure that he was not there and found out that he played possum to avoid her in school. Henry would head in another direction whenever he saw Kat. Eventually, she gave up trying to get an explanation out of him. All Kat wanted was a potential mate lined up, and she dreamed of being like Ozzie and Harriet, June and Wallace Clever, and having a family similar to Father Knows Best.

Ed attended Gladstone grade school, and later transferred to Marshall High School. The funniest thing was that Kat was at Gladstone with Ed. They also attended Marshall High School together, and they would meet at a skating rink on Madison and Albany and later became an item. Ed eventually became a ticket to emancipation for Kat, a strategy gone wrong.

* * *

After searching for the baby for hours running around Ed's head pounding while his heart beating fast, tired after hours he leans against the wall closes his eyes because he is dreading the inevitable. Ed slips into a flashback of Vietnam. He thought the more time someone is missing, the likelihood they are dead.

The men of the hood gather around Ed as he stared at the lifeless, headless body being placed in a body bag and carried away.

"Oh man. I don't believe this," cried out one of Ed's friends, Ned.

Ed is on his knees with his arms dangling at his side in the mud. Ned offers comfort by putting his hand on Ed's right shoulder. Ed sprung to life by jumping on his feet with his gun and began pointing it at his friend's head. Ned stood there in shock. The guys around them waved their hands and walked backward to get away from Ed.

Ned quietly said, "Ed it's us. He took a pause. "Man, it's us. Put the gun down, man."

Ed walked two steps forward as if he still did not understand, and the guys walked a couple of steps backward, but Ned stood his ground.

Ed looks in Ned's eyes, and Ed falls to the ground as a brick meets the back of his head. Ed's commanding officer dethroned and deactivated the soldier from behind.

The commanding officer ordered, "Now pick him up and take him to the infirmary. Get'em outta here. That's an order."

The soldiers dragged Ed out of the foxhole. Dorothy, the office clerk, delivered the latest casualty report so that she can contact the military police, who can then notify the families of the fallen soldiers. Guy told her that Timothy was in the foxhole with Ed when he lit a cigarette and Mr. Charlie blew his head off in front of Ed. Ed told him not to do it. Timothy's beef was that it was pitch black, and nobody was out there. "Nobody gonna see nothing, out there," Timothy said. Well off his head rolled. Timothy was Ed's best friend, and last friend from Chicago.

Ed saw all his friends killed off one-by-one in a strange land. They all joined the Army to protect their country. Now Ed was the lone survivor. Yes, he made friends while in the Army, but he lost his homeboys. Ed was on the psychiatric ward in a catatonic state, no one knew if he would pull through. *Geeze,* thought Dorothy, the psychiatric nurse, *another one bites the dust.*

"SNAP OUT OF IT!!! Niggas!" *Why won't they listen,* thought Commanding Officer Jeff Martin. I have lost half my platoon to either gun fire or the loony farm." Whatever the case, all was washed up and sent home, honorably discharged. It's been difficult to get men to answer the draft. Many in droves ran off to Canada to avoid the senseless war.

* * *

The baby was found. Kat walks through the front door and leaves Riddy on Big Mama a/k/a Anna White's bed interrupting a conversation between Big Mama and Madea who never knew that the baby was ever missing.

It was a long crawl from the deep dark hole. Riddy had finally made it out! Riddy looks back, amazed. The dark tunnel ran deep and far, and there was only one way out. She found it. She found it by following the light in God, and in her heart. She traveled through mirth, crawled over stones, and was bruised by the sharp obstacles of life.

There were times when she could hardly breathe. She even remembered when the rain from above drenched her until chills ran through her thin, weary frame. Her moments of sunshine were few and far and in between. And she could recall, throughout her childhood, feeling stifled by life. And though she may have wanted to die, those few sunshine glimmers kept her in faith.

Riddy remembers the times of being entrapped in quicksand. She remembers the dirt storms, feeling cramped and smothered in a hole.

Riddy remembers the times when the water rose up, while in the black hole up to her nose, then suddenly descended, but she did not drown. It was a mystery as to how she survived.

Baby girl met all sorts of creatures in the crawl. You see, the tunnel was narrow and there was no room to stand. One could only crawl.

Some of the strange creatures would ask Riddy where she was going. She would always reply, "Out of here!"

Some of the creatures urged Riddy to tell her story. "If you get out, come back for me." They begged, while others cursed, jeered and mocked her systematic crawl movements.

Then, there were the sorrowful, bitter ones that wanted her to remain stagnant in her lacuna of her childhood. But something internal was calling her like a magnet. Inside, she was being summoned.

Now, Riddy made it out, and lies on the ground after being soaked from the rainfall. The rain felt good on her body. And, Yes. If you are thinking, this is metaphorically speaking, it is.

Riddy had five nations flowing through her veins. She is Hebrew, African, Arab, Native American, and a hotheaded Irish woman. Each multicultural gene fought to dominate her. Each wanted full control.

Riddy's hair was to her hip, black, and thicker than a raven's coat with a hint of a reddish sheen that showed as an overtone in the sunlight that shined in between each rain storm. Her high cheek bones commanded attention. They were commanding and felt the pounding of the rainstorm. The thick, sloped, nostril descended between her narrow sequined eyes. The melanin skin was filled with cuts, scrapes and wounds from head to toe. But the rain washed away the blood and emotional debris.

The rain felt good. As she lies on the cobblestone pavement then a pain struck her. She grips her chest in agony, rolling her head from side-to-side. Her body grew lifeless. Riddy's body grew lifeless because of the exhaustion of the crawl to escape then her body jerked. *I am emancipated*, Riddy thought. As she lies there, her thoughts traveled back in time.

Anna, Riddy's Great Grandmother a/k/a Big Mama, had great delight in her new baby. Although she did not have to endure birth pains or be bothered with pushing exercises, this was still her baby, three months old.

Riddy's mom could not keep her. She said the baby cried too much. Maybe she was crying because of too much dissension in the home, who knows. Riddy's head stopped rolling to the left side of her body. She stopped moving and her eyes came wide opened, staring.

Every day Kat would always drop off the baby in the morning. After work, Ed, the father would come by to take the baby home. This went on for three months. As time went by, Ed did not come for the baby, any more.

Yes, Riddy was an orphan whose parents were very much alive but seemed dead.

This is another chance from the Lord! It's another chance to get it right, thought Big Mama as she powdered the baby after a diaper change.

Months later, Riddy was one years old when she began to learn how to walk. She had a big bald spot in the back of her head.

Big Mama proclaimed, "By Christmas, my baby is going to have a ponytail."

The kinfolk laughed. Even though no one saw how that was going to be possible, everyone believed it because whatever Big Mama said, it came to pass.

It was time to capture a still photo for memory. A week or two later, a thick pair of big hands cuffed Riddy under her arms standing her up in a clothed double-stitched green rayon chair while her legs presented how strong she had become. Riddy tilted forward. The camera flashed. The occasion was Father's Day, and it was his paternal right to join the ceremony in his honor.

Riddy would always remember him as long periods of time passed by. As Riddy got older, visits from her dad became fewer. From the age of five, Riddy could remember her dad's visits, and she remembered when they stopped. The next visit was on her twelfth birthday, and the television he gave her was his apology for those many absent years.

The black and white television was presented to Riddy by her paternal grandmother, Johnnie Mae and father. Riddy was elated because she could view her favorite action super heroes instead of sports and those cowboy pictures that the boys at the house who were distant cousins would be eager to watch after their daily sacrifices of letting Riddy watch what she wanted. Houston, Dwight, and Thurman are Riddy's cousins and their parents were Big Dot and Erns.

Chapter Two

It seems like yesterday when Kat marched into the unlocked front door of the house and interrupted her conversation with Madea by laying a three-month-old babe on the bed with no explanation—no good evening, howdy or nothing. Kat did not utter one word, but turned on her heels and abandon her crying child, screaming her heart out, nonstop. Well into the dawn of the night Kat went.

Big Mama picked Riddy up off the bed. "Hush nawl, little one," Big Mama softly spoke into the baby's ear, holding her close. "Rock-a-bye, baby..." she sang and pleaded, and cuddled. In a straight path between the crib and the rocker in the corner, she wore the carpet thin beneath her bare feet. The baby's cry was so pitiful. It took months of constant love for it to fade.

Kat would visit her mom Madea from time to time. She never held the baby. She never even looked at the baby. She never talked to the baby. To Kat, the baby did not exist. As the young child grew and could answer the phone, she knew her mother's voice and would try to talk to her, but Kat would coldly ask to speak to Madea. This made Riddy feel unwanted and disconnected.

The child would cry and her little heart would ache. Whenever Kat came by, Riddy would sit in a corner stealing precious glances of this beautiful woman who would never look her way.

Ed on the other hand was the opposite. He showered her with kisses and hugs, but as she got older the visits grew few and far and in between.

Riddy was five years old when her dad proceeded through the door; she clung to him and would not let him go. Ed and Riddy had begun to roll a red ball back and forth to each other. The ball would roll from the living room into the hallway, which led to the big brown door, which led to the outside world. With each roll, unknown to Riddy, Ed grew more and more distant from her. *This game is fun*, Riddy thought. The ball rolled back to Riddy, and the door shut. She cried hysterically, a cry that would go on for hours, the second she realized that her daddy had disappeared.

She enjoyed the times when Ed would come to see her and became sadden when he left because she never knew when she would see him again.

One visit was traumatic when he came by and Riddy ignored him because she had not seen him in so long and was really hurt by his malingering.

He snapped at her and pulled a piece of paper out of his pocket to show her. He spoke harshly about how he owned her and would take her away from Big Mama. Then he stormed out the house. Several years went by before she saw him again. He was strung out on alcohol and had fallen victim of the harsh heroin epidemic of the '50s.

Ed swung through the revolving door, in and out, of jail. He could not hold on to jobs. And the only thing that kept him from a life of homelessness was Johnnie Mae and Nate, Ed's mother and step-father. Johnnie Mae was under five-feet and was a bow-legged, mean heifer of a woman. Johnnie Mae took no mess. She ran off with her son, Ed from her husband, named Hiawatha, Riddy's grandfather, who used to beat Johnnie Mae, silly. Hiawatha, who was a full-blooded American Indian, was also a womanizer and Johnnie Mae refused to let Hiawatha talk to or even see the youngster.

Ed, although young, remembered those beatings. But when Hiawatha lost his mind and lunged toward Ed, enough was enough.

Johnnie Mae ran away with her child. She had to leave Mississippi. Johnnie migrated to the north like so many of her generation. It was in Chicago that she met Nate Dolle who was the opposite of Johnnie Mae.

Johnnie Mae was born free from slavery but escaped to Chicago to hide from an abusive husband and father of her only child, Ed. She ran from another kind of slavery. Hiawatha was a drug addict, womanizer, and would beat Johnnie Mae, but now he started beating Ed, so Johnnie Mae planned an escape to Chicago.

Johnnie Mae had relatives in Chicago, quite different from Nate who had nobody but God. Johnnie Mae stayed with a girl cousin for a while. Then she met Nate one Saturday night at a club on the east side of Chicago on 47th Street. They danced the night away and on the first night Johnnie Mae slept with Nate. Afterwards they were inseparable. Nate asked Johnnie Mae to marry him and they did. Nate and Ed got along just fine.

Nate a man who was darker than a cast iron skillet had been a former slave who ran off from his master and made a life in Chicago. While living in Chicago Nate met Johnnie Mae, a young attractive mulatto colored skin woman and her son Ed. Nate did not have any children. Ed was at the age of seven by the time they married.

Although Nate and Johnnie Mae was both born and raised in Yazoo Mississippi, they did not meet until they lived in Chicago, Illinois. Nate was twenty years Johnnie Mae senior. He landed in Chicago not knowing anyone and having left all his family in order to seek a free life for himself. Nate had to have a low profile and blend in with other Negros from the south. Nate's escape was perfect timing. Well *kinda sorta*.

He fled slavery in 1865 as congress was in the midst of abolishing it, and it took three years to get to Chicago by foot mobile, and when he made it to Chicago, an opportunity opened for negroes to be trained to peddle Watkin products in 1868.

Nate had tough skin literally. It was either do or die and sink or swim. After being told no so many times, he came across a yes. Nate determine to make it would clear $500 per week. This was a lot of money for his generation. Nate would buy $500 shoes, and pay hundreds of dollars for suits to look the part. He would deliver products in one hand and hold a pistol in another hand. He had no problem pulling the trigger. No one could overpower him but Johnnie Mae.

Nate was most fortunate than most Negroes. Although many had escaped both slavery and Jim Crow, racism was up North, but in a different form. Although they were not chained, Negroes were allowed to be educated. Often times upon graduating with a trade such as secretarial, teacher, or mechanic most ended up with jobs as domestics, wash women, cooks, and porters. Very few of them could break out of these pigeon hole positions designed especially for them.

Another form of slavery existed. Both a white and colored girl that took the same secretarial course could go on an interview. Although the colored could type faster, the job went to the white. Big Dot, Riddy's aunt was turned down for a position, and it is to be believed that it was because she was too dark. Only mulatto colored skinned blacks were favored. Another person that Nate knew was turned down for a job because she was a divorcee.

The opportunities for Negro men were butlers, porters, cooks, and a railroad worker. Nate got favored along with a few others by the boss' son, at Watkins, who had the mentality that a dollar was a dollar no matter where it came from, so he trained a small band of Negro men to go after the Negro dollar bill, and after the bills they went. Nate was the top sales man.

They moved into an apartment building even though Nate had the money to buy a house or an apartment building but no one would sell to Nate, so he just used the money to lavishly furnish the place called home, and shower his family with gifts. He did not have a strategy like Big Mama. Big Mama felt you can have anything you want in life if you have a strategy. There is always a way to go around anything or anybody.

Nate and Johnnie Mae never had children together. Maybe he was all bucked out. During slavery time the buck was used to impregnate females.

Johnnie Mae would get bored sitting at home as a house wife. Then she started noticing after years of being married to Nate, there was a mean side, even a stingy side of the man she loved. Johnnie Mae found a job at a neighborhood cleaner's and worked for a Jewish man and his wife for many years. Johnnie Mae developed rheumatoid arthritis and her legs would bend for standing long hours pressing clothes at the cleaners.

Although she loved Nate, she did not trust him fully. She was not going to allow herself to end up like she was with her husband. They were never officially divorced because no one knew where Hiawatha was, and she was not looking for him and did not want him to know her whereabouts.

Years later Nate became ill and Johnnie Mae heart was broken as Nate would begin to spend up his savings with the intent of leaving Johnnie Mae with nothing. After all it was his money. While Johnnie Mae stood in the doorway of the hospital room, Nate demanded that Johnnie withdraw money from his account to bring to the hospital.

Johnnie Mae said, "I know what you doing. You do not want me to have anything. That's alright I will bring you your money."

What a pitiful way for a marriage to end. Johnnie Mae still loved Nate, although, he was a bitter angry man that still wore slavery on his back and in his soul. Johnnie Mae was another piece to him and a good cook.

Nate had trained Ed, his step son, when he was younger to be a good abiding citizen, but when Ed got older he was headstrong. Nate grew weary about keeping Ed on the right path. He did not want to leave anything to Ed either.

Chapter Three

It was Riddy's first day of school. Madea was bent on Riddy learning to spell her name. Every time she missed a letter, playtime was cut out. The two wrestled nearly the whole summer over her letters. It was not until Riddy got a lick that she finally remembered how to spell her name. Madea won.

At the start of kindergarten, Madea took Riddy to the doctor for a physical. Riddy had to take off her clothes and put on a long white dress. Then a pretty lady in white grabbed her thumb to stick it with a pin. The gush of blood alarmed Riddy, but she tried to keep calm.

A friendly white man gave her a poke here and a poke there. Then he asked Big Mama a lot of questions. Riddy even had to urinate in a cup.

Riddy was always sick. Every week, Madea and Riddy would be at the bus stop and on their way to the doctor's office. Because Riddy was so sickly, Madea bought a car to get her to the doctor, quicker and easier.

Riddy was a picky eater. She would turn her head to pig feet, pig tails, oxtails, chicken feet, and chicken heads. Howbeit, when it was discovered that Riddy liked something, it was fed to her until she gorged out.

Riddy lived with Madea, and her husband Sid, along with Big Mamma, who became her legal guardian. Big Mamma represented everyone's Big Mamma in the neighborhood. She was five-feet one inch tall, and tilted the scale at four hundred pounds. She had a mess of tight salt and pepper curls all over her head and she wore cat-eyed glasses. Big Mamma had a gold tooth right dab in the front of her mouth. It glistened with every smile. She had a warm and gentle nature, too. Everybody loved Big Mama.

Madea was Big Mama's daughter. Who was the opposite of her mother. She was funny especially seeing her sandy brown hair blowing in the wind, and her drawers showing and exposing her big behind every time she went upside somebody's head in the backyard.

"Mannnn, what's wrong with your wife?," one of Sid's friends asked, "She sent Luella home crying." Sid just shrugged his shoulders and offered no reply for Madea's actions. Actually, perhaps, because of her actions, he was interested in drinking himself into a stupor.

Riddy six years old started having a series of sore throats. Dr. Kaye said that it was her tonsils, and that they had to come out. One day, Madea and Big Mama took Riddy to a strange building. Riddy knew that something was up. There had never been an occasion for both of them to take her to the doctor.

The three of them were in a room until Big Mama and Madea said that they had to use the bathroom. In the meantime, a nice lady had Riddy put on a long white dress, and the nurse tied it at the neck where her two French braids met. Riddy looked up and time was ticking away; neither one had come back. Riddy's heart suspended as she stared at the door while expecting them at any moment.

The nurse took Riddy by the hand and led her into a room. In the room, there were hundreds of large playpens with mattresses. The nurse picked up Riddy and assembled her body into an empty playpen.

Riddy stood while clutching the bars, and while her head was wedged through the slits. Silent tears began to flow down her cheeks. Riddy was too hurt to make a sound; she was abandoned once again.

The next day, the same friendly nurse came and put Riddy on a hospital gurney, and it felt hard and uncomfortable. Riddy was wheeled into a very cold room and it was there that they told her to start counting. Nervously, Riddy started counting. You could hear a shiver in her voice. She was finally under and Dr. Kaye started the procedure to remove her tonsils.

When she woke up, both Big Mama and Madea were at her bed asking, "Would you like some ice cream?" Riddy was so happy to see them. She could just pee on herself. Someone brought Riddy a bowl of ice cream. Every spoonful she took burned her throat and it had an awful taste. Riddy thought, *ice cream tastes a lot better than this*. Since she was feeling well, Madea and Big Mama took Riddy home.

The building Big Mama and her family stayed in at 3165 West Monroe was a three-story Greystone building in Chicago. Riddy was happy to be home, although, it was over crowded. Big Dot (Dorothy), Madea's baby sister, who is married to Ern, their three son's Houston, Thurman and Dwight who are Riddy's cousins also, lived with them. Big Dot grew up to be a fine young lady.

Riddy loved Dwight; he seemed like a brother to her. Every morning, she would wait by the bathroom door to greet him. She was a real pest.

Dwight's legs were shaped like baseball bats and had a lot of hair spouting out of them. This fascinated Riddy to no end. It intrigued her. Click. The washroom latch would open and out would come Dwight every morning at the prey of his cousin rubbing his hairy legs. And every morning, she would be slammed into the white wall in the hallway. Every morning, she cried, "Mama, Dwight hit me". Every morning, Big Mamma yelled, while stirring food in her pot, "Boy, you better leave my baby alone."

The two were stubborn and they each were determined to have their way. After three months of getting plastered into the wall, Riddy gave up.

School was cool as long as Riddy was inside of the classroom. However, every week, Riddy was at the doctor's office or the doctor visited her house. It was nothing for Riddy to pass out at home, outside or inside the school's bathroom or hallway.

One particular night, Big Mama sent for Dr. Kaye. Riddy was burning up with a fever and too weak to leave the bed. Riddy got a shot. Dr. Kaye and Big Mama scratched their heads because no one knew how sick the little girl was or how long the illness was going to last, for goodness sake!

It was by the fifth grade that Riddy always knew what grades she had before the teacher passed out the report cards.

The card never held anything above a D in all her subjects. This was because she missed days, and sometimes, weeks, out of school. It was difficult for Riddy to master the three R's, reading, writing and arithmetic, before she would become sick, again. The class would be at chapter one when she left school, and upon her return, she found her classmates on chapter three.

One hot summer at school, Riddy met a boy. He was cute. She even fantasized about kissing him. But she remembered how Big Mamma said, "Never let a boy kiss you. If you let a boy kiss you, you'll come up pregnant." Well, later in life Riddy would find out that Big Mamma had left out a lot of details—on purpose.

Anyway, the boy chased Riddy all the way home. Riddy slammed the door and leaned up against it while heaving heavily to grasp for breath. The kiss came.

Coincidentally, not long after, Riddy's stomach began to cramp. She went to the bathroom to find a red spot of blood. Riddy panicked. She changed her underwear, but spots kept reappearing. Soon, Riddy was out of underwear—completely.

It was time for Riddy to tell Big Mamma about her condition. Big Mamma was sitting in the midst of a women's family POW WOW council in the kitchen. It was their usual thing to do. In the midst of the solemn amen corner, Riddy eases upward to Big Mamma and whispers, "I got blood in my panties." "Mama, I'm pregnant," Riddy confessed.

Big Mama breaks out with a joyful laugh and announces, "Hey everybody, Riddy got her period." All eyes in the room narrowly stared at Riddy. The kitchen was filled with laughter about the idea of Riddy being pregnant at the age of eight because a little boy named Johnny chased her home.

Madea was sitting snapping pole beans then started standing at the sink to wash the beans for cooking. Big Dot sat at the kitchen table across from where Madea was sitting. Every fifteen seconds, Big Dot started with, "Well, I guess I'll go," while clutching her car keys, but never getting up.

Madea's daughter Ms. J a/k/a Bell, Kat's sister stood in the doorway talking about her eldest wayward daughter, Deb, who was bringing human litter home. Ms. J had just set up an appointment with Big Mama to beat the living day lights out of her for disgracing the Christian family's name with her heathenistic ways and her life style as a fornicator. Kat's head drooped with empathy.

Riddy was shocked, embarrassed and befuddled. She took a step backward, away from all the laughing faces and thought, *period, period. What's a period?* The women-folk swooped in on her and began to congratulate and welcome her into womanhood. To Riddy, the whole thing was a blur. *Womanhood*, she kept thinking and wondering, and accepting hugs, *I am a woman now?*

Big Mama pulled Riddy into the bathroom. She pinned a sheet around and between her legs like a diaper. Big Mama gave Riddy a note with the words sanitary belt, and Kotex written on it. She instructed her to go to the drugstore for the belt, and then to the Certified Grocery Store for Kotex.

Finally, Riddy made it to the drugstore. She told the sales clerk who was a woman that she needed a belt. Then Riddy enters Certified Grocery Store and saw Diane with her huge French roll, ringing purchases on the register. She glanced at Ned at the liquor section. Bobby, the butcher was rinsing down the greens, and other vegetables.

Riddy went from aisle to aisle looking for this other item. She was going into another circle a third time when she finally noticed a box of Kotex on a top shelf in the back of the store. Riddy stood on her tiptoes and made several attempts to get the Kotex box down, and then stopped with a deep sigh. A long arm came out of nowhere. It was the butcher Bobby. He smiled at Riddy as he gave her the box. Riddy dropped her head embarrassed and quickly walked away.

Upon returning home, Houston was in the bathroom washing out the tub when Riddy entered with the box behind her back. He smiled and reached behind her and grabbed the box. Riddy began to cry, helpless and embarrassed. When Houston spied the pitiful look on her face, he gave the box back to Riddy, patted her head and left her with a sympathetic smile on his face.

After an inspection by Big Mama, Riddy was led to her custodian bedroom where she stood to watch Big Mama remove a book from the back of the drawer that was covered with a brown paper bag. Riddy was given the book and told to sit on a milk crate outside the house on the back porch and read it to herself. This was her introduction to sex education.

Riddy followed Big Mama's instructions. She opens the book and screams when she saw things that she had never seen before. However, she did recognize a few body parts that resembled hers.

Back in the day, women did not share about menstrual to the younger girls or about sex.

Riddy returns the book and attempts to revive herself after the shock. Big Mama and Riddy's eyes met, but not one word was exchanged. This experience amounted to Riddy's education about sex.

Chapter Four

Monroe community in Chicago, was a beautiful and prime property, especially in the sixties. It was only ten minutes away from downtown Chicago. There was beautiful green grass on both sides of the street. The view of the church could be seen directly across the street from the front of their house. Riddy spent many summers participating in the Vacation Bible School programs at the church across from the house next to the City of Chicago's parking lot.

The church was operated by a middle-aged pastor who had twelve children. The pastor's wife died ten years beforehand while having their one and only son. The doctor had warned them both, but neither took his advice. Their son's name was Marshall.

Marshall and Riddy spent some time together. Later in life he would become a doctor and a leader in the Civil Rights Movement in the new millennium.

Monroe community had rows of beautiful houses and a few apartment buildings at Kedzie and Fifth Avenue. The community leaders sent out an alert of a rapist that had raped a mentally ill little girl named Gwen. She and her family moved out of the community after this happened. This made Riddy afraid to walk down the street in fear that he might snatch and rape her.

Riddy took a walk down the street and saw the apartment buildings that she would have to eventually run pass because everyone thought the rapist lived in one.

Riddy's world when not traveling downtown or riding in the family's car consisted of Monroe, Madison, and Kedzie Street. Kedzie was filled with stores, the bus barn, and a restaurant that the bus drivers hung out at.

East of Madison had a huge movie theater, a Certified Grocery Store, a music store, an eye doctor and a doctor who was a general practitioner. The west of Madison had an old Henry Hamburger joint that was lined with beautiful trees, and it had stores that led twelve blocks to a shopping center. All the way to Cicero, you could find a venue cheese cake bakery, and clothing stores. Madison was beautiful before the rioting and looting after Martin Luther King, Jr. was assassinated.

Sometimes Riddy would leave out the back door and walk down the stairs into the backyard that had rows and rows of flowers and bushes. Big Mama took special pride in her rose bushes. Riddy helped Big Mama in hoeing the ground, raking the grass, and collecting berries from the mulberry tree. During Christmas time, Big Mama crushed the berries and made wine.

Big Mama's family became share croppers in Terrell County located in Dawson, Georgia like so many other families after the great emancipation toward the end of the civil war. Big Mama just could not get with the program. A man name Cherry had shamed her in the family. She got pregnant out of wedlock.

She began to prepare to go to Chicago. Every time she heard the train rushing and whistling through the town she became more and more anxious. Big Mama vowed that she would, one day board, a train northward to Chicago. Big Mama's dream came true.

Chicago began to experience an influx of oppressed people being strangled by the Jim Crow era. Of course, they were seeking a better life.

Big Mama did what so many others did, she worked as a domestic. She also baked and sold sweet potato pies, snow balls, starch dollies, and even did some babysitting.

Madea remained in Georgia, and taught grammar school after graduating from eighth grade at the little red school house that lay on top of the red Georgia clay. That red Georgia clay dirt was famous for being baked and eaten by pregnant women. The shift in the women hormones caused them to become nauseated and strangely the Georgia dirt settled their stomachs.

Big Mama left Georgia in search of a new life. She left Madea with her Grandparents, Mollie and Amos Thomas. She planned to send for Madea as soon as she got settled. Big Mama was in search for a new life and would send for Madea later. Big Mama arrived to the Promise Land of Chicago, that was filled with overcrowded boarding houses and the Negroes were only allowed to only dwell on the South Side of Chicago.

Madea grew up and married a man named Will McClain. They had two children. The marriage was filled with violence. The final straw came when Will, in a drunken stupor, molested their youngest daughter, Kat (Riddy's Mother). Madea cried all night and then snuck out of the house, barefoot, while Will slept.

She ran to a neighbor's house to use their phone to call her mother, Big Mama. The two women planned Madea's escape. Big Mama wired money to the train station and instructed that the ticket not to be cashed in, but only used to board the train by Madea. If her daughter did not show up, she instructed, the money was to be sent back to her.

Madea got on the train, the next morning, after Will went to work. In a hurry, she could only manage to gather a few of their items. In a rush, Madea, Ms. J, and Kat left Georgia with the clothes on their backs and barefooted. And Madea was pregnant with Howell, soon to be born. Madea never went back to Georgia. As far as she was concerned, that part of her life was erased from her memory.

A few years would pass before Madea could trust to love again. Madea worked at the factory where she met and married Sid. They remained married for over fifty years until death, did them part.

Big Mama married a guy name Maynard Roger years before Madea came to Chicago. The marriage failed as did her marriage with Georgie White and Mr. Cherry in Georgia. Georgie White was her last marriage.

Georgie was a womanizer, a drunk and a miser, and he rarely brought any money home. When he did, Big Mama could only buy beans and a little pork. Georgie had a beautiful daughter from a previous marriage named Alice. Alice brought Big Mama great joy, and she was a great playmate for Big Dot who was Maynard's daughter. Big Mama got a part-time job and swore the young girls into secrecy.

She brought groceries for a day at a time and they all ate high off the hog. There would be days of pork chops, ham, roast, and bacon. You name it, they had it. However, every crumb had to be eaten with nothing left so that Georgie would never know she had a job.

Big Mama kept a pot of beans on the stove for Georgie. They would all sit at the table to eat, and it was hard for the girls to eat on a full belly, and hold a straight face. They picked at their food, and fought their giggles. Big Mama would cut her eyes at the girls whenever they snickered as Georgie fussed about how the kids were wasting their food, and how tired he was of eating beans. Big Mama sat there putting on a shame-face look. She replied, timidly, "I'm sorry, but that's all I can buy with the money you give me."

It was becoming more unbearable to live with Georgie. Big Mama began to plan the great escape. The only thing she hated to leave behind was Alice. Alice was not her child and she knew that Georgie would hunt her down. Big Mama had to make a clean break from Georgie. She told Alice and the secret was kept with hope of one day to be rescued by Big Mama. She was merciful in disappearing on an unknown day when Alice was in school so that the departure would not hurt so badly.

Big Mama found a flat in a six-story tenement and she moved herself and Dorothy in. Madea would join them later. Big Mama had shipped her middle child, Georgia, to her mother after being in Chicago, and she had made another mistake with another no-good man. Once Big Mama settled in her new place, she sent for Georgia and later Madea and her children, Ms. J, Kat and Howell, would join her.

Sid moved in after Madea and the children had settled.

A few years later Georgia married and had a son named Jon. So Georgia and her family returned to the South.

One night Big Mama got a tragic phone call from a hysterical Georgia that her husband had died defending his sister who was being beaten by her husband. Jon Sr. opened the door the night he heard his sister's screams and was met by a double barrel shotgun that tore through his intestines and left them hanging and dangling. Jon, Sr. died instantly. Georgia and her young son moved to Chicago.

The love bug struck Big Mama again. But this time she shacked and repeatedly refused to marry Bill. Big Mama was no longer the marrying kind, and she was treated very well. Bill was a great provider and friend and everyone liked Bill but Georgia caused a wedge between Bill and Big Mama. The common-law couple eventually went their separate ways, and afterwards, Georgia started partying and hanging out at all times of the night.

Georgia and her young son lived together in their own place until one day Georgia contracted tuberculosis. She was hospitalized and died. A week went by before Big Mama found out. She had a 30ish daughter to bury and a grandson to take home to the building on 12th and Wilcox which was the heart of Jew Town where she previously lived before purchasing the new building at 3165 West Monroe Street.

The City of Chicago, upon the requests of the University of Illinois, did an eminent domain where they seized all the houses and buildings in the area for the purpose of a school expansion. It displaced people from their homes, leaving them to scramble for shelter. It was difficult to find a place to live in Chicago during this era. Chicago was overcrowded due to the migration of oppressed Negroes spilling in from the southern states. Fortunately, everyone in the house who was over eighteen, had worked and saved money. They were willing to pool their money together.

Big Mama met a Jewish lawyer and took a chance on allowing him to purchase a three-flat building at 3165 West Monroe in a white neighborhood. It would be a wing and a prayer that this man would not run off with the money or purchase the building and claim it as his home. If either happened, she knew that there would be nothing she could do about it. But Big Mama felt at peace about it, because of a special twinkle she saw in his kind eyes. The lawyer signed over the deed to Big Mama and gave it to her.

The family had a new place to live. They would be the second Negro family to move in the neighborhood after the matriarch Lucille and her family. Big Mama, Madea, Sid, Houston, and Dwight moved on the first floor. Big Dot, Ern, and Thurman moved on the second floor front, and the back rooms were rented out by a married couple who had no children. On the third floor was a Cuban couple with their children.

Everybody upstairs and downstairs shared the common areas. After a few months, the married couple moved out and Big Dot and her family moved as well.

Big Mama had a hard time accepting the day that Big Dot and Ern moved. She took it personally. Big Dot assured her that the move was not targeted against her and that she could visit whenever she wanted, and they would still come over for the holidays, BBQs, weekly women POW WOW, and breakfasts. Nothing would change and everything else would pretty much remain the same.

Chapter Five

During the early '60s, teachers would have up to forty to fifty students in a classroom. There were no tutoring or special education programs.

Riddy had to take speech therapy due to a hearing loss of high tones because of the numerous fevers that she encountered as a very young child. She had speech therapy two times a week. It was rather embarrassing, seeing Ms. Sullivan's face through the glass window of her classroom door because all the students walking pass could see inside. Everyone knew Riddy's business.

There was a time in the sixties when kids had to go home for lunch, and it was expected for children to have had breakfast before coming to school. There were no free breakfast or lunch programs, and parents back in the day did not have much money in order to feed the family.

Riddy loved to go home for lunch. Sometimes Big Mama would give Riddy a break from eating chili, every day, and surprise her with a burger and French fries from Old Henry's restaurant on Madison.

However, Thurman and Houston's girlfriends, Peg and Dee, all met at Marshall high school and enjoyed gorging out on Big Mama's chili, every day.

* * *

One year back to back, Riddy contracted chicken pox, measles, small pox, and mumps. She felt awful like death scratching and bleeding while waiting for each disease to run its course. This was a terrible year.

Riddy had Thurman, Dwight, and Houston scratching her back for some relief, while they sat on the piano bench watching the black and white console floor model TV. Riddy had made up in her mind to run bath water to cool off from both the itching and the burning. Big Mama caught Riddy as one foot was being lifted to get inside the tub.

Screaming, "Do you want live?" Asked Big Mama.

"Mama, I am on fire; I am burning." While crying profusely.

"Riddy you will die if you get in that tub. I will rub you down with calamine lotion."

The lotion stopped the itching and burning temporarily, so it was used often.

Riddy put her clothes back on, and then, it was time to read with Big Mama. Riddy loved to read, especially to Big Mama. It would be years before Riddy would find out that all Big Mama had was, a third grade education. They would travel to faraway places through their reading sessions. During their reading time, they would go back to Georgia, then the deeper south, the Delta, and back to Chicago.

Literally, every year Riddy and Big Mama traveled to different places during the hot summer months. Riddy remembers traveling to Momence where she saw dusty roads, Illinois that has the best scenery, Florida near the ocean, Ohio where the weather is damp and raining, Canada where it is cold, Detroit the deserted communities, and they even took the Amtrak to Macon Georgia. Riddy got her love for travel from Big Mama. She also took Riddy to a Rolling Stone's concert. Big Mama had gotten front row seats. The two of them were a strange pair, an elderly woman with a ten year old child.

Big Mama also took Riddy to church. Riddy's childhood church was located on 12th Street and Hastings. It was beautiful in Riddy's eyes. However, the middle-aged pastor had ventured out and found a cathedral on 99th and Justine. Riddy could not understand why they could not go to the church that was across the street where cute Marshall directed the choir. Because she knew Christianity would be her foundation for survival and Marshall was a great incentive.

It was at the new church that Riddy watched the church services from the back pew in her junior usher's uniform. Oh how Big Mama would go into a frenzy when she heard the song "Leaning on the Everlasting Arm". Big Mama would get on her tiptoes and strut with her head held back. Then going from person-to-person and shaking hands, she would sing, "Oh what a fellowship! What a joy divine,... leaning on the everlasting arm!" Then everyone would jump into the chorus.

Riddy loved how church made her feel. She loved when the senior choir marched toward the choir stand while singing: "All Hails the Power of Jesus' Name". The choir members wore long sparkling white robes. They looked like angels. Riddy always felt something moving above her head, but she was never afraid because it gave her a good feeling.

Everyone stopped going to church because the family's car broke down, and it was too far to walk, so every now and then, she ventured across the street to Shiloh Church. The church Riddy wanted to attend.

Riddy, throughout her entire life had never ever seen Big Mama angry. Riddy never heard her say an unkind word to, or about anyone. Riddy often wondered why there was such a big difference between Madea and Big Mama.

Another milestone event occurred when Riddy turned eight. She got godparents, Pennie and Les. One day, Big Mama was talking to Riddy about what would happen if she died. She wanted Riddy to be taken care of properly. Unbeknownst to Big Mama that she would outlive her godparents.

Anyway on the way to the back porch at 3165 West Monroe upon walking up to the banister was a white woman. Riddy was shocked. She jumped and her eyes opened wide. Big Mama laughed, and explained that the woman was just high-yella. Pennie was not white or uppity. The woman and Big Mama talked, and she welcomed Riddy into her family, so it was Riddy's goddaughter duty to visit Pennie once a week.

Pennie introduced Riddy to Les, her husband, and she also met her new god-brother Les Jr., sister-in-law Gwen, and their children Geno and Venus. Everyone was one big happy family.

At thirty-nine years old Les Jr. died a slow death of kidney failure. He had been a police officer for many years. Pennie was devastated. They had great times together, and that was all Pennie could hold on to. It broke Riddy's heart to see that sweet woman having crying spells over a long period of time. This affected Riddy.

After Les Jr.'s burial, Les Sr. began to drink himself to a stupor. Every time you saw him, he was drinking. He even began to yell at Pennie. He became a very rancorous and unpleasant man. This whole scenario went on a whole year.

Gwen still kept close contact with Pennie, and Pennie's grandchildren visited all the time and spent whole summers with her.

Riddy saw how great of a family they were and felt a little out of place never having a mother that really cared about her and a father who was lost. Now, the evil begins of Riddy acting out of rejection.

One day, Riddy got jealous and messed up Venus' party dress, Pennie's granddaughter. *No one had ever given me a party dress*, she thought as she worked at the hateful deed. Pennie sweetly told Riddy, "You are a pretty little girl. You don't have to act like that." Riddy dropped her head in shame.

Both girls wore a pretty dress to the party. Riddy's was a pretty pink party dress while Venus' was cream with sparkling gold ruffles.

Pennie and Les lived on the third floor and had a huge swing on their back porch. Riddy loved being up there on hot, sweaty summer days. One could catch a cool breeze on that swing.

Riddy also made friends with the lady who lived on the first floor named Gracie Finley. She was sweet, too. Gracie had never married nor had children. She did raise two of her sister's sons whose names were John and Marvell Campbell.

John used to ride his motorcycle up and down Monroe Street. He was endearing. Sometimes he would let Riddy ride, too. Marvell could not because he was in diapers. Gracie's sister Bernice was a drunk and the city wanted to take the kids away from her, but Gracie fought to keep them.

While going through the mail, John finds that he received a letter drafting him to go to Vietnam. Everyone on Monroe Street was sad. Everyone admired John's mannerism, everyone.

One day Riddy was sitting in the kitchen with Big Mama. Big Mama suddenly jumped up and looked out of the window. Riddy ran to look, too. They both saw two uniformed men park their car behind the Finley's tenement building. Big Mama shook her head. Riddy nudged her head, wanting to know what was up. Big Mama told Riddy, "John is dead."

John had stepped on a grenade, and it blew his body in half. He had nothing from the waist, down. Miraculously, he made it to a hospital, alive. But when he found out about his condition, while no one was around, he managed to unplug himself from all the tubes that kept his body functioning.

John had never married, nor had children, so Gracie received ten thousand dollars to assist her during her time of bereavement.

It had been rumored that John was gay. Gay or not, Riddy loved him like a brother. She would always remember him in her heart.

Riddy was fortunate to visit the Vietnam Wall in Washington, D.C. It had scores of fallen soldiers' names on it. Riddy checked the wall twice, John Campbell's name. It was not on the wall. Riddy was sadden not seeing John's name. She will keep John in her remembrance.

Gracie sat many days and nights in silence. Riddy did all she could to cheer her up. Big Mama even started taking care of Marvell. Gracie was out of it. Eventually, Bernice came around and took Marvell back. The death of her older son had sobered her up.

Since Gracie was all alone, Riddy made it her business to visit twice a week. She would walk into the kitchen with a smile, look into the pots as if she owned the place and said, "So what's for dinner," laughing, hoping to cheer up Gracie. Sometimes it worked, but most times it did not.

Riddy had begun to notice Les Sr. coming out of Gracie's house when she would enter. A strange feeling came over her. Then one day he came to the house and Riddy refused to leave because she felt that he was up to no good. On this particular day, Riddy dropped something, and as she straightened up, she saw Gracie and Les Sr. kissing.

Riddy was flabbergasted. At that moment, Pennie was walking down the stairs. Riddy yelled, "I'm going to tell."

Then Les Sr. shouted, "Like I care!"

Riddy ran and told Pennie, and Pennie doubled over in tremendous pain. Riddy was so hurt for her and then ran home to Big Mama and told her everything.

Riddy just could not believe it. This hurt her more than it hurt Pennie. It would be weeks before Riddy would venture back to see either Pennie or Gracie. When Riddy finally showed up, again, everyone pretended that everything was okay.

Les Sr. continued to drink. He developed high blood pressure. But he would not stop drinking nor would he eat the right foods to bring nutrition to his body. Eventually, Les had a stroke that left him partially paralyzed, and using a cane to try and get around. Les Sr. threw tantrums, and would even curse God. Pennie would always sweetly say, "Don't say that Les. Don't use God's name in vain." That would throw Les into a tirade of goddam-its.

Riddy still visited him, even though he was mean. Les would always manage to squeeze out a smile for her.

Riddy visited Pennie and Les, one day, wearing her pink corduroy hat and coat. Big Mama had also made a matching coat and hat for her favorite baby doll. Les took a picture of Pennie and Riddy with his one working hand. Riddy was still his girl. Of course, Les was not able to rendezvous with Gracie any more. He was in his sad physical state until he died, not long after his stroke.

Gracie bought a house in Battle Creek, Michigan and moved. In Battle Creek, she worked as a cashier at a store with the military insurance money from John's death. Riddy lost contact with her through the years. Pennie sold the building because she wanted a fresh start, too. She bought a three-flat building on the South Side of Chicago.

Gwen had remarried. She married a military man and traveled. They lived in different parts of the world such as Spain, Germany, and Italy. She would always send for Pennie. Finally Pennie died. Everyone came to the funeral—and everyone would stretch the truth like they usually do about keeping in touch.

Chapter Six

One evening nearing bedtime, Riddy always saw Madea reading a big black book, so Riddy came up with a plan to uncover the mystery of what her grandmother was reading. Once the house was quiet and the queens of the house were snoring, she would put her plan in action.

Sid was always asleep from alcohol. The boys had moved with Big Dot and Ern, and all Riddy had to do was to tiptoe, open the kitchen door, quietly click on the kitchen light, sit in Madea's chair and open up the big black book she read every night.

What's in this book? She thought. The plan worked. Riddy was sitting at the kitchen table in Madea's chair. She discovered it was the Bible. The B-I-B-L-E. Riddy started reading Genesis, chapter one. Then she moved on to reading about Abraham, Isaac, and Jacob. She read a little about Joseph. Suddenly, a noise startled her, and she looked up to find Madea standing in the kitchen. Riddy's heart pounded and she broke into a cold sweat.

Oh now a whipping was in the making, she knew.

Madea smiled and said, "Continue reading a little more and then go to bed."

Riddy answered, "Yes, Madea." Riddy swallowed hard, but with relief.

Riddy's attention was then turned to a passage of scripture that mention how "Enoch walked with God, and then was translated and he did not see death." Riddy then wondered *if she could walk with God.* She closed the Bible and went to bed.

Soon thereafter, one morning, Big Mama announced to Riddy after reading the movie section in the newspaper that they were going downtown to see "The Bible". George C. Scott played the dynamic role of Abraham.

The bus trip downtown was awesome. Tall buildings were everywhere. White people were everywhere.

Inside the movie theater there were so many huge pillars trimmed with gold, and Cherubims painted on the ceiling. The two sat in the middle of the movie theatre, and blacks and whites were scattered throughout.

Two weeks later, while Riddy was in her room and quietly sitting on the floor when she heard a voice call her name. She had been playing with her doll, combing the doll's hair. It was a siesta time in the house. Big Mama was in her own room, napping in a chair with her head bowed—her chin touching her chest. Madea was in her bed with her bedroom door partly closed. High-pitched snoring sounds were flowing from the room.

Riddy ran into the room awakening Madea. "Ma'am, you called me?"

Madea answered, "I did no such thing."

Riddy distinctly heard her name again and returned for a second time with the same accusation, "Ma'am, you called me?"

"You keep breaking my sleep. What is the matter?" Madea asked.

On the third attempt, Riddy held fast to her guns and said, "You did call me!"

"I did not!" Madea insisted.

Riddy was eight years of age and knew she heard a voice calling her name, so she just shriveled and stared at the door that led to her room.

Riddy would not go back into her room. Big Mama could not get Riddy to go back to sleep in that room. She would sleep with Big Mama until she turned twelve and was forced back into the room but with the door open. Riddy thought that it was probably the God that Big Mama told her to talk to when she made bad grades, and He is now answering back. She would run pass the room to go outside to play because she thought it was weird hearing a voice and no one was there.

From time-to-time, Riddy liked to go outside to play IT, Red Light/Green Light, Simon says, dodge ball, jump rope, Chinese rope, and Hop Scotch. However, she was not allowed to go pass the front of the porch or stay out once the street lights came on. Whenever she was called inside, she would grumble. Then she would hear a voice say, "Do you want a whippin'?"

A few weeks later, Riddy met a gal named Lydia from next door. The building that both Lydia and Riddy lived in was really one building, but white folks sold the building as two pieces of separate real estate.

Lydia and Riddy became good friends. However, her sister, Diane, was annoying. She always picked at Riddy because of her long hair. Diane was practically bald. One day, a fight broke out between Riddy and Diane. Riddy pulled out the remaining strands of her hair clinging to her head. She was about to lower a brick upside her head. Big Mama grabbed Riddy. Diane was never a problem, again.

Lydia's mother's name is Alice who removed her from public school, and enrolled her into a private Catholic school. Riddy begged Big Mama to let her follow Lydia to the new school. It was a brief stint because one day Riddy grew too quiet for Big Mama.

Big Mama opened the door and there was Riddy on her knees before a white doll with a blanket on her head. Big Mama calmly explained that the family could worship only God, and kneel to him alone.

Although Riddy was pulled out of the Catholic school system, Lydia remained. Lydia and Riddy would see each other after school and played in the back yard.

On one particular hot summer day Lydia nudged Riddy while the two of them were playing in the yard and Lydia said, "Look." Sid was sitting on a crate with the basement door open, and exposing himself. The girls screamed and ran up the stairs and into their own houses. Riddy ran and told Madea. Madea believed Riddy, and ran out of the house in a rage.

Riddy quietly followed behind Madea as she walked toward the basement. Madea turned once they got outside and told her to stay put. Madea entered the basement and closed the door.

Riddy never found out what happened behind the closed door, but she had no problem with Sid any more, and she never respected him, either.

* * *

However, many years later God put forgiveness in Riddy's heart to the point where she led Sid to the Lord Jesus on his death bed. Sid repented of his sins and wrong-doings in life. At first, it was tough.

"Sid, this is a great time to give yourself to the Lord and ask for forgiveness for the sins you committed in your life. Let us pray a repentance prayer." Riddy explained.

Sid was reluctant to pray the repentance prayer because he felt that his sins were too harsh to receive forgiveness.

"I am not sure if the Lord would forgive me." Sid exclaimed.

But when Riddy and her only child, Sweetie, left out of the room, Riddy felt led to return and asked her daughter to lead Sid into salvation.

Sweetie held Sid's hands and asked him would he accept Christ to be his personal savior. She explained how the Lord was sent to the earth to be our example on how to live, then the Lord died shedding his precious blood, and resurrected giving us the right to salvation. Riddy stepped in to help Sid pray the repentance prayer.

After Sid prayed the repentance prayer repeating every word after Riddy, Sid accepted eternal life, and on the next day, he died.

* * *

The year that Riddy returned to the Chicago public school, she did not return to the school system alone. Riddy's companion was a pair of tan hideous, dinosaur-looking orthopedic shoes that would accompany her to the fifth grade.

It was during an annual physical that the doctors noticed problems with Riddy's feet, ankles, and calves. She had a limp.

Madea proudly announced to her baby girl about the new pair of shoes. Riddy thought that the shoes were cute until she met B.J.

The first day of school was exciting, and everyone was happy. Ms. Harper, Riddy's teacher, had given everyone their seating assignments after making out a seating chart. Once the class settled, and after going over several lessons, Mrs. Harper called Riddy to her desk. That is when B.J. called out attention to Riddy's shoes. Riddy was very hurt and embarrassed. The whole class burst out in laughter. The teacher finally settled the class. But for the next six months, B.J. and her gang teased Riddy before and after class. Riddy's only refuge was in class or at home. It seemed that everywhere Riddy turned, the gang would appear.

Riddy once pretended to have lost the shoes hopeful that Big Mama would let her wear her sneakers. But Big Mama would pull out her strap, and Riddy would magically find the shoes. Then on another occasion, Riddy scraped them up until black marks appeared, but Big Mama cleaned them up with kitchen cleanser and then shined them.

One day B.J. and her mom came to class to return her books. Mrs. Harper signed B.J. out of class. She was moving out of the school district or something. *Who cares*, thought Riddy. It was the end of B.J. and the gang's constant terrorist attacks against Riddy.

Through the years, Riddy wondered, what happened to B.J., and how could such a beautiful girl be so ugly? B.J. was a gorgeous, high-yella, gal with blondish, brown hair, but she was a mean heifer.

The rest of the year was a breeze until the final marking period. Mrs. Harper gave Riddy her report card, and had a sympathetic look especially since Riddy missed half the school year because of illnesses. Riddy thought, *Here we go again, more U's and F's.*

Riddy was socially passed to the sixth grade; she knew that she was not going to pass academically. The pressure of not doing well in school was on Riddy's mind as well as when the kids gave her a hard time.

A month before school let out for the summer break, Riddy had a fight with two girls, who seemingly just wanted to torture her. A note was given to Riddy that she was going to be beaten up at 3:15 p.m. All Riddy had to defend herself with was her leather purse that had a very long strap. The two girls surely kept their promise and were waiting for Riddy to walk through the door. She remembered the story about David and Goliath, and whooped the girls until they ran off.

Riddy did not get away without being punished. Mrs. Newman, the school's counselor, grabbed and dragged her to the office. She got suspended for five days. The girls were left unpunished. Big Mama understood the punishment, but not the unfairness of the other girls getting off, free. But the suspension was really a vacation.

Riddy got to watch television and have fun. She played outside, and she even helped Big Mama work on quilts. Big Mama made right, Mrs. Newman's unfairness by allowing Riddy to enjoy the week out of school. Big Mama was not going to punish Riddy for protecting herself. This was the same Mrs. Newman that thought Riddy was anti-social and pairs her off with a girl named Jerry to be her friend.

Jerry did not want to be bothered, the two girls were thrown together by Mrs. Newman because they were budding and were the only ones in fifth grade wearing a bra. The parents met and decided that the two girls should become friends. Jerry was a snob. Mrs. Newman always got the wrong ideas about people, and things.

Anyway Riddy was surprised to even have a report card. Riddy slowly approached Big Mama with her head down and gave her the report card. It was while her head was down that Riddy said that she was tired of making bad marks on her report card. Big Mama said, "Well go to your room and pray and ask God to help you". This was not quite the response that Riddy expected. She thought a whooping was coming to her.

Riddy immediately went to her bedroom and knelt. Then she looked up at the ceiling and told God, "Big Mama told me to talk to You about my grades. If You are out there, please help me. I'm tired of getting bad grades. Amen."

* * *

Sometimes Big Mama and Riddy would hit the road to travel out of town off the money that Big Mama earned from cooking special meals, baking sweet potato pies, starching doilies, quilting, babysitting, and snow ball sales.

Big Mama always had money, but it puzzled Riddy as to why Madea always begged Big Mama for money when she was working a so-called job.

Madea had gotten a better job when she worked at a factory and lost the tip of her third finger on her left hand. It was due to this injury that she left factory work, obtained her high school diploma, and qualified to take the city crossing guard exam. Madea passed and the money that she made on a part-time level was twice her old factory job.

Riddy loved the fact that Madea worked as a crossing guard because the family received huge discounts at the cleaners. Crossing guards had to get their clothes cleaned and was able to get them done at a discounted price, so Madea included other clothes which made laundry easier at home.

At the end of the year, a huge party was thrown with lots of food for the crossing guards and their families. The festivities would start with a program, food, and then raffle ticket numbers would be called. Riddy would win the raffle every year.

It was during one particular year when Riddy won an egg in a hatching chicken game that Riddy discovered a devastating secret. Riddy found out that there was no Santa Claus. This made her think that everything someone told her up to that point was not true.

The crossing guard festivity was a few days before Christmas, and Riddy wanted to show Madea that something was wrong with her game. Riddy went tearing into Madea's room without knocking, and found that Madea was not home. It was as Riddy was leaving the room that she noticed the closet door was open, and she saw shopping bags that contained the exact items, she told Santa about at the Sears Department store.

They were downtown doing a little Christmas window shopping when Madea and Big Mama suggested that they go inside and talk to Santa. They had had a ball looking at the animated manikins, and afterwards eating at Wimpies. But now, here Riddy stood with her mouth dropped open. So, it was at the tender age of twelve when Riddy found out the raw truth that there was no such thing as a Santa Claus. It was the beginning of Riddy finding out other raw truths, and when life would dispel and dissect the Cinderella syndrome and the happily-ever-after-life lie, too.

When they got home from window shopping, Riddy then played outside for a while after changing into her play clothes. Big Mama called her in for dinner. It was at the dinner table that she felt sick. She laid her head down. Riddy felt something moving inside her head then to her nose, chest, and then something was pressing on her stomach. Riddy had an urge to go to the toilet. At this time she was a virgin, so it could not be pregnancy. Riddy's body opened up and a huge round slimy green mass, the size of a dinner plate, departed out of her body with a bang in the commode. Riddy yelled. Big Mama ran into the bathroom. Riddy leaped off the toilet and there was a green slimy mass. Big Mama and Riddy looked at each other. Riddy looked to Big Mama for an explanation.

Big Mama said, "It is cold."

"That's all, it's cold?" Riddy said with disbelief.

"Flush the toilet; let's go eat," Big Mama said.

Chapter Seven

Sixth grade was a great year! Riddy made a lot of friends with both boys and girls. She met Debra a/k/a Deb, Edith, Bev, Joann, Cecil, Johnny, Dwayne and Gwen. All the girls liked Dwayne because he was athletic. Deb liked Dwayne, but Dwayne liked Gwen, so, Deb settled for Johnny. Riddy and Edith liked Cecil, but Cecil liked Bev. Bev didn't like anybody.

Periodically the group would sneak off to Edith's house. At first, sneaking off was fun until one day Edith told Riddy,

"I love Cecil, and if I can't have him, life is no longer worth living and I am going to kill myself."

"Girl you are crazy," Riddy told her.

One day, the group was at the house. Deb and Johnny got lost in the house. Edith suddenly appeared on the top stairs wrapped in a long white sheet. Edith announced, "I'm going to jump" Deb and Johnny came running from a room after the sounds of screams followed the crash. Edith had leaped forward and went plunging down some stairs. She survived, but the group did not. Everyone began to go to classes. It was devastating to see someone trying to commit suicide. Edith was transferred to another school and no one ever saw her again.

Deb invited Riddy to her house. Deb's mom worked for the Post Office at night to support herself and her two kids. She lived with a boyfriend. Deb periodically begged Riddy to come and spend the night. Whenever Riddy saw this man, it gave her a creepy feeling.

One day Deb came to school, smiling. It was a rather peculiar smile. She told Riddy that she and Johnny were going to have a baby. Deb and Johnny kept in touch during the summer months. Deb was getting bigger each month. She was happy, for it pricked her mother's heart and shamed the family. Then finally, Deb had someone that she would call her own especially, since Johnny had suddenly stopped visiting and calling. Deb had to stay home until the baby was born.

Bev's mom died, and she moved to Washington to live with her big sister. Bev's mother had thrown a birthday party for her daughter one month before she died.

Bev's mom was a kind and soft-spoken woman with light brown hair and eyes. She was a very petite woman who wore a French roll. *Life can be so unfair*, Bev thought. Bev's mom died of a brain tumor.

Johnny was talking to another girl. Riddy never told Deb. Deb and Johnny had a little son name Dana. Deb found out about Johnny and went to another school. Riddy saw Deb twenty years later. She too would be a mail carrier like her mother, but married and kept Dana, her son, by her side. Things worked out. Riddy never saw Deb again after running into her at a mall.

Now, Riddy had crushes on two teachers during her elementary, but nothing like Arvella's crush on Mr. White. It was when the seventh grade school year had begun that Riddy secretly liked Mr. Matthews. He was a white man with dark hair and green eyes. All the girls thought he was cute.

The seventh grade girls of room 204 would always circle him before class got started, but Riddy always ran straight to her seat. He would glance at her from across the room with a strange look on his face possibly wondering why Riddy was not like the others. At least that is how she saw it.

Mr. Matthews mysteriously disappeared during the middle of the school year with no explanation. Not long after, the principal entered the classroom with a teacher named Mr. Michaels. Now, Mr. Michaels moved Riddy with his blond hair and sky-blue eyes. On one particular day, when her hormones must have been raging, Riddy decides to let Mr. Michaels know that she liked him.

Riddy was standing at his desk, and he was positioned in front of his desk. Riddy told him that she liked him. She waited for his response. But when he placed his hand on top of hers, she got an eerie feeling and abruptly dashed away from him, and sat down. The eerie feeling, she knew, was her inner being dispatching an alarm warning her that she was crossing a boundary—entering into uncharted waters. And that is all it took to make her sit down and check herself. *Thank God*, was her thought about it, later.

It would be twenty years later while on a bus headed downtown when she would catch sight of Mr. Michaels again. Riding and deep in thought, she glanced out the window to see him entering a building. She zoomed in to get a good look—he had gotten a little older, yes, but he was still fine. She chuckled about what might have been—had her young world gone completely haywire.

Cecil started working at a drycleaners. The gang had become disconnected, and Riddy found seventh grade to be a lonely year. Occasionally, she would be with Gwen and Dwayne, but felt like the third wheel. Then she found out that Gwen was just as athletic as Dwayne and they did not like each other but decided to remain friends.

The seventh grade ended with both a bang, and with a bittersweet taste in Riddy's mouth. The bitter came in non-acceptance by the ones she thought were her new friends, but the sweet—the bang—came with her fantastic grades, E's and G's on her report card from the sixth grade, on.

* * *

Riddy was intrigued with the eighth grade girls. The group wore heels, stockings and make-up. Riddy admired a girl named B.B. who later went on to be a famous Chicago designer. She was a home economics' major. Riddy tried to learn how to sew, but Ms. Thomas would pull out all her stitches from her potholder and skirt.

Riddy seventh grade teacher Mr. Faraday would allow her and one other girl friend to be in the drama class with the eighth grade girls. Riddy was so happy whenever she could quietly hang around, especially with B.B.

One day B.B. noticed her and included Riddy into the conversation. Riddy felt accepted among the new gang of friends. She felt a part of the upper classmen that would soon graduate in royal blue caps and gowns.

One day, before drama class started, a girl named Vivian asked Riddy to do a skit with her.

"Me?" Riddy asked endearingly.

Viv gave her the lines.

Drama class started. The two of them was called. It was a Listerine commercial. Vivian, however, conveniently left out one line, unknowing to Riddy. Vivian recited,

"Riddy, you have bad breath," and laughed out loudly.

No one responded. It was so quiet you could hear a pin drop. The drama teacher looked in disbelief. B.B and the other girls looked in shock while Vivian's voice roared and got louder and louder. Riddy swallowed back the tears. She dropped her head and went downstairs.

* * *

Riddy saw Vivian in the 1980's as she visited a hospital to check on her work-study students at CCH. A housekeeper lady struck up a conversation with her. Riddy was polite, but did not recognize the lady. It was not until Riddy had walked down to the end of the corridor to exit and get to her car that her memory was jogged. As she opened the car door with one hand and clutched her briefcase in the other, Riddy had on her navy-blue and white pinstripe suit, with matching navy blue shoes, and Jerry curls. But, a pain of sadness struck her heart and Riddy felt bad when she remembered the past incident with Vivian because this was all she amounted to, a housekeeper carrying a mop and a pail. It does not pay to treat others badly.

* * *

Deb was graduating from grammar school and Ms. J did not have the money to buy a graduation suit. Riddy just got this pantsuit and Deb is wearing it before her. So what, she gave Riddy used clothes. Riddy stood on the front porch with her lips poked out and arms folded while asking Big Mama,

"Why does Deb, teasingly call her Ms. Ann has to borrow my two piece mint green knit pantsuit with the double breasted jacket and big gold buttons when I haven't even wore it yet?"

Big Mama told Riddy, "Don't be selfish. Debbie always gave you her clothes when she grew out of them. I will make sure you get your suit back in the same condition as before. Now, straighten up or else."

Riddy stomped her way into the house.

The next week, Big Mama and Madea took Riddy shopping for clothes because school was starting soon.

Chapter Eight

Finally, Riddy's dad returns to be in her life. Riddy had an opportunity to spend time with Ed. Ed came by to pick her up for a ride and a promise of a movie with Serena and Ed Jr. at the local movie theatre. Serena and Ed, Jr. are Riddy's brother and sister.

Ed had to stop by Cody's house, one of his childhood friends, who owed him money before going to Johnnie Mae's to get his other children, Serena and Ed Jr. because they were not ready. He had planned to take his children to the movies so that they could spend time together. Ed picked up Riddy from Big Mama's house before heading to Cody's.

Ed had forgotten something in the car, and when he was out of sight, Cody chased Riddy around the cocktail table in the living room and asked her for a kiss. Cody is the same age of Ed in his thirties. Since Ed was asking for his money Cody wanted his shoes that Ed borrowed and Ed left them in the car, but did not want to drag Riddy down stairs with him helping her down stairs along the way. It was after kicking him in the shin that Riddy knelt on the couch while looking out the window hoping that Ed would hurry up and get upstairs before any molestation took place.

Cody was lying on the floor trying to get himself together after the kick. Gradually, Cody stood up and began to chase Riddy around the cocktail table again, and just when he was about to lunge toward her, a key was heard through the door, and they both sat down as if nothing happened.

Eventually, the family of four saw "Fantastic Voyage". It was about a diplomat that had a brain tumor and it is located in an unreachable area of the brain. So, the scientist shrinks a ship with doctors and sends it through his body. The scientist has so many hours to perform surgery before antibodies form and attack them. The movie was great, even though Serena lost a shoe.

Riddy refused to accompany Ed anywhere anymore even though he kept his promise of a movie with her sister and brother.

* * *

The eighth grade was exciting and the year zipped by. There was Iowa testing, filling out high school applications, the class luncheon, class trip, and then the grand day, which was the day of graduation.

Riddy was a lanky string bean, five-feet two inches tall and weighing in at one hundred pounds. Riddy's hair was so beautiful against her high cheekbones. This helped her feel great about herself.

Riddy always thought she was ugly with buck teeth, but now she transformed into a beautiful teenager and looks just as good as her peers.

An upper-grade school carnival was planned. The eighth-grade fundraisers, which consisted of a carnival and other events, were used to defray the cost of graduation.

Riddy chose to be a psychic during the carnival. She foretold people's future, what a foreshadowing event. She dressed as an American Indian. Madea gave Riddy a white suit to cut up and design fringes. Riddy parted her hair down the middle, and put a headband across her forehead. It was a lot of fun! This inspired Big Mama to share the little that she knew of their heritage.

Big Mama told Riddy,

"Your great-great-great grandmother was taken from Africa and had a little girl named Mollie in America. Mollie grew up and married an Indian named Amos."

Madea's grandmother which was Mollie was a slave. Big Mama was born five years after the great emancipation of the slaves by Abraham Lincoln. In addition to that, Big Mama told Riddy about her experiences with Jim Crow.

Big Mama even mentioned to Riddy about her baby sister named Viola. Viola was born to their mother, Mollie Thomas, with a full set of teeth and came out of the womb talking.

"One day, papa went into the woods and came back with a squirrel," Big Mama said, while telling the story.

As she continued, "Viola, as a baby, told her mother, 'do not eat the squirrel. If you eat the squirrel, you will die'."

Mollie refused to have anything to do with it. Then, three days later, Viola died. The famed, full set of teeth, talking, infant died as mysteriously as she entered into the world. A few years later Big Mama was born. Riddy also learned that Big Mama's real name was Lily Anna.

Riddy always spent her summers alone on the porch. Besides Lynn and her cousins (Winnie and Neecie), there was no one else to play with. On one particular summer day, she met a gal down the street named Arvella. Eventually, Arvella was in eighth-grade along with Riddy. Big Mama was reluctant to let the two girls hang out because Arvella was sixteen and in the eighth grade. Riddy was only thirteen.

Arvella lived at the end of the block near Albany and Kedzie. Riddy lived on the opposite end near Kedzie. Riddy began to explore more of her world. Her world expanded out the back door across the porch through the yard into the alley.

There used to be a Chevrolet dealership that existed before the rioting of the assassination of Dr. Martin Luther King, Jr., she would have to walk down Kedzie on Jackson stretching onward to 5th Avenue to go to the social room and for hot dogs and a lot of times she visited Arvella.

Arvella was exciting and full of life. The two of them took turns visiting each other. But it never failed that every time Riddy visited, something would go on at Arvella's house like the time, Arvella and her big sister got into a fight.

Arvella's sister was mentally ill. The police had to be called and she was carried away in a straightjacket.

Arvella and her sister Shirley had an argument earlier over a guy. Riddy was on the couch with Arvella and she started rubbing Riddy cheek. Riddy felt strange and then all of a sudden the sister Shirley came running down the stairs and jumped on

Arvella for no apparent reason. At least Riddy thought the reason was not valid.

On another occasion, Arvella was smoking a cigarette and was trying to get Riddy to take a smoke. Riddy slapped the cigarette out of her hand, and went home mad after announcing,

"You can't make me do nothing!"

On a day when Arvella and Riddy were on their way to school something else happened. In the eighth grade, Riddy's favorite subject was history. Mr. Robert White made history exciting. The only complaint that Riddy had about Mr. White was that he wore too much cologne. All the girls loved Mr. White. Riddy saw him as a father figure.

It was on the way to school that Arvella revealed her hair-brained scheme. Inside her big black purse was a black lace negligee. Arvella told Riddy,

"I am in love with him."

"With who?" Riddy asked.

"Mr. White," Arvella answered while giggling. Arvella further informed Riddy that,

"I'm going to sneak into the bathroom and put this on for my man in between classes."

"How are you going to do that without anyone noticing you?" Riddy inquired.

"With my coat silly," Arvella said.

"I'm not the one," Riddy retorted.

Just thinking about what Arvella had cooked up caused beads of sweat to pop up across her forehead. Her hands grew clammy as the class period was about to end. Sure enough, Arvella's lustful nature could linger no longer and she got a washroom pass from Mr. White. She returned with her black shiny coat on with leaving little to the imagination underneath.

The bell rung and the class emptied out. Arvella and Riddy's eyes locked as Arvella was leaving out of the classroom.

It was ten minutes later when commotion was heard throughout the hall. Riddy stuck her head out of the door and Arvella was standing in the hall, but not alone. The principal, assistant principal, counselor, and Mr. White were all in a panic and screaming at Arvella. She was dragged down the stairs by security. Arvella was crying as she was escorted away.

Big Mama told Riddy to stay away from Arvella. Arvella was troubled. It was just as well because strange things started happening the last few times that they were together.

When the two of them were alone, Arvella started rubbing and twisting Riddy's hair. Then Arvella rubbed Riddy cheek lightly. Riddy slapped her and ran once again out of Arvella's house. Then the grand finale took place, and the straw that broke the camel's back occurred. Arvella's brother Victor had tried to rape Riddy. Riddy got away with her clothes on.

Riddy later found out that Arvella had been expelled from school. Arvella could not live it down. Arvella's Mama and daddy gave her a whooping, and the neighborhood boys were after her like dogs in heat. Eventually, the family moved away. Riddy tearfully found out that Arvella would be going to another school.

Years later Arvella met a nice man named J.C., got married, and had children. She also became a nurse, and then a minister. Arvella's life turned around.

Riddy was the only one to miss Arvella and her family. The neighbors considered them as pests, and would call them the foot family because of the way all of them walked, swaying back and forth, and acting as though their feet hurt.

Lynn had gone boy crazy and was sneaking guys into her house, but Big Mama caught her, and told Alice and Lucille. Alice had been working nights. That's when her three children began to roam the streets.

The last time Riddy spoke to Lynn, it was about her future. Lynn wanted to be a nurse. But Lynn had now fallen, head-over-heels in love with a guy named Ricky.

Riddy's cousins Winnie and Neecie had their own circle of friends. Ms. J would include Riddy in her family outings to the beach, White Castles, and to her church. Ms. J was very popular with the young adult, and the adult choirs. She was a mentor to people like Cornelius, Maurice, Marie, and James. This bunch was always coming over to the family building for the holidays.

All of Riddy's cousins were in the choir at a church that Riddy was invited to visit. Riddy met a lot of interesting people. She later stopped hanging around Ms. J because Riddy just did not fit in no matter how hard she tried.

The eighth grade was Riddy's year! She played in the school band, although she would have to go across the street to another school name Faraday that had a partnership with Marshall Upper Grade Center to share resources including its Music Department. Riddy had to leave out in rain, sleet, and snow to be yelled at by an overworked Mr. Garfield who was the band teacher.

Riddy wanted to play the flute, but Mr. Garfield said that Riddy's lips were too thick. No one was allowed to play the flute. According to Mr. Garfield, "One must have thin lips to play the flute." In other words, he was saying that she had to be white to play the flute.

Riddy spent every evening since the sixth grade on the back porch. Big Mama assigned the area for Riddy to practice playing the alto saxophone. Mr. Garfield would not even let her play the clarinet—big lips, again. Riddy's only comfort was her upcoming graduation, which was only two months away.

Mr. Garfield was always yelling and calling his class dumb. And the closer they got to graduation, the worse he acted. One day Mr. Garfield went too far with his insults. Riddy walked out and refused to practice or to play with the band for the eighth grade graduation. Mr. Garfield later apologized, and Riddy got back in the band before the eighth grade graduation.

At Faraday there were two teachers everyone always whispered and wandered about, and they were Ms. Palace and Ms. Ellen. Ms. Ellen was a big boned gal from Texas who was over six feet tall and had blonde hair. Ms. Palace was the opposite. She was a shorty, who wore three-inch spike heels. She had dark features for a white woman. Her hair appeared to be dyed black, and she wore heavy black eye liner, black mascara, and black lipstick. She also wore black, every day. The kids spread a rumor that Ms. Palace was a witch. The kids even commented that Ms. Palace had a fake behind.

It was one month before the school year ended that the two of them were asked to leave, and substitute teachers were placed in their classrooms. The school officials did not explain their departures.

A class trip was planned for the eighth graders to go to Springfield, Illinois, a luncheon, and an award ceremony. Riddy was only interested in the luncheon even through Big Mama tried to talk her into going on the eighth grade class trip to Springfield, Illinois.

Riddy had heard a month before from different classmates who signed up for the trip that they were planning to act a fool while away from home. Riddy did not want to be dragged into it. Riddy sat on the porch with Big Mama and watched down the street as the bus drove off, and Riddy had no regrets, none.

It was exciting taking eighth grade class pictures and being measured for caps and gowns. Riddy felt ugly. She was thin, lanky and had buckteeth. She looked like a rabbit. People told her that she was pretty, but inside, she just would not bring herself to believe it.

Riddy remembered when the three of them Big Mama, Madea and herself went to a studio to have professional pictures taken in her graduation cap and gown. Big Mama had to threaten Riddy to get her to smile. She demanded to see teeth.

The big day came when Big Mama, Madea, Big Dot, Kat, Kat's second husband named Ed, and Johnnie Mae attended the graduation ceremony. Ed, Riddy's father, had to work and Riddy was heartbroken when she heard because he was the love of her life.

However, another Ed came on the scene and Riddy did not like him at all. He wanted Riddy to call him Dad, but she felt that step-dad was suitable. Besides he had the same name as her father.

Ed, Kat's second husband tried to buy Riddy by giving her an expensive silver-toned locket that could hold two pictures. The locket had rhinestones, and military ribbons. Ed was a military man and a chef with Uncle Sam. Kat was crazy about him.

He wanted Riddy to sit on his knee. Big Mama got huffy and demanded Riddy to get off his knee as if she had wanted to be on his knee in the first place.

Big Mama had some strange house rules. And Riddy noticed them when she got older. Riddy could no longer lay on the floor, pants or no pants because testosterone hormones were raging, Big Mama explained,

"And I'm not talking about your hormones, Riddy."

Madea attended Riddy's eighth grade graduation, and she would be graduating the next week from night school, herself.

Riddy's luncheon dress had sheer, long dusty rose sleeves and an empire waist. Riddy's graduation dress was a beautiful white lace, knee-length dress with long double puff lace sleeves.

Thoughts of the graduation also brought about thoughts on what high school to attend. Riddy ran home many days because of the shootouts that took place between the Vice-Lords and the Disciples on the school grounds.

The elementary school that Riddy attended also had a high school. Riddy was doggone if she was going there after having to dodge bullets for three years to have to dodge bullets for another four years.

Riddy heard of a school named Lucy Flowers, and she was eager to attend because there was no swimming pool on the premises. Although it was an all-girls school, the boys would be the first ones on the school grounds before the attendance bell rang. Riddy really wanted to go to Westinghouse, but she did not meet the entrance exam requirements by four points on her reading score. Nevertheless, Lucy Flowers was the ultimate high school experience.

Riddy and Madea attended a freshman orientation which was held in her new school's auditorium. It was so exciting to soon be attending high school. The principal, Mr. Krammer, opened the program, and teachers introduced themselves and their programs. The students were allowed to meet their division teacher and were given their home-room numbers, and paperwork.

Ring! Riddy glanced over her class schedule and began to look for each class as the school bell rang periodically under the watchful eye of hall monitors. The school was enormous compared to her elementary school, and there was no teacher to follow around like she was a baby chick. Freedom!

It was during midday, Riddy went into the school cafeteria. After getting her lunch, she took a deep breath and entered the lunchroom. It was filled with girls all over the place. It was very loud and bursting with energy.

Riddy looked and there was Arvella with a group of girls. Although the family moved from off Monroe, Arvella was allowed to attend Flowers. Both Riddy and Arvella smiled and acknowledged each other. It was when Riddy looked to her left that she saw Lynn with a group of girls. They nodded in acknowledgement of each other, too. The two girls had chosen other friends, who were like-minded, boy crazy, so Riddy thought hard about whether or not she wanted to sit with either of them.

Riddy spotted a table where a girl was sitting, quietly keeping to herself. She walked over and asked if she could join her. Mary smiled, and the two introduced themselves. Both girls were freshmen.

Riddy thought Mary was too old to be a freshman, but said nothing about it. Mary voluntarily explained that she had a child and missed a year or two out of school. But now she was back on track. Mary spent the lunch period talking about Harold her man and Krystle her daughter. The bell rang then it was off to English.

Chapter Nine

Ms. J, Riddy's aunt, played for The Pilgrim Rest church's choir and was in charge of the young adult choir. A young man named Cornelius sings lead and sometimes solos under the direction of Ms. J. Everyone enjoyed listening to Cornelius singing. It was as if he could do no wrong.

Riddy would attend church with her aunt where she met Cornelius. At some outside church activities Ms. J would chaperone the young adults. While Riddy and her best friend Ronnie, who came along to the Starrock State Park beach outing, walked away for a minute, Cornelius tried to make a pass at her.

She slapped him and said, "I am going to tell."

Cornelius begged, "Don't tell, don't tell," because he was eighteen and Riddy was only a teenager.

It was also while all the fireworks were going on when Riddy's sister, Serena was drowning at the beach.

Serena had to be rescued, and thank God, it was by a nearby lifeguard. Unfortunately, this would be the beginning of the deterioration of their relationship as sisters. Riddy and Serena were kind of close in their teen years; however, when Riddy was younger, Big Mama would ship her off to Johnnie Mae's.

Riddy is the oldest. She ended up with big Mama. Kat did not show up in court and the judge gave Ed custody of the other two children.

Johnnie Mae was meaner than a rattlesnake. She was very bitter because Ed's father, Hiawatha, did not know how to treat her. Riddy eventually told Big Mama that she did not want to visit Johnnie Mae ever again.

Johnnie worked at a drycleaners and was very bow ... or rather ... woooa legged. She had rheumatoid arthritis and constantly rubbed her hands and knees with Bengay, and took aspirin for relief. Riddy went to work during the summer months to help Johnnie Mae at the cleaners. She got to meet Johnnie Mae's boss, Heiman.

Riddy looked forward to going downtown grocery shopping with Johnnie Mae. They returned with that famous Hillside coffee cake with the pecan icing.

Johnnie Mae was cool to be around until she started talking about Kat. Johnnie Mae's outbursts of,

"The heifer didn't even show up in court to claim you all,"

or

"That's not a mother, that's a mammy," would run rampant.

Riddy grew tired of her outbursts and never returned to visit Johnnie Mae, her sister, brother, or not even her love for fried tomatoes and eggplants with rice — the dish that Johnnie Mae cooked so well. Enough was Enough. *Good bye Johnnie Mae*, was Riddy's thought cemented in her heart

Johnnie Mae would always talk about the children's mother in their presence. One time, Johnnie Mae told Riddy while striking a match and smoking her pipe,

"Your mother, Kat, is nothing more than a heifer, a mammy, and a female dog."

Johnnie Mae even mentioned the times that Riddy, Ed Jr., and Serena all got drunk when Ed and Kat lived together.

Now Riddy vaguely remembered when the three of them were supposed to be asleep, and their parents were having a card game. The three of them crawled out the room, and under the table. My dad before the divorce would get me from Big Mama and force me on my mother for a visit. It felt weird.

They opened the refrigerator and pulled out a huge bottle of beer, and drank it until they had passed out on the floor. Ed and Kat found them intoxicated. Kat wanted to take the children to the hospital, but Ed asked her,

"Are you mad? Do you want to get locked up?"

So, the children had to sleep it off.

Riddy did remember the room spinning, and hearing Ed Jr. complain to Ed.

"Daddy, make the room stand still." Ed Jr. cried out. Ed told this story over and over throughout life.

Riddy could not take it anymore. She also did not feel safe in the house with Johnnie Mae and her second husband, whom she called John even though his name was Nate. These two pistol-packing lovebirds never had children together.

Johnnie Mae kept Ed tied to her apron string. He could never keep a wife because of Johnnie Mae. Although Ed was a grown man, Johnnie Mae always hung out the window looking for him late at night.

Nate would yell at her, "get out the window. Ed is a grown man. Take your titties out his mouth, woman! Nawl, c'mon to bed, Johnnie Mae."

Ed would always come home mugged, and without the rent money. It continuously caused a financial strain on the family. Johnnie Mae always believed that some man, a thug, robbed her son instead of a sweet talking woman disarming him. It made her feel better about it, anyway.

The only time Riddy saw her father was when they slept together. It was very crowded in Johnnie Mae's apartment, so Ed would take little Riddy downstairs to his place on the first floor. Riddy would awaken in the morning to a back turned to her. Ed loved his daughter, and nothing happened. Ed was a good father when one could find him.

Ed moved up to the third floor after getting married for the fourth time. Riddy remembered during the summer of 1966 in which wife number four had jumped out the window from the third floor because Johnnie Mae was getting on her nerves.

Ed and his wife had a fight. He went to work and returned home and started beating on her. He blocked the door way, so she jumped out the window. She broke her legs and was hospitalized. From the hospital, she called the police and he was arrested and denied bail. After recovery she moved back with her folks and divorced him. Johnnie Mae eventually got money to get him out.

Nate died first, and Johnnie Mae's last years on earth was in a nursing home, with her mean self and eventually died.

Riddy was sure that Johnnie Mae was burning in hell. The only thing that Riddy has to remember about Johnnie Mae is her love for eggplant and a polarized picture of her and Nate. This is the legacy that was passed on from Johnnie Mae. *Sad*, she thought.

As for the rest of the kinfolks, Riddy stayed away, especially after a cousin tried to kiss her on the mouth. Riddy was about seven years old and her fourteen year old pervert cousin tried to kiss her.

Riddy had a cousin named June Bug who tried to make a pass at her and wanted her to hold his private part. Yuk. This happened in the living room, while Big Mama was in the kitchen stirring a pot. The Bug had sat in Riddy's rocker and motion for the seven-year-old to come and sit on his lap. Then he unzipped his pants and tried to get her to hold his penis. But seven-year-old Riddy would not cooperate. Riddy grew uneasy, she began to cry, and was rescued by Big Mama when she heard Big Mama's voice call out from the kitchen.

"Riddy, baby, you all right. C'mere, child."

June Bug had to turn her loose for fear he might get caught. Riddy leaped out the chair, off his lap and ran to safety. She never told, but hated June Bug ever since.

* * *

Riddy sat in English class behind a queer looking, triangular face, light-skinned, girl who had stunning light brown eyes named Wanda. The two hit it off. Riddy was slowly making friends. She then met Trafalgar in History, and Barb in gym class.

Trafalgar is a class mate that Riddy met in the Cooperative Laboratory Program (CLP) in her junior year in high school at Lucy Flower Vocational. Trafalgar lived in the Henry Horner Projects on the west side of Chicago.

Wanda came along with Riddy to the lunch room and sat there with Barb who had just met Karol, Lynnette and Rory. This completed the clique. This would be the group that would spend four years and beyond studying, laughing, and crying together. Some would become athletic; some would become scholars; while others would still be trying to find their way to get the feel of their life, and the world. This core group became inseparable, unstoppable and an unbeatable force in high school.

Riddy also made friends outside the core. She was very popular. She met Deb, Mary, Tresh, Jo, Del, Rory, Linda, and Arlene. Riddy pretty much communicated with them on an individual basis. She enjoyed them too.

The biggest events during her freshman year were the big sister/little sister get together, parties, and assemblies. Everyone wanted Vicky Dickens to be their big sister.

Vicky was a very popular senior, poised, and with a good head on her shoulders. However, she had archenemies that were jealous because Vicky had long, wavy hair, and looked white rather than high-yella. The entire freshman class was sad when Vicky had got into a fight and got suspended. If that was not enough, she suffered a broken leg due to the fight.

The school counselor assigned seniors and freshmen. Riddy ended up with a senior who name was Vicky, but she was not any Dickens and the total opposite of the Vicky Riddy knew.

The seniors were supposed to show the freshmen the ropes. However, some showed the wrong ropes. It was everyone's duty to talk over the phone, meet, and study together. The seniors were told that they could give advice, but if something was more than what they could handle then they were instructed to report it to one of the freshmen school counselors.

During Riddy's time at Lucy Flowers, there were twelve hundred girls occupying the school. In its heyday there were still whites attending as well as Latinos, and Blacks. It was three to a locker, and two to a gym locker. You were left with ten minutes for lunch once you got out of the long lines.

Vicky Matthews was always sleepy, and had a strange odor about her. Eventually, Vicky got caught with marijuana, and she was pregnant. She got expelled from school, so much for a mentor.

The core spent the summer visiting each other, playing basketball, and shooting the breeze. Summer was great. The core would go to the park often and shoot hoops and neighborhood boys would challenge them in a game of basketball. The girls always would snicker and win. Then the core took turns hosting get-togethers at each other's houses.

Riddy was excited when her turn would come around. They would follow the same format and that was to hit the living room and everyone would lie on the floor and stare at the ceiling talking about their boyfriends, school, and future plans. Although they took turns, most of the get-togethers were at Karol's.

Karol's living room was bigger on Polk Street and the core would practice dance steps to prepare for Flower's open house and school orientation day. They had recently practiced the funky chicken and the robot off of Billy Preston blasting instrumental song. They were always listed on the program and would be a big hit each and every time. Plus the group would also sing in the gospel choir.

Ding Dong, September rolled around and the school doors swung open. It was Riddy's sophomore year.

In the mid-year, the core was sitting at a table. Everyone but Riddy was talking about their boyfriends they had met over the summer. Riddy was not sure if she wanted a boyfriend. She had a bad experience that involved a boy, and her friend, Mary. She thought Mary was her friend, but found out that she was not.

In December of Riddy's freshman year, Mary invited Riddy to a party. She begged Big Mama to let her go. It was against Big Mama's better judgment. Riddy did not want to be treated like a baby.

Madea took Riddy shopping for a knickers set. It was a black silvery gray set. Riddy wore a huge Afro around this time.

At the party, she met a man who claimed to be only nineteen. The dark shadow that hovered over Riddy at three months old near the swing that she was left in has appeared again. This shadow would not go away.

Chapter Ten

Mary's mother had about twelve children. Riddy only met one of her sisters and two of her brothers, Ronnie and Ernest. The brother named Ernest was interested in her. Ronnie was a friend who attended the church outing where Serena almost drowned.

During school, in the lunch room, Mary invited Riddy to a party that was happening on the weekend. Everyone could not wait because this party was going to be *jumping*. Smoking, drinking, dancing, card playing, food and some other activities.

Now to convince Big Mama, Riddy had to beg and plead for a week to go to the party and begged Madea to take her shopping for an outfit.

The day of the party, Riddy put on her new outfit, made sure her hair was beautiful, and everything else was together. Madea was in the car waiting because she already told her that she was coming at a particular time to take her to the party and would be picking her up at mid-night from the party.

While at the party, Ernest came over and let her know that he was Mary's brother and they both sat on the couch talking for a while. Riddy was almost staring thinking to herself, *he is talking to me?* He looked really really good. She did not want him to know, this was her first party. The conversation continued. One thing led to another, and the two snuck off that night at the party to talk because the music was loud and other people were talking. After having a great conversation, they exchanged phone numbers and stayed in touch.

Two months later, he called and they met. The relationship continued at different locations so that they could spend time together. It became a one-sided relationship. Riddy was young, only fourteen years old. Ernest was eighteen so he said.

One evening on the phone Ernest convinced Riddy to cut class and come by his parent's house. Riddy fell in lust. She found herself cutting classes and forging notes to get back into school, undetected by Big Mama. Also, for a period of time,

Riddy separated herself from the group. This man became her world.

Then Riddy's art teacher talked to her after her art class, one afternoon. She told Riddy that she was a beautiful girl, and did not need to be with that older guy who was only after one thing. The art teacher had seen them together in a park, after school. And, immediately the teacher knew what was up. Then Riddy's history teacher whom she admired gave her the same speech, but Riddy would not listen. Before long, Riddy and Big Mama began to have disagreements.

Riddy met Ernest (nick name Ern) at his mother's house. He wanted Riddy to prove her love for him. He took her into the bedroom. It was an awful painful experience. Riddy was thinking, *why did I go this far and lose my virginity at such a young age*. It seemed right at the time.

Ronnie, Mary and Ern's brother Riddy's best friend, was in to fashion. He was very stylish in his attire and a great dancer. He and Riddy would practice dance moves together. She met him through her classmate Mary at Flowers. Ronnie and Riddy had a platonic relationship. He was a really great friend. They spent lots of time together.

Then Riddy found out through Ronnie that Ern had two girlfriends and each one of them had babies by him. One girl had seven children by him while the other had five. Riddy was shocked, and hurt.

If Mary, Riddy's friend, knew all about this, then she did not care about Riddy, either. Only Ronnie cared. Ronnie respected Riddy and told her that she deserved much better. Ronnie never ever tried anything with Riddy. The day that Riddy found out that Ern was no good she called it off, walked out the house, and walked across the school grounds back to her home.

Riddy walked through the kitchen, dining room, and onto the front porch, where Big Mama sat alone in meditation. Big Mama missed her companion. She was praying, while trying to give her great-granddaughter some space to come to her senses.

Riddy came behind Big Mama and told her she was sorry, and they both cried. Riddy never saw Ern again nor spoke to Mary.

The group was glad to see Riddy and welcomed her back. No one asked any questions.

She went home and thought about praying instead of leaping out there again. She did not ask God about Ern. It had been a rough freshman year, so Riddy prayed that she would meet someone, especially before junior and senior proms.

In the sophomore year, the school threw a half-cap day celebration. Everyone in the group, but Wanda, would learn a dance called the robot. Wanda did not have any rhythm.

Madea allowed Riddy to buy a lace white body blouse that snapped underneath the crotch, snug black pants that split on each side, and white go-go boots. Riddy had to work on her Afro.

Riddy was also in the color guard and was co-captain with Barb. The two of them had to open up the assembly, and had the other guards to post the flags. The American flag and the school flag had to be posted.

Riddy remembered how Ms. Stayack, the Color Guard teacher, had a group to audition for a position in the color guard. Riddy was nervous, and sure enough, although she was last on the list to be chosen, she rose to the rank of co-captain. They wore a uniform and opened up all school assemblies with the American Flag, and the School Flag in a march from the rear of the auditorium where both the co-captains would take turns yelling, "Color guards attention". The guards would march in place then the co-captains would yell, "Forward march," and the guards would move down the aisle then up the stairs onto the stage and they would receive instructions to lower the flags into the ports on stage. Riddy was a color guard from sophomore to senior year, and it was then that she became a captain.

On half-cap day, a celebration of being mid-way through high school, all sophomores received a paper graduation cap in the school colors brown and gold. There was also a program and a luncheon immediately afterwards. Riddy was so happy that both Big Mama and Madea came.

Riddy and Barb had to hurry up and change from their uniforms and into their outfits for the dance. Well. Riddy lived during the time before panty hose where women and young girls wore girdles and stockings. When panty hose came on the scene women wore panties under the panty hose so Riddy thought. As the core was racing up the stairs to hurry to the stage to dance after changing out of the color guard uniform except Wanda who could not dance and was off beat and was not on the dance team, Riddy was alarmed that Wanda had no drawls on with the panty hose just naked meat with lots of hair. It was alarming.

* * *

It would be at the end of the sophomore year that the core would talk about how they plan to spend their summer. Then someone yelled out in September, we will be juniors and prom will be coming up. Everyone had a boyfriend except Riddy. The bell rung and Riddy was left wondering how she was going to get a boyfriend especially for prom. Then she remembered that Big Mama said, "If you ever had a problem or needed something, talk to God." Well God had a pretty good track record with Riddy. After all, He healed her from illnesses and healed her from a learning disability, too. Now, surely God can give her a boyfriend.

Riddy saw Steve at a school dance held at Cregier High School, which was an all-boys school. Then she would see him again at Flower High School. Riddy had begged to go to the dance and glad she was able to go. It was at Cregier that he saw her across the room and asked her to dance. They danced off of The Four Season song, "I Love You For All Seasons" that would definitely be prophetic for them for the next 40 years.

Anyway Steve had a friend named Danny. Riddy liked Danny but to get to Danny, she had to go through Steve. She invited both Steve and Danny to the house. They brought another friend over to Riddy's. She invited two girlfriends and tried to put one off on Steve, but he was not having it. After a few phone calls Danny kind of disappeared. She later found out that Steve had something to do with the disappearing act. However, Steve got Riddy's attention, and she fell in love with him and that love would be eternal.

Steve did not look so bad now with Danny gone. He matured. From then on, the two became an item. Steve was Riddy's life. She had someone to go to the prom with.

Steve gave Riddy his class ring and a pillow with his picture on it and she showed it off to the group who nodded with approval. Riddy met his parents and siblings over dinner.

Steve, Flo, Riddy and Dan sat at the dinner table.

Flo, Steve's mother said, "Steve talks about you all the time. Here is Dan my baby and all my other children are grown and on their own. My oldest daughter is named after me and lives in Flossmoor with her husband and children. I have a son name Joe and he is married and lives on the South side as well as my daughter Della who is a military nurse that travels and have been all over seas. Then there is Rebie who lives out south with her husband and family. It's just myself, husband, Steve and Dan. So tell me about yourself Riddy."

Riddy said, "Well. I live on Monroe and Kedzie and go to Flower High School. Steve and I met at a dance. I love to dance and majoring in science. I live with my great-grand mother, grandmother, and grandfather."

"Do you travel? Do you like to read?"

Riddy answered, "I love to travel. Big Mamma and I go south, but it's been awhile since we been anywhere."

"Yes, I enjoy reading. Now, I am reading 'Gone With The Wind' and find romance novels to be interesting."

Steve introduced Riddy to fine dining. She was used to eating at home or with friends. He took her to plays and candlelit dinners. Steve was romantic. He learned his trade from his mom who wanted to teach her sons to give what she was not getting because her husband was a hermit.

* * *

Another big event during Riddy's sophomore year was when she walked home from school. Madea always dropped Riddy off at Flowers on her way to her job as a crossing guard. She used to let Lydia ride, too, when Lydia was not dragging her feet about being on time or shuffling around with an attitude. Madea would tell her off because Lydia had adapted the attitude that Madea was supposed to do for her.

Since Riddy got rides to school, she would walk home and used her bus fare to purchase butter cookies and chocolate milk. And sometimes she would stop at a restaurant called Coleman and buy chicken wings or a foot-long polish sausage.

Well, it was another hot summer day, Riddy was dressed in her yellow and white hot pants set and sporting her white go-go boots. Riddy heard her name being called, and turned around into her biological dad's face. She was so happy to see him. Riddy had not seen Ed since she was twelve years old.

She was jumping up and down hugging him, when a short plump woman with her hands on her hips asked Ed what was going on. Ed chuckled and introduced his daughter to Mary, Riddy's new stepmother.

Mary embraced Riddy, and Riddy found out that they lived two doors down from the restaurant where she was about to buy a foot-long polish. Riddy was invited upstairs into their cozy apartment.

Ed said laughing, "This is Riddy my daughter. Riddy this is Mary. I got married again. Meet your stepmother."

Mary said, "Let's go inside."

Everyone walked inside the apartment after climbing a lot of stairs. Ed was out of breath when he got to the top.

Mary said, "Excuse the place we just moved in. Riddy you are welcome to move in and live with us if you like."

Riddy said, "Nawl. I like where I am."

"Well come and visit us anytime."

Riddy noticed although Mary was an older woman at least twenty years Eddie's senior, she had a beautiful personality.

Riddy kissed them both, excused herself because it was getting late, and she did not want Big Mama and Madea to worry about her. Plus no one knew she had gone over to Ed's house. Big Mama and Madea would have killed her if they knew she walked home.

Chapter Eleven

Ed and Mary had plans to buy another home and move the children, Serena, Ed Jr., and Riddy, in with them.

Mary invited Riddy to live with them. Riddy declined. This was about the third time someone tried to take Riddy away from Big Mama.

The first time occurred when a couple that were relatives, invited her to their home. They lived in Wisconsin, but came to visit Big Mama, Madea, and Big Dot. Upon Riddy entering the room the lady started throwing her wealth around.

She asked Big Mama if she could talk to Riddy. Big Mama said to her, "Well, you can talk to her, but she is not going to go with you." The lady explained how she could buy Riddy a car when she turned sixteen. Riddy, at the time, was ten years old.

The lady told Riddy about the beautiful house that she would live in. "And Riddy," the lady said, "You could attend a private school. Wouldn't that be nice? etc., etc., etc."

The lady told Riddy that she could live with her. But she promptly and politely said, "No thanks," before turning on her heels and heading to go outside to play. Big Mama sat silently, holding on to, *I-told-you* grin.

The second time was when Riddy was eight years old, and visiting Johnnie Mae when her father was still living with his mom. He had gotten mad because she would not give him a hug. Ed pulled out some court papers and shoved them in Riddy's face.

"You belong to me," Ed said, waving the court papers around,

"And, I can take you away from Big Mama any time I want to, young lady."

Riddy's heart fell. It trembled because she did not want to leave Big Mama, and because she did not want to hug Ed not only because it had been such a long time in between visits, but also because he had the nerve to show up drenched in the stench of liquor. His eyes were redder than hell, itself.

* * *

During high school, Ms. Barto, a German woman with masculine features asked Riddy if she would like to be a science major. Riddy's friends had already declared their majors. Karol, Lynette, and Rory were all business majors. Viv and Barb were home economic majors. Riddy made very good grades in biology, so she agreed to become a science major.

Ms. Barto had a hard time finding a lab for Riddy to do her laboratory internship. Riddy was always picked over.

Being a science major, Riddy made a couple of friends within the CLP circle. She made friends with another girl named Linda who was a year ahead and worked at a neighborhood clinic.

Linda was crazy about a guy named Rob. Riddy went to visit Linda in the hospital, and she was told that her friend was on the abortion floor. However, when Riddy questioned Linda, she was told that, that was not true. Riddy was confused. Her mind went back to the reason why she met Linda. I met her in the Lab Program at Flower High School. When a girl got pregnant in high school, she got married but Rob dumped her. He did not conform to the social norm.

Riddy had hoped that she would be accepted at the neighborhood clinic that Linda worked at, but it did not work out for her. Riddy's friend outside of the core group named Tresh was hired instead.

Riddy learned to always be happy for other people when they got a break. However, Riddy began to feel bad because after going on a number of interviews, other people were accepted. She even had laboratory experience from the previous summer.

In the summer of Riddy's junior year, Ms. Barto told Riddy about a fantastic opportunity that was being offered at the University of Illinois. Madea drove Riddy to University of Illinois to complete an application, take an exam, and participate in an interview.

Riddy was interviewed by an East Indian man who really wanted to hire Riddy for the summer, but commented that her math scores were too low. So, after debating with himself, he gave Riddy a chance.

Riddy was given her start date, and she did well at the microbiology laboratory. While Riddy was there to get experience as well as a check, and in addition to that, she had a deep love for science, she did notice how some of the others were only there for the money. How unfair, she thought.

The training that was given to the students was superb, but one day a male peer got obnoxious and disrespectful. Clift, a student, shoved and bullied the teacher while everyone looked on with fear and disbelief. Clift was terminated from the training, and another instructor finished up the summer institute.

So, even with that experience under her belt, it seemed as though Riddy could not get her CLP internship anywhere, not even for free labor! Now Ms. Barto explained that some would get paid for part-time work, and some would not, but to keep their mind focused on acquiring credits so that they could graduate.

Riddy even had an interview at Cook County Hospital and was turned down. Riddy's next stop was an interview at Bethany Hospital, where she met and was interviewed by a really good looking laboratory director. God made sure that she did not get placed there.

However, another babe named Artis ended up there and became his mistress. Oh girl got the chance to go on trips, shopping sprees, and always had a pocket full of money. The man even bought the girl a car.

Artis was the envy of all the CLP girls. Everyone made a code of silence to make sure that Ms. Barto would not find out. It puzzled everyone how did Artis get all the attention, when Eva, her sister, worked there before her.

Thomas only had eyes for Artis. The fun had to end when Artis started coming to school with shades on and sleeping a lot during classes. Her great life was catching up with her. Artis was pregnant and chose to keep her baby. Thomas refused to leave his wife to be with her, and the romance ended.

However, Artis continued to work at Bethany until it was closed down, and of course she was forced to make a career change.

Ms. Barto wanted to talk to Riddy after class. She told Riddy to be encouraged, and she had a place to send her, but Riddy could not tell anyone. At the time, it was Riddy and JoAnne who were left without a lab. So, Riddy got Madea to buy her a white lab coat, and placed it in a brown bag, and Riddy hid it in her hall locker.

Ms. Barto placed Riddy at Mary Thompson Hospital after training for one year in the school's CLP. Riddy was interviewed by a petite lady named Ruth. She liked Riddy right away. Riddy felt good about her interview with the lab supervisor and the pathologist.

Riddy did get the job at Mary Thompson hospital and felt excited about working in an actual hospital's laboratory. She made friends with two sisters that were very attractive, Precious and Priscilla. It was hard to tell the difference between the two. One sister had red hair while the other had black hair. If it were not for the hair color, anyone could have thought that they were twins. Later they both lost their jobs due to being involved in a prostitution ring.

One day Riddy was driving Madea's car, and after stopping at a light she saw the two sisters working the street. They saw Riddy, and waved, probably because they did not know what else to do. Riddy never told anyone about what she saw the sisters doing, but you could see the fear on Precious and Priscilla's face whenever Riddy came around.

Riddy was too shocked to say anything. Well, someone else saw them, and before everyone knew it, the police had handcuffed them and removed them in broad day light from the premises of Mary Thompson Hospital.

Chapter Twelve

Riddy was the baby of the lab. Everyone took to Riddy even Bill who was a stone alcoholic. Bill taught her how to do a venipuncture "how to draw blood". At first she was afraid then it was fun to see blood flowing from people's veins like how music flows from the notes on a page.

Bill was the laboratory chemist. Then there was Geri, the hematologist, and Eartha the urinalysis technician. Every day after one o'clock in the afternoon, Riddy dashed with excitement to the laboratory.

Riddy's high school, Flowers, was on Lake Street. She would take the Lake Street bus to Ashland and be at work in a snap. Riddy met a lot of interesting people and even got paid for her work. At lunchtime she shared as much experience that the core could stomach. The core had jobs as secretaries in offices, and law firms. Then there were those who worked at Jewels, the largest supermarket chain in the Chicago area.

It was near the end of Riddy's junior year, and everyone looked forward to the senior year. Steve was already a senior and asked Riddy to be his prom date. Riddy was excited. She hurried to buy her dress and shoes. Steve bought Riddy a corsage. On the day of Steve's prom, his sister Theresa did not like Riddy's dress or hairdo. Theresa felt that Riddy looked too plain, and not trashy enough. Theresa did try to spice up Riddy's look every time she and Steve would visit.

Theresa lived on the south side of Chicago. She was a part of the Section 8 program, and got a house built from the ground up. She was very temperamental, and her marital problems ran rampant, off and on.

Steve and Riddy even began to talk about getting married. But every time they would talk about marriage, Riddy got an unexplainable, funny, gnawing feeling in the pit of her stomach that she just could not shake. And on top of that, the core did not like him anymore.

The core all began to say that there was something about him that they could not put their finger on. The first year, they liked him; but as time ticked by, the dislike began to surface. Everyone in the core had someone now. Riddy wanted to keep her someone, too.

Wanda in English whispered that she needed Riddy to go over to her grandmother's house after school. Wanda was so giggly. After school the two entered the house. In the living room, Riddy glanced at the picture of Wanda's mom in a military nursing uniform with a cape. Except for the thick horn-eyed glasses and a slight aging in the picture, one would think that the woman in the photograph was Wanda. It never made sense to Riddy why Wanda never lived with her mom and two brothers.

Wanda spilled the news about Mr. Bate. A man! He was a full-blooded grown-tail man. She met Mr. Bate at her church and he was not only single, but also handsome and available. Mr. Bate was twenty-five years old. Riddy was shocked. Wanda said that she did not want a boy. So here, now, was a man. And the strangest thing was that it was okay with Wanda's maternal grandmother.

You see Mr. Bate was buying expensive things and household items. He was very charming. Wanda was jail-bait at the age of sixteen, but only if someone would have reported him. Mr. Bate resembled Ramsey Lewis a little, and he was a computer operator at Mercy Hospital.

Karol who could pass for white except for her nappy, dyed red hair was short and she was built like a robot. She always won dance contests, and taught those who had rhythm in the group how to boogie down.

Karol formed the dance group and the core would perform on the school stage, at parties, and other functions. Karol met a guy named James who was a mechanic and who also was twenty-something. He always picked up Karol from school. He was her chocolate milk dud.

Barb met Melvin, but it was not clear what he did. He was the love of her life. Barb was high-yella and a good dancer. Melvin was Blue-black and was a contrast to Barb's color tone. He was short and stocky and butt ugly. Well to each his own and beauty is in the eyes of the beholder and the goal was to have prom dates. Get a boy in a tux and make a man out of him.

Viv met Elbert. She seldom talked about him. Viv became awfully clumsy in her junior year. She began to run into doors. Fall down stairs and always insisted on wearing dark glasses. We would find out later, what that really meant—that Viv was being physically abused.

Wanda was having weird experiences, too. She was always wearing scarves around her neck. One day a scarf fell off and red bumps were all lined up around her neck like something or someone had been chewing on her. Riddy spied it, and nervous Wanda hurried to put the scarf back around her neck. Riddy knew they were hickies and that her boyfriend rather twenty-five year old man friend was gnawing on her neck.

Then there was Candy whom no one knew anything about. She never talked about men. She was the most mysterious of the members of the core.

Lynnette topped us all in the category of having-a-man. In their freshman year, Lynnette told Riddy how she lost her baby by her teen boyfriend. The baby was born premature and could not survive. Lynnette was heartbroken.

Lynnette had a bad temper. Her and Riddy would fight almost every week because of Lynette's attitude. Riddy tried having a pep talk with Lynette, but she took it the wrong way. Lynette fought so much that she knew how to fight and won every single fight she had. She was eventually suspended from school. While on suspension, Lynette met Nelson at a party.

Nelson was TWENTY-EIGHT years old. Lynnette's mother wanted Nelson for herself. Lynnette was not having it. There was a fist-fight and she moved in with Nelson. The two became a common law couple. The two were still together during Lynnette's senior year.

Back when Riddy was at Marshall and in the eighth grade, she had sat in front of a guy who liked her named Darryl. Well, Riddy would not give him the time of day. He was always pulling her hair. So, Riddy turned around one day after getting fed up and slapped the mess out of him. The two fought inside the classroom, and the fight ended outside in the hallway. Riddy took Darryl's big head and banged it against a locker several times, before teachers ended the fight. Now, how she lost to Cleo is a mystery. She whooped Darryl, but could not beat Cleo. Riddy had four fights in her entire life. There was one fight she had with Lydia's sister and won.

* * *

Riddy's junior year ended with her going to Steve's high school graduation. Steve did not go to college. Steve's ultimate dream was to be a mailman like his big brother, Joe.

In the meantime, he worked at places like Churches Chicken and Burger King. This was in contrast with Riddy's para-professional job. On top of that, Steve was always quitting. Every other month he would get a new job. Riddy would just stare at him.

In her core, all of their men-friends had their own places, drove their own cars, and always had money. Steve was still living at home, driving his mom's car, yet he always had money. Steve was definitely a hustler, but he was not stable and it was driving Riddy crazy.

Riddy grew impatient with him. Steve made promises that he could not keep, especially when it came to Riddy's time to go to the prom. Steve promised to rent a car for the prom.

Riddy was dressed and ready. Steve was late and came with no car. Madea told Steve that he could drive her Impala. Riddy was crushed, but got over it, yet something was gnawing at her.

Riddy's senior year was superb. Riddy was ranked twelfth in a senior class of one hundred and twenty students. Some of the core was in the top ten like Karol, Barb and Wanda with Riddy trailing close behind. Everyone had someone to go to the senior prom with. However, most of the core was not interested in the luncheon—with their grown selves.

Riddy had developed a relationship with Del. They went shopping together and wore the same outfits and hairdos at the luncheon. Del was a friend she met in the CLP that she did things with whenever the core had nothing going on.

Dr. Alpana at Mary Thompson Hospital had sent for Riddy one day. A week earlier, Riddy had presented her with a box of chocolates from Fannie Mae. Dr. Alpana talked about how her little girl liked Riddy and Del. Dr. Alpana wanted to know Riddy's plans for the future. Riddy had none. All her life Big Mama told Riddy two things, "Don't get pregnant; and get your high school diploma."

Well the staff at Mary Thompson Hospital had a family atmosphere and everyone knew everybody. Ruth and the other women had grabbed hold of the mission for Riddy to finish school without a baby. Ruth pulled Riddy's coattail and told her to use birth control pills. She warned Riddy how soon she was going to have to start giving it up in order to keep Steve.

Riddy started taking the pill and began to gain weight. She dropped the pill, and started using the diaphragm. The people in the lab kept a close watch on Riddy. After all, she was the baby of the family.

Riddy's guidance counselor nor the division teacher spoke to her about college. Riddy stood before Dr. Alpana's desk and was told she could become a regular employee and could get a raise. She then explained that there were lots of opportunities for women. At this time, Dr. Alpana encouraged Riddy to further her education. She was the only one.

Dr. Alpana leaned forward with her thick black ridge-horn glasses and with a stern look on her face, she told Riddy to check out colleges. Then Riddy was dismissed from her office. Riddy filled out scholarship applications, and an opportunity presented itself for her to win a scholarship as a debutante in a cotillion.

Ms. Barto had read during the summer months about the Lawndale Youth Commission that was looking for Debutantes. Riddy and Rory, a non-core group member, decided that they would represent the school. So, Riddy took a flyer home and showed Big Mama and Madea.

On the first day, Madea took Riddy to the meeting. It was in the basement of a raggedy building. Riddy was not impressed. She told Madea it was time to go, but Madea told Riddy to hang around and see what would happen.

Shortly afterwards, a short stout middle-aged man, who was the dance teacher, using a walking cane entered the poorly heated room and following him was the president of the commission. The president explained the mission and talked about previous cotillions.

He also explained how the contestants would be responsible for selling ads and getting patrons. Those who did well would receive monetary scholarships for college. This sounded good to Riddy, and it was good enough for Madea.

There were approximately thirty females. He told everyone that they needed an escort. A smile came on Riddy's face as she thought about Steve. It would be six weeks of grueling dance rehearsals, catwalks, and selling ads.

The dance coach promoted dirty dancing before they made the movie. Riddy had a problem with intimacy. Riddy's problem with intimacy would become Steve's problem, too. Riddy could not stand for Steve to touch her. His lack of ambition nauseated her.

Every girl was assigned a sponsor for the cotillion and this person's job was to make sure everyone was selling, and knew what was going on. Toward the end, each debutante was expected to write and give a short speech, which would entail their school, status, grade point average, career goals, and aspirations.

The fathers were solicited for a special rehearsal to help their daughters practice their debutante bow. Boyfriends were expected to be at every rehearsal where they would learn the tango, fox trot, waltz and the Charleston, which would conclude with the soul train line.

Now time was to the wire. Everyone was told that the cotillion would take place at the Pick Congress Hotel, and the day and time was given. The girls were told to get white dresses and shoes and not to forget to get their hair done.

Riddy went downtown to search high and low in the heart of winter in December for a white dress. She did not know to go to a bridal shop. Riddy's friend Linda made her own dress for the cotillion.

She found a long sleeve gown, her first, with real fur at the wrist. It was simple, yet elegant with its scoop neck. Big Dot let Riddy borrow her enamel mother of pearl barrette to be worn as a tiara. Riddy found a pair of white platform shoes, too.

The big day came and Big Mama was proud of her baby. Big Mama got so inspired that she bought herself a full-length gown, which was teal blue, and she pulled out a sharp fur coat that was a Hudson Seal.

At one time furriers used to kill baby seals to make coats out of them. Big Mama bought one back in the day. The coat was gorgeous. Big Mama showed Riddy what she was going to wear a few days before the Cotillion.

Riddy asked Big Mama if she could have the coat one day. Big Mama told Riddy that when she died the coat was hers. Big Mama even got her hair done for the cotillion.

Riddy went to Ms. Brown who gave her a fabulous hairstyle. The whole event was like getting ready for a wedding. It would be about as close to a wedding that she would have in life, perhaps.

Steve and the other fellows had to wear a tuxedo with tails and a white ruffle shirt. The girls were kept in a suite separate from the guys, just like a wedding.

The time came when everyone got dressed and met in the hallway. Riddy was crushed when all of the other girls pulled out their elaborate dresses bought at bridal shops. Then to top it off, the director had told the mothers of the girls not to wear white. Somehow one of the mothers did not get the memo.

Well, one brick-headed woman decided not only to wear white, but also she had on the identical dress that Riddy had on.

The mother kept repeating how sorry she was. The director and sponsor comforted Riddy.

It was then time for a group photo. The guys took their pictures first and then the girls.

The fathers escorted the daughters onto the dance floor. One by one, the fathers brought their daughters in. The girls would do the debutante curtsey and the fathers would bow.

Once everyone got on the floor, the fathers and daughters danced the waltz. Then there would be a drum roll, and the escorts marched into the ballroom, tap the fathers on their shoulder to take over dancing with the debutantes. The crowd roared with appreciation and laughter.

Then the announcer cosigned the glorious move, instructing the fathers to move over.

The ladies and their escorts waltzed. The evening moved into the tangle, fox trot, the Charleston and on to the immortal soul train line. Finally, each Debutante glided on to the stage like a Ms. America pageant queen to model their formal wear, and to give their small speech. Each was critiqued by each girl's sponsor.

Then finally the moment came. It was no secret that one of the Debutantes in the cotillion was the daughter of the chairman. So everyone knew that she would become queen. But a weird thing happened, Riddy's sponsor gave her a big hug and said you were supposed to win. The sponsor said I did what I could, then dropped her head and walked away.

Names were being called. After the announcement of the fifth runner up, fourth runner up, and third runner up, Riddy began to fret. Steve comforted Riddy, and whispered to her, "You are going to be called. You are going to get a scholarship for college."

Then the second runner up was called. Then a drum roll was played and Riddy's name was called as first runner up and a glaring spot light beam was shone upon her. She was stunned. Riddy's mouth dropped open. Steve pushes her forward. The announcer who was a white man shook Riddy's hand and gave her a piece of paper.

Debra was called and crowned queen, the one, who said that she wanted to be a doctor. Later on, she ended up being a special education teacher. Life is so strange. Riddy would become a Doctor with a Ph.D. in Pastoral Counseling, Deb did not. Life has lots of ups and downs with twists, turns and curves.

The cotillion was over and concluded with lots of photos with guests, friends and family members. Riddy had a grand time. She felt like a queen and went to sleep with a smile on her face. Sunday was church, and then Monday morning could not come fast enough.

Riddy told the division teacher about coming in first runner up and winning a college scholarship for $750. It was announced later that day over the intercom, and printed in the school's bulletin.

A few months later it was time to be measured for caps and gowns. The prom drew nigh and Riddy had picked out a green gown with a diamond cut outline with pearls at the waist. But one day she was at Marshall Fields and saw a gorgeous peach colored formal gown as she was riding up an escalator. The gown had a turtleneck with white and peach orchid feathers at the sleeves.

Although Riddy bought the second dress, the first gown did not go to waste because the hematologist at Mary Thompson invited Riddy to participate in an Operation Push dinner and fashion show for graduates.

Riddy had to have the other dress for her senior prom, so Riddy bought both dresses.

Riddy's friend Rory almost did not go. Riddy was trying to be Ms. Helpful. Rory had broken up with her boyfriend, Lawrence, who was her escort at the cotillion, so she did not have a date for the prom.

Riddy asked her maternal cousin June Bug "Junior" if he would escort her. Junior was very handsome with naturally curly hair that fell at his shoulder and was parted on the right side. He agreed. "Why not?"

Rory wanted to save money, so she used her white dress from the cotillion. Junior rented a green and white striped tuxedo with solid green pants. Rory made a short dinner jacket out of the identical material, and bought a pair of green shoes to match.

The food was okay. The dancing was great. Then there was the famous soul train line. People told Riddy that she looks like she was shouting in church. The way she was dancing it look like she caught the Holy Ghost.

Lynette said to the core, "Okay after the prom Nelson and I will have the after set at our house. Don't bring no clowns. Don't worry about food or drinks it's all on Nelson."

Everyone chimed in talking about their dates. Riddy asked, "Can we invite people outside our group?"

Lynette answered, "As long as they ain't stupid."

The core and their men went to the after set. Linda and Junior were permitted to come because of Riddy. There was drinking, dancing and partying.

Prior to all that, Big Mama said to Riddy, "Don't let the sun beat you home."

Well, it was three o'clock in the morning when Riddy glanced at a clock, then frantically began searching for Rory. Junior sat in a chair looking amused.

To Riddy's surprise, Rory had gotten sloppy drunk and had climbed into the middle of Lynette's bed. Lynette was busy trying to get folks to go home. Nelson had crashed on the bed as well. Lynette laughed when she saw Nelson slobbering on his cheek and his eyes bulging.

Riddy yanks Rory out of the bed and began slapping her around. Steve and Riddy poured water on her and walked her around. Riddy thought, *c'mon, girl. You can't go home like this*!

Lynette and Nelson made coffee. Riddy peeked out of the window and to her horror it was seven o'clock in the morning. Both the moon and the sun beat her home.

Riddy used the telephone to explain to Big Mama what happened. Finally, Rory came to herself and Steve and I drove her home. Riddy apologized to Junior especially after giving him a speech before prom convincing him not to take advantage of her friend.

Riddy scared out of her wits. "Oh lardy." Riddy said, "Mama, Rory got drunk. Sloppy drunk. We are trying to sober her up. She done got in the bed with Nelson and Lynette. Oh God. She's a mess. Her mother trusted me and Steve with her."

Big Mama said, "It's okay. Get her straight."

June Bug had been the perfect gentleman. Riddy found out that Rory had tried touching him, and he refused her.

Riddy thought that she knew Rory even though she was not in the core. Rory was really a stranger. Upon returning to school the two were walking in opposite directions. They both stopped and looked at each other. Riddy paused then kept walking.

There were lots of graduation rehearsals. Great news of being accepted into colleges and scholarship awards were announced. Riddy had a college to go to and lots of money that would help her get there. She was headed to college. Big Mama, Madea and even Dr. Alpana were so proud of her.

Chapter Thirteen

The next evening, Riddy graduated. It was exhilarating to march in and then to hear Jackie the valedictorian's speech, "It's our time. We are entering the world so let's take it over." Karol was the salutatorian who would later marry her childhood sweet heart and have children.

Years later, Karol graduated from Northwestern University with a business degree. Wanda would go to court reporting school, and open an office of her own business. But the demand would be so great that she would take down her shingles, and become a legal secretary with a prestigious law firm in the Chicagoland area. Barb would be a penal system librarian. Lynnette would become a special education teacher. Lori left Chicago to attend a college out-of-state. No one would hear from her again.

After both the Valedictorian and the Salutatorian addressed the graduating class, and the class president gave her speech, the seniors stood to sing the Hall of Ivy. Riddy got all choked up singing with tears streaming down her face. She wondered what would lie ahead for her life.

Riddy thought she and Steve would marry and have children. Perhaps, she would work in a lab, and Steve would do whatever.

After graduation it felt strange. Life changed after graduation. High School was over. Now, Riddy has to make decisions that would impact her future.

Steve gave Riddy a dozen red roses. Big Mama, Madea, and Johnnie Mae were there. Big Dot was not feeling well, so she did not attend the graduation. Kat did not make this graduation because Riddy refused to give her a ticket.

Before graduation, Kat called demanding a ticket. Riddy told her off.

Riddy's response, "You got to be kidding. Where is your ticket? So you gave me a stereo set and think you should have a ticket. Where have you been all these years??? I am 17 years old and received one present from you. For years you have ignored me and act as if I did not existence. I tried to get to know you and you looked through me. NOW, you want to be my mother?

With a deep sigh and a very low and soft docile mumble Kat said, "Okay."

Riddy slams the phone into the receiver and says, "It felt good telling her off. Yes. It felt very good."

After hearing Riddy hang up the phone, Big Mama dealt with that spirit of pride and self-righteousness.

Big Mama told Riddy, "Always respect your mother. No matter what, your mother will always be your mother."

A few months after graduation, Steve proposed to Riddy and Riddy accepted. The day she accepted his proposal, he took her to Sears and let her pick out any ring she wanted. Steve bought the ring, and the two of them showed Big Mama and Madea. They smiled with approval.

A few days later they were intimate in the tiny apartment that he found for himself and Riddy would visit from time to time.

However, Riddy felt something was very wrong, but could not quiet put her finger on it. Riddy started spending a lot of time alone that summer between her high school graduation and heading to college. She spent a lot of time working in the lab.

* * *

Riddy was an avid reader, the summer before college she dived into a book called the "Brave New World". It was an awesome book. The book covered events way before they took place. The book talked about men traveling to space, and eventually trying to live there. The book had information about a birth control pill for both men and women. The writer of the book spoke of a society that would disrespect the elderly, and approve mercy killing.

She learned that mercy killing is when people are terminally ill or in this case society wants to get rid of the elderly. They are hooked up to IVs and a solution flows through their bodies to end their lives. It is also known as euthanasia.

Riddy remembered looking up toward the sky, and asking God for a daughter one day, and that they would be so close.

She reflected upon a time when Big Mama always showed her lots of love but never hugged and told her she loved her.

Steve pulls up. He and Riddy went inside the house. Steve was visiting and came to pick Riddy up to take her out on a date. Big Mama was inside of Riddy's closet inside of her bedroom. Riddy realized that Big Mama was getting older and would die one day.

Riddy went inside the house and into her room and found Big Mama in the closet. Big Mama was feeling low. She tried to hug Big Mama. She asked Big Mama did she love her. Big Mama would not answer. Riddy ran and told Steve. Both Steve and Riddy entered the tiny closet and hugged Big Mama against her will. Riddy planted a big juicy kiss on her cheek and ran off with Steve, the love of her life so she thought.

Big Mama had a lot of bad relationships and she had married abusive men and it was very difficult to outwardly show affection but Riddy knew that Big Mama loved her.

The night was full of escapades. Steve and Riddy started with a nice quiet romantic dinner at a restaurant near the movie theater. After dinner, they stopped to see a movie and then took a long walk together talking about their future before Steve took Riddy home.

* * *

Summer was a breeze. Riddy began to work full time in the lab to help with the short staffing during the vacation season. Steve went from one Church's Chicken job to the next. Toward the end of summer, Riddy began to wonder where this relationship was going. They started arguing and fighting. Unknown to Riddy, they had outgrown each other.

Riddy thought back to her sophomore year in high school when Steve and his childhood friend Daniel were in the band and they both were musicians. One day they came into the library, and Riddy's eyes met Daniel and her eyes fell on him. Riddy liked Daniel but Daniel never chased her. Then one day she was downtown and ran into Daniel who was all grown up and invited him to her house.

It was late in the evening when there was a knock on the door, a familiar knock. Steve! Daniel and Riddy were sitting together talking about all sorts of things.

Riddy met Steve at the door to tell him that she would see him later. Steve got suspicious and rushed passed Riddy; he saw Daniel on the sofa.

Steve snatched his arm from Riddy and yelled, "I don't believe you."

Big Mama came running out of the kitchen and screamed, "What is going on in here. "The boy done punched a hole in my wall."

Steve leaned forward breathing heavily, "I am sorry Ms. White. I am so sorry."

Steve then dashed out the door with Riddy following behind trying to explain but Steve was not hearing it and drove off. Riddy returned to ask Daniel to leave. Riddy then realized that she never wanted Steve but Daniel.

The next few weeks Steve and Riddy began to talk, again. Riddy finally made amends, but things were not the same between them.

Steve and Riddy drifted apart because Riddy was in college studying and working part time then she was studying for her state board. Then the situation with Daniel occurred which caused an even greater distance between them. They were losing each other.

In the fall, Riddy started college. It was new, exciting, and fun. She met people of all races and nationalities. She was very attractive, and had come into her own, but still, kept to herself.

She met an older guy named William who drove a corvette, and would drive her to work, every day. He never made a pass or invited her out. Somehow he knew she was stuck on stupid.

William was a guy that spotted Riddy in a humanity class and would chat with her afterwards but Riddy would always be in a hurry. So one day William wanted to know why she was rushing after class and she explained that she had to go to work at the hospital. It was from that point that William would take her to work in his yellow sun roof corvette with his fine self, but all Riddy would talk about was Steve, Steve, Steve. And this engineer with a yellow corvette was trying to get to know her so when the semester ended William ended as well.

Riddy had gone to a junior college and in two years finished and graduated with an Associate's Degree. At the graduation, Steve demoted her from red roses to yellow roses, and Riddy did not see the handwriting on the wall. Big Mama was so happy for Riddy and her accomplishment but was not able to attend the graduation because she was not feeling well. She saw her baby in her cap and gown with a radiant smile on her face.

In December, the year before she had to give up her job at Mary Thompson Hospital in order to do an internship, Steve and Riddy started seeing less of each other. When she would call his house, he was always downstairs or at a neighbor's house. Riddy really did not pay attention to what was going on because she had a state board exam to take. So, Riddy spent months studying and preparing. Since Riddy was working in the laboratory without her certification, her pay was less until she passed the state board exam.

Riddy solicited the help of her cousin, Arenda, who was studying to be a Medical Technologist. Riddy went over her house and Arenda helped her review the chemistries and biological sciences that Riddy had to study. But every time she made a visit, Arenda's mom asked her, "Didn't they teach you that in junior college?" She did this every time, but Riddy only attempted to respond to her, nicely, without showing any hurt feelings. She did tell Big Mama about her sister's behavior. Arenda was sweet, but Tillie was something else.

Riddy decided to go on a fast for one week before taking her examination. She asked God to help her. Yes, the same God that helped her learn, get a prom date, and now surely He can help her pass this big four-hour state board examination.

At night Riddy sat at the kitchen table, studying. Big Mama would be right there until she finished. Finally the day came, and Big Mama wished Riddy well.

* * *

Big Mama became awfully sick. Riddy had started having dreams in her senior year in which she saw Big Mama in a white casket, white dress, and with a lilac corsage. Riddy had these dreams for three years.

Although thin and aged, Big Mama wished her Godspeed as she left with Madea to take the test. The test was to be conducted at Michael Reese Hospital. It was mandatory to bring identification, diploma and her transcript.

The room was predominately filled with whites, Asians, and with a few blacks sprinkled about. Everyone's guest had to remain outside of the testing area. Riddy was nervous, but she bowed her head in acknowledgement that God would have to help her.

The test booklet and answer sheet was distributed to everyone. Riddy opened it and proceeded to take the test, only to find out that about thirty percent of its content was not covered during her course of study. She softly prayed and asked God to give her the right answers.

Finally, after four hours Madea and Riddy left. As soon as Riddy got home she went straight to bed, and did not awaken until the next day. Riddy was grateful that she was already scheduled for the day off. The next four weeks were tormenting because it took that long to receive the results of the exam.

Riddy thought she would see Steve more, but the opposite occurred. One day, the two of them got together to visit Steve's mom. Upon leaving, Riddy noticed a young woman who stood in the hall right over Steve's floor watching the two of them, intensely. Riddy felt very strange.

She did not like to be intimate with Steve. It felt weird. She often wondered if this was how people became neurotic.

Steve took Riddy out for a drive and told her he had something to say. It had begun to storm and as the rain drops came down, Steve told Riddy that he was going to have a baby. She ran out of the car.

Steve followed Riddy and grabbed her arm. He said that he only wanted her. After a cooling-off period, the two tried to patch things together.

Steve joined the Service to set Riddy at ease. Steve sent money to her to save for their wedding ceremony and marriage. Steve was expecting Riddy to marry him, but Riddy felt that something was missing and wrong with that picture.

One night Riddy prayed and told God that if He wanted them to get married, then so be it. But if it was not God's will, she wanted Him to separate them. But deep in her heart, she really wanted to marry Steve. Riddy was deeply in love with Steve. It's just things were not coming together. She was expecting God to fix them. After all God had answered all previous prayers favorably.

During the month of February, an envelope arrived from the American Society of Clinical Pathologists. Riddy was nervous. Riddy opened and read the results. The letter started off congratulating her. Riddy was now a certified and registered Medical Laboratory Technician, and had the authority to use ASCP after her name. The credential would give her preference for jobs, and authenticity. Big Mama was beaming with joy.

Tillie and Jon, Arenda's parents, came over. As they were preparing to leave, Big Mama told them to wait a minute because she had something to show them.

Big Mama told Riddy to bring her the results. She handed the paper over to Tillie and she began to read. Tillie's countenance changed.

Big Mama asked her, "Isn't that the same test that Arenda had to take three times and still didn't pass?" Tillie went running out of the room with egg on her face with her husband slowly walking behind her. Big Mama chuckled. Riddy stared in amazement. Big Mama gave Riddy the letter back.

Later that day, the family was having dinner. Big Mama leaned forward and was perspiring profusely. Riddy and Madea helped Big Mama into the car and took her to Dr. May's office.

After the examination, Riddy and Madea entered the room where Big Mama and Dr. Mays were. Dr. Mays announced, "I have sent for an ambulance." Big Mama was in heart failure. Madea and Riddy followed the ambulance to Henrotin Hospital.

Riddy rushed home to tell Steve of Big Mama's plight with a phone call to New York. Steve went off and said that he would be home for the weekend, and he did not care what was going on nothing and nobody was to interfere with the wedding plans this time. Then he slammed the phone on Riddy.

The doctor discharged Big Mama with medication the next day. Sure enough, on a hot summer Thursday, Steve was sitting on the living room couch after Riddy got off work with a strange look on his face. He was not alone, for heartbreak and heartache both sat beside him.

Steve jumped up off the couch and told Riddy that he was tired of her canceling their wedding over and over. Riddy told him that she loved him and was just trying to find the right time. Steve shot back, "If you don't marry me this weekend, we will never get married. I'll marry someone else."

Riddy felt the Irish portion of her heritage flare up inside of her. Riddy had never liked being bullied, intimidated or given an ultimatum. Riddy told Steve that they could not get married at this time, and that she could not leave Big Mama.

On that note, Steve turned his heels, walked out, and slammed the door. Riddy thought, *he'll call later tonight after cooling off.* But then nine o'clock passed, ten o'clock passed, eleven o'clock passed, midnight passed, and then one o'clock in the morning passed. Steve did not call. It started raining hard.

Riddy's stomach began to turn. At ten o'clock in the morning on the next day, Riddy called Steve's house. Steve's mom answered.

"Hi Mrs. Jones."

"How are you, Riddy?"

"I am feeling uneasy with where Steve and I stand."

Mrs. Jones queer response, "I will always love you Riddy. Steve decided to marry Sheila. I tried talking him out of it."

Riddy screams, "WHAT!"

Riddy slowly hung up the phone without saying goodbye and became violently ill. Big Mama was sitting in a chair and saw the look on her face. Riddy climbed into Big Mama's bed and began to cry. She told her what happened.

Riddy told Big Mama, "This is the hardest pill I've ever had to swallow."

Riddy cried into a pillow, and cried herself to sleep. Big Mama sat by the bed with her head hung down. Big Mama was always there to support Riddy, but felt helpless. Howbeit, to Riddy, Big Mama's very presence was comforting. Her presence was soothing even in the midst of emotional pain.

Riddy would have rather been slapped, kicked, hit or even stomped. She felt her insides being ripped inside out, the stuffing knocked out of her. A sharp pain in her stomach, Riddy began to moan. The pouring down rain on the cobber stone ground intensified, and there was no one to help her out the street as she lie next to the hole that she crawled into. This dark shadow continues to follow her even when she thought it was gone because she had not seen it in years.

It was night fall, dark, and wet. She caught glances of neon signs flashing and the headlights of cars. Riddy's hand rubbed her stomach and her head tilted to rest on her right side.

Riddy awakened to go to work the next morning numb. She just went through the motion of the day. After work, at home, Riddy would find herself in the kitchen staring in space, while everyone else would be in the living room, having fun and watching TV.

A dark cloud hung over Riddy's head. THE NEXT DAY, the telephone rang. Big Mama yelled for Riddy to pick up the phone.

Steve was on the other end sobbing, "Riddy, I did not know what I was doing and made a wrong decision. Please forgive me."

Riddy quietly said, "You made your choice," and hung up the phone.

She did not give him time to really tell his side of the story and the reason why he made a hasty decision. It hurt so bad that she did not want to hear his voice.

Steve called long distance from New York. Every day, Riddy took his calls just to hang up on his pitiful pleas.

Riddy called Steve's mom and told her the problem. Mrs. Jones assured her that she would speak with him, so the calls would end. The calls stopped, but then letters started coming to Riddy. She would steam them open to see what he wrote. They dripped with regrets and apologies. Riddy resealed the letters and wrote on the front "return to sender". To make the letters stop coming, Riddy spoke to Steve's mother, again. Finally, they stopped.

Riddy was so distracted by all that was going on concerning her breakup with Steve that she could barely stand to be in the lab, performing the job that she loved. One day, she took an early break and sat in the phone booth talking to her friend, Del, who finally had gotten tired about hearing of the Steve's drama episodes.

Del told her, "Riddy, it sounds to me like Steve just wants to be married—to anyone."

"What!?!"

"Yep. Accept it, Riddy. And just leave it at that," Del said.

"Well, I—"

Del interrupted her, "Stop takin' it is so personal. And stop eggin' on the drama."

"Huh," responded, Riddy. She took a breath. "Gosh, I never thought of it that way, Del. But you know what?"

"Yeah, I know what—life's too short?" Del said. She cosigned with a laugh.

"I think you're right," Riddy said. Her emotional fog was clearing. "This is some madness, Del," she added. And with that revelation, Riddy dropped the Steve drama and all notions of him. She never talked about him or allowed anyone to bring him up in her life.

Men have always been a real pain in Riddy's life. Riddy loved her father, Ed, who was a womanizer. He was too busy chasing women and wine to spend time with his children. Ed's children were always with their grand and great-grandparents. He got caught up in the cycle of the grandparents, and great grandparents raising the children's off springs because the adult children jumped the gun and got married too soon and wanted to relive or try to recapture their childhood.

Sid, Madea's husband, was a flasher before the term became popular. Junior wanted to be felt on. Thurman was gay. Houston and Dwight could not commit to marriage to anyone. They were too much in love with themselves. Riddy thought, *so much for male role models*.

Steve was gone, and Riddy worked on combating her feelings of abandonment and loss or feeling unloved. After Steve, there were rendezvous with men who were mentally or emotionally disturbed. Well, it has been said that you attract what you are.

Curtis from down south came on the scene one summer. He was five years Riddy's senior. The two of them would talk and enjoy each other during the summer, but Curtis had to return and start his senior year in college back down south. All Riddy had to remember him by was a picture.

Men were constantly in and out of Riddy's life. At one point, Riddy counted that there were only five married couples in the history of her family other than the women in the family which was headed by single females. Now Riddy must face an uncertain future. She would have to learn about the love and the protection of God. God's love supersedes any individual, and this is certain. It was before marrying Erle that Riddy was in ten weddings. It got to be pretty embarrassing. Would Riddy always be a bride's maid and never a bride?

Chapter Fourteen

"He's fine. Super fine, but he's not mine," laughed Riddy as she explained the reason behind ordering the ER's laboratory supplies every week instead of monthly.

Stockler, her supervisor, just shook her head, okay, "I do understand that you are trying to get in thick with ole boy, but draining the laboratory account is not okay." Stockler said, chuckling.

"Just cut back a little. I'm just saying."

"Yes, boss," Riddy said.

Fifteen minutes later, Riddy grabbed the steel cart and a requisition list because she was still on her mission to capture Erle's attention, but this time she only ordered half the amount than usual. *Oh that man is gonna be mine*, she thought, *and soon*.

Riddy worked at Mount Sinai when she was in her last year of junior college and was required to do an internship. The program director would not let Riddy stay at Mary Thompson Hospital because they had the hospitals set in which their students could train and was not interested in adding a new site, so Riddy had to resign and accept her clinical internship at Mount Sinai where she remained for two years after graduation and was later hired by Cook County Hospital (CCH) as a Medical Laboratory Technician for the Pathology Department.

Upon finishing her clinical training and part-time stint there were no full-time opportunities in any labs at Mount Sinai Hospital. Riddy talked to Big Dot who retired from CCH and had been its first black supervisor. She told Riddy to contact Ola in HR.

Riddy met with Ola at CCH and saw about ten lab jobs available. Ola sent her on all ten of them.

Riddy's favorite lab was blood bank work, but she did not have the experience, and her clinical did not count as experience. So it was onward to the gastro analysis lab. As soon as Riddy opened the door a pungent odor met her nostrils, and she almost vomit.

She met the chef tech, and just stared at him. This was her out and she blew the interview. She decided after walking in the gastro analysis lab that she did not want to work in that area. Playing crazy was her game plan.

Ola was irritated, and reviewed with Riddy the various comments that were made about her. "People are saying that you are not talking with anyone, and you just sit there and stare."

Ola had a disgusted look on her face when she added, "Well, I got only one last place to send you."

She handed Riddy a slip with the name and address on it, and said, "So make an impression—a good ... impression. Go to the Hecktoen Building, and see Mr. Martin."

Riddy took the slip of paper, but thought, *What's the point.* She had been to surgery, gastro analysis, hematology, chemistry, microbiology, Fantus clinic, and other labs. All that was left was Hecktoen.

Very discouraged, Riddy entered the lab with an attitude, and shoved the paperwork at Mr. Martin. Then she sat down and stared at a wall, and glanced only once at the man because of an unusual odor swirling about him.

Mr. Martin was smoking a pipe at work? *Ahhh, nawl. Can't be. Yep.* He smoking a pipe. Mr. Martin towered over six feet, and had a full head of hair—at 50ish. *But he would be considered handsome,* she thought, *if you like that type.* The strangest thing that happened that day was that Mr. Martin asked only one question.

"When can you start?"

"Huh," was Riddy's first response as she swung around in her chair then she said, "In two weeks."

"Good. It's a done deal," Mr. Martin said, while extending his enormous hand to seal the agreement. Martin gave Riddy her paperwork and before turning around to head back to the HR office, he said, "Take a ride to the basement and go to room Basement Number Three next to the morgue."

"MORGUE?" Riddy asked

"The morgue," he said, not responding to her shock.

Really??? Was Riddy's thought, but she held it in.

"Ask for Gaston." Mr. Martin said, "That's your supervisor, and she will sign-off on this paper work."

Riddy left Mr. Martin's office, and shot down to the basement below his office and scooted, nervously, pass the morgue. *Hmmm, that's what kept me from becoming a Registered Nurse*, she thought.

In school, she had the grades, stamina, and the interest, but was scared of dead people. Of course later on in her life, she would discover that it was best to watch out for the living. The dead cannot do you any harm.

Riddy opened the screen door and entered the laboratory. The room was six hundred square feet in diameter. There were several lab technicians there, who welcomed Riddy after she introduced herself to Gaston.

The new supervisor was five feet, eight inches, husky built with brownish red hair. She had a Jamaican accent with beautiful gold jewelry from her country. They both agreed on the starting date and that training for the ER lab would consist of two weeks under Gaston's watchful eyes. Riddy could hardly wait. *A full-time job*. It was more money, but with the same job title—Medical Laboratory Technician.

Tears came to Riddy's eyes after the grueling two weeks of back-to-back interviews.

Ola congratulated Riddy and gave her a photo ID, key card for the parking lot, and the employee's benefit package. Riddy had tons of papers to sign. Next on her agenda was to quit Mount Sinai Hospital and enjoy the couple of weeks, prior to the start of her new job.

The time went by fast. Before she knew it, Riddy found herself parking in the employees' only parking lot. She got out of the car and took a deep breath. It was June, 1977. The landscape was well manicured and the day's sunshine was bright. Riddy wore a white uniform, white stockings and shoes, and she carried her white lab coat over her arm. She grabbed her purse off the front seat, and unfolded herself out of her brown Ford Granada—that she would purchase with her leftover tuition reimbursement from college.

The hospital took up the whole block. It had been built in the early 1800s from limestones that has a circular pattern. It has nine floors, and next to it is a clinic. And there were three more buildings behind it. The buildings were simply named A, B, and C.

Her mind went back to when she was visiting Big Dot's son, Thurman, at that hospital when he broke his leg. What she recalled is him sitting outside in a wheelchair, getting some sun. Riddy never dreamed that one day, she'd be working there. Now at twenty-one, she is employed there as a Medical Laboratory Technician.

Riddy walked pass the hospital to cross the street onward to the Hecktoen building to be trained before being cut loose in the ER which is in the main hospital building.

The two weeks went by fast and Riddy made friends with all the gals in the labs. She met Lisa, Theodora, Linsey, and Linda. No matter what hospital or clinic in which a person worked, every new employee had to go through an initial training. It does not matter what degrees, certifications or experience, every lab had its own system of doing things.

Another supervisor by the name of Stocker completed Riddy's training by showing her how to order lab supplies and where to pick them up from which is Central Supply where Erle worked.

Dave chuckled and elbowed Erle in the rib. "When you gonna make a move?" Dave whispered

"You know she want you," he added.

"Man, she's a baby," Erle, whispered back, "I'm so much older than her. She'll run. Let's bet."

Riddy got on her tippy-toes to get a good look at Erle. He had not been there in a few weeks.

"Where is he?" Riddy said, talking to herself out loud. Suddenly, Erle came from the back, and took her requisition. He began filling the order, while Riddy quietly waited. He then made his move.

"My name is Willie Erle," He said, stopping what he was doing to say it. "But people just call me, Erle." He smiled. "What's your name?"

"Riddy," in her gentle sweet voice.

This was great, Riddy was thinking because all the other times she came his way, he always used to hold his head down or not give her eye-to-eye contact, but today was different. Erle looked in Riddy's face, they were eyeball-to-eyeball—at last. And then he asked her an unsettling question.

"How old do you think I am?" Erle asked.

"Twenty-five?" Riddy answered.

"Nope," he said, satisfied, "I'm thirty-five years old."

Riddy could not believe that this fine specimen of a man was pushing forty. *What a handsome creation of God*, she thought. Then Erle jotted down her number, and the phone calls began. They became inseparable.

Riddy was very popular especially after Mabel got fired. The ER required two techs on all three shifts. But Mabel barely came to work, and when she came to work, she was sloppy drunk.

Mabel would come in late, climb through the lab window from the alley, work a few hours to get paid, and then she was gone. Riddy would be stuck with the majority of the work. She took it for a while, but then got fed up and reported Mabel as well as the ER administrator who let her get away with it. Martin had no choice but to fire Mabel. It was the right thing to do, but it would be several months before Martha would be hired. So in the meantime, Techs from other labs had to come and help with the heavy workload, or so Riddy thought.

One of her first experiences was with another Tech in the hospital named Charles. It was revealed otherwise when Charles visited the lab as a spokesperson and ambassador to explore her sexuality.

Charles sat in a chair all laid back grinning from ear to ear looking like he swallowed a canary. Finally, Riddy could not take his weird expression and silence any longer. She asked him what was up. Charles asked her had she ever wondered why people were so helpful to her. He said it was because she was really liked. Riddy smiled.

Charles laughed out loud and said it again, "Yes, Riddy, you are really liked."

He leaned forward and repeated with great emphasis, "YOU ARE REALLY LIKED."

"Haven't you noticed that Monroe is always coming around, and so are the others?"

Riddy looked at him, incredulously, but pleased.

Charles continued, "Have you ever wondered why?"

Riddy replied, "To help out?"

"Sure you, right," Charles agreed, "Monroe really likes you."

"That's nice," Riddy answered as she began to catch on to what Charles was really trying to imply.

"I hear you, Charles,"

"But you ain't g'tting' it!" Charles exclaimed.

Riddy added, "What are you tryin' to say, Charles?"

"Monroe is a bull dagger," Charles summed up. "She sent me to ask you, directly, do you go that way, too."

Charles seemed to be enjoying being the bearer of strange news. He said to Riddy, "She's been throwing you hints, but you never act like you get 'em."

Riddy responded, "What way?"

"Do you like women?" Charles came right out and asked.

Riddy was stunned, and Charles began to explain the subculture at CCH. Charles then asked again, "Monroe wants to know do she have a chance with you?"

"Not at all," Riddy said, and proudly added that, "Erle is my boyfriend."

The ambassador stood up, sighed and explained to Riddy that most of the Fantus' gals went that way, "They all had a bet about which one of them would crack that nut—meaning you." Charles said.

He chuckled on that last part. And it was on that note that Charles left the laboratory—and the help stopped. However, shortly afterwards the new hire came on the scene, Martha.

After several weeks, Martha gave up being helpful, too. She stopped splitting shifts with Riddy. People do not want to work? After a hard sell, Riddy agreed and the arrangement worked well. Martha would work from 7:00 am-11:00 am, and Riddy would pick up at 11:00 am and get off at 3:00 pm. This unapproved schedule worked out well for both women.

Well a few months later Riddy met Anne and Connie who were married women with children. Hmmm, possible female friends, which Riddy did not have any because all of her high school friends went their separate ways.

In between shifts they would visit the lab and they would discuss their lives, and their men. Anne would share with Riddy a game that they would play with other men. They would bet they could lose so many pounds with men other than their husband that was interested in them. If they won, the men had to give them money, and if they lost, they had to give the men sex.

"Really?" Riddy asked.

Whenever Riddy had lunch she would talk about the women to Erle. He would just sit and listen.

One day Erle visited her in the lab, and it looked like he had something on his mind and was trying to decide whether or not to tell Riddy. Then Riddy mentioned them gals again. Erle bowed his head and said, "They are not your friends. Anne propositioned me."

Riddy's mouth fell opened, "What?"

The next day Anne came to the lab, and Riddy let her have it. She threw her out the lab and told her to never come back.

Chapter Fifteen

In the meantime Big Mama was sick. Very sick. Riddy helped Madea with her care, every day, right after work. Big Mama was assigned a home health visiting nurse named Marvette. Marvette befriended Riddy with Big Mama prompting.

Marvette would greet Riddy whenever she would be there when Riddy came in from work. They started having small talks, and she even invited Riddy to parties in Chicago. Then one day Marvette asked Riddy if she like to travel and that she was planning a trip to New Orleans and that they were going to party on the train all the way to New Orleans. Riddy was game.

She agreed to go to the Mardi Gras via Amtrak and they would party on the train. Unknown to Riddy, Big Mama told Marvette about Steve and what he had done to Riddy. She wanted Marvette to be a big sister to Riddy.

Marvette laid out the game plan that they would be sharing a room with Lydia and would only be in the room to lie their heads on a pillow other than that they would be gone club hopping. Sounds good to Riddy, but what did not seem right to her was Marvette was dealing with a married man and was planning to meet him in New Orleans.

When they got there Marvette stayed with him in his room at another hotel, and Lydia had her man at another hotel. Riddy was alone yet not alone. Marvette was like Dr. Jekyll and Mrs. Hyde. Riddy thought, *Cannot judge a book by its cover.* In spite of it all, Riddy had a great time and met a great romantic guy. Riddy needed to be romanced again.

During the day, Marvette was mild and docile, and at night she was a party animal and going with a married man. What a mess. This sweet daytime angel grew horns and a pitchfork on their trip causing Riddy's jaw to drop open. This is a case of Dr. Jekyll and Mrs. Hyde. Lord, have mercy.

New Orleans was Ronay's hometown. A guy Riddy met who was an off-duty police officer doing security at a jazz club, and he took a liking to Riddy. But there was something about that Erle guy that Riddy could not shake. She was hooked.

After several visits to the Jazz club, and having fun, on their last night Ronay asked Riddy to have breakfast with him after he got off from work. "I'd just like to talk to you," he said. The two met at the Crown Point hotel by the train station, and they had breakfast together.

Ronay told her that in a few months, he would send her an airline ticket, so that she could come back to visit him.

"I'll send it as soon as you can get away from your job," he said. Ronay was a perfect gentleman to Riddy. He never tried to make out with her or have sex with her. Ronay was special, but there was something about that Erle she could not let go.

When Riddy returned home from New Orleans, she could not wait to see Erle, so she called him to let him know that she was back in town. They went back to business as usual seeing one another daily and going out.

Several months later, Ronay held true to his word, and sent the airline ticket when it was convenient for Riddy. She parked her car at the airport and boarded the plane, southward to Dixie. Ronay wanted Riddy to meet his mother. Now things were moving too fast. Well, Erle was seeing a girl, named Breen who had a child. They were not in an exclusive relationship, and they had agreed to have an open relationship.

Ronay picked Riddy up from the airport. She stayed at his house and kept busy during the day and in the evening they toured his beloved city, and they talked about his ex and their two children.

Ronay was very romantic and attentive. They had a picnic lunch on the shore of the Mississippi River and watched ferries glide downstream. Ronay even took her to the well-known Popeye's Chicken® that was destined to become a franchise and obtain national fame. Once you cluck, cluck their chicken there was no going back to the other contenders.

Ronay was very hospitable, easy to talk to, also. On his off days, he cooked Riddy breakfast. He even made gumbo for her. He was also comical. The two had lots of laughs. One day Riddy visited his mom and thank God, she was there because Big Mama did not know she was staying at Ronay's house. Whew!!!

Riddy's two weeks' vacation was coming to an end, and she was not home. Big Mama thought that she had lost her mind, and she wanted the details about Riddy's trip once Riddy got back to Chicago where she belonged.

"Get your tail back up here, girl," Big Mama told Riddy on the phone. "You don't want to wear out your welcome."

"But I love it here," Riddy said.

Ronay smiled a mischievous smile as he munched on a piece of celery. His mom, also listening in on the phone call, her eyes widen at the strain of the conversation. Ronay's eyes twinkled as though he knew something that Riddy did not.

Riddy's curiosity was pricked. After the heated phone conversation ended, Ronay drove Riddy to the airport in silence as though he was in deep thought. He put her on the plane bound for Chicago. Riddy returned to Chicago reluctantly.

Big Mama chewed her out. Big Mama wanted her to make new friends and forget about Steve, but this took the cake. Big Mama probably would have had a stroke if she knew that she was with Ronay at his house.

Riddy and Ronay talked every week, and she continued to date Erle. Finally, Ronay popped the question. She did not answer. The phone went silent then she hung up.

Riddy wanted Erle. She immediately called Erle and told him about Ronay's proposal. She asked Erle what he was going to do. The phone went silent. Riddy hung up immediately. A few days would pass before Riddy would hear from Erle. He asked her about them moving in together. Riddy wanted a ring. She politely told him, "You got to get papers on me." The phone went dead. And a whole week went by before she would hear from Erle again.

Riddy stopped going to his Department and asked Martha to pick up the supplies. Then she would interrogate Martha on Erle's appearance and behavior. Martha would just laugh and tell Riddy not to worry.

"Erle's gonna come around," Martha laughed, "Eventually, you're gonna get what you want."

Riddy was a bold heifer, and she felt like her boldness had gone too far. It was going to cost her. She remembered many visits to Erle's place as well as their dates. One day Erle got a phone call, and she knew that it was Breen. He acted like Riddy was not there. So she pulled the phone cord out the socket and snatched the phone out of his hand. With him chasing her, she ran and threw it in the garbage then bolted out the door. Erle never tried that again. Other than that, they ate at nice restaurants and had good conversations, but he would never take her dancing. Erle did not like to dance, but did not mind watching Riddy.

Riddy remembered her favorite place to eat, it was The Tropical Hut located far south on 95th Street in Chicago. One week she had the waiter for all three dates scratching his head. She had been brought there by Erle, Ronay, and another guy in her hay days. Shame. Shame. Shame.

Riddy just sat, grinning and winking at the waiter. She would give each one a hush-money tip when her dates were not watching. Getting a man was never a problem. She had been proposed to four times and engaged three times. Now, maybe Erle would marry her.

She had tried the pregnancy lie routine that women of her era used. He did not budge. Then she tried the miscarriage lie and that did not work. *Now, would Ronay be the leverage that would force him to drop Breen, and marry her?* She wondered. Erle was dating Breen before and during Riddy. Their relationship had run its course.

Riddy had not nor did she expect to hear from Ronay. She really did not expect to because her silence to Ronay was a silent, **no**—he understood that. Ronay and Erle knew about each other. Ronay was a great guy, but it was something about that Erle. She wanted Erle who was involved with Breen.

Finally the lab phone rang and when she answered, to her surprise, it was Erle. He was inviting Riddy to lunch. She was so ecstatic, but she fought not to reveal it in her voice. He told her to meet him in the hospital lobby at high noon. Riddy was there and she followed his lead.

The two crossed the street and walked through the green park. Riddy thought it was odd because they usually had lunch at the restaurant in the park, but he led them beyond the park. They crossed another street and walked to the train station and she followed him to the train station. *That's odd*, Riddy thought. No lunch at the sandwich shop either. The two of them boarded the train heading east to the loop and got off at State Street, and they did a long walk to Jackson Boulevard.

They entered a jewelry shop. Erle asked a sales person if he remembered him. The man answered, yes. Erle asked him to pull out an item and to show it to her. It was a set of rings. Wow. *Well hush my mouth*, thought Riddy. Erle then asked if she preferred another ring instead. Riddy was so touched and thrilled that he thought enough of her to pick out something, himself. He made his intent for marriage although he never officially asked. No knee bending. He put the rings on her finger and that was the end of Ronay and moving to New Orleans. Erle shut it DOWN. Well.

The two spent the next few months planning their lives together. Neither wanted a wedding, and they decided to elope. Erle told Riddy to find a place for them to live and then give him the information, so he could take it from there. He was not going all through Chicago looking for a place and besides, if he did, she was gonna have to like it.

"You're gonna be the woman of the house," he explained, "I'm gonna be working—hardly there, so you do the picking."

Sooo she checked the south side of Chicago, west side, and even Oak Park.

Erle favored Riddy's uncle Ern. He had his mulatto complexion, height, and weight. They looked like brothers. He was very handsome. Ern would smile at Riddy whenever she came upstairs to visit him and Big Dot.

Her mind wondered back when there were times when Riddy was younger, Big Mama would send her upstairs with a pot of food the back way where the pit bull would be yapping at her, leaving Riddy close to wetting her underpants.

Eventually, after much whining Big Mama would let Riddy carry food and sometimes a garment that had a zipper stuck for Ern to fix up the front way, therefore, avoiding the pit bull. The orphan, with living missing parents in action, never knew when to go back downstairs with Big Mama. Big Dot and Ern were like bona fide parents and was as close as she was going to get to having parents.

Big Mama would bang on the pipe like banging on a set of African drums that vibrated the upstairs' apartment as a signal to bring her tail back home. Nothing doing. Big Dot would gently tell her it was time to go downstairs, and Riddy would turn her head and would not move.

After Ern finished fixing a broken zipper from one of Riddy garments, he and his wife would dress for bed. They would turn the light out as a hint and a sign for Riddy to go back downstairs. *Nothing doing* was Riddy's thought. She would jump in the bed with them, under the sheets, right between the both of them. They would all look and snicker at each other.

Riddy was the daughter that they never had. And they could not bring themselves to send her downstairs. Then suddenly a booming voice in the hall could be heard calling her name from the first floor to come home. And it was not God's voice either.

Big Dot would tell her, "Mama calling you."

Riddy would not move until she heard a repeated threat from Big Mama, yelling, "Girl, don't make me come up there." Key words.

Then Riddy would jump out the bed and fly down the stairs faster than a speeding bullet pass Big Mama quickly to avoid a lick. This was a weekly routine, played out every weekend. Thank God.

How she felt about Ern could be one of the reasons why she liked Erle. He had many of Ern's qualities. Unfortunately, too many that Riddy did not know about, but would soon find out.

Riddy then went to one complex, but you had to be low-income to qualify to live in the beautiful place, which was weird. Finally, Riddy found an apartment building across the street from the hospital where Riddy worked in the ER lab, and Erle was an administrator of Central Supply. Yes!!! Erle made an appointment to get a tour of the apartment. His fine looks paid off, and they moved up the list of availability. Erle moved into the apartment in September. The two agreed on an October elopement date.

Erle and Riddy stood before God and man in a Baptist church to become man and wife. Riddy moved in that night, and called Madea from her new home phone with excitement while wearing a one piece blue and white stripy footsie PJ jumpsuit.

She wondered why Erle stared at her so hard. She had on a one piece pajama set on their wedding night and was not looking sexy. She did not have a clue because she lacked intimacy.

Chapter Sixteen

"Oh Mama, you got to eat," Riddy begged Big Mama.

Big Mama refused to eat the hospital's food. She had been feeling ill and nothing they did helped.

"Well," Riddy said, frustrated, and putting the spoon down on the tray "I got to go and meet Del at the hotspot club. I will see you tomorrow," Riddy said, and she gave Big Mama a kiss on the forehead. She walked to the edge of the doorway, Big Mama's eyes met hers, and a chill ran up Riddy's spine. Big Mama's eyes told her good-bye.

"Big Mama Big Mama," Riddy repeated. A tear rolled down Riddy's face and she felt a lump in her throat. "Oh Mama." Then she left and headed on her way.

Riddy had to meet Del at the hotspot club for disco night. It was hard to have fun thinking about Big Mama. Riddy drove home after dropping Del off at home and there sat her cousin Nonnie who was visiting on the front porch in tears.

"Riddy," Nonnie said, "Mama's gone."

Riddy felt a knife in her chest. Big Mama died one year after Steve walked out. Here is this dark shadow showing up again. Riddy told Erle that Mama was gone. Big Mama wake and funeral was held on a hot summer evening before Madea's birthday.

Big Mama was loved. There were over three thousand people in attendance, standing-room-only. There was a line of people even stretching around the corner, waiting to pay their respects. A queen had passed. Riddy was amazed because Big Mama was pretty much a homebody except when she and Riddy would go on their trips during summer vacations. There were people that Big Mama had loved and helped throughout the years. She housed many people who called her Mama or Mama White. What a testament of life. What a legacy.

Erle was there and Riddy rested in his arms seated with her head on his shoulder. The inevitable had happened. Big Mama had told Riddy that she would marry Erle. Everything she ever said came to pass. Big Mama liked Erle and said he was a good man.

Although she said Riddy would marry him, she did not say that they would stay married. No one stayed married in her family, and the women in the family were known to marry three to four times. The men of the family rarely married. They liked to shack up. *This time the cycle will be broken*, thought Riddy. *This time things will be different*, she declared in her heart. Everyone went to their perspective places.

In late November, close to Thanksgiving, the ER was slow. Riddy had nothing better to do, so she decided to do a pregnancy test. In the '70s a rectangular glass onyx cover slide with three circles side-by-side each had one drop of urine, one drop each of two chemicals of the HCG hormones, then the slide had to be rotated and rocked manually side-to-side by hand.

The slide allowed for three tests to be done at one time. You could test the urine specimens of three women at the same time. A negative result would be the formation of clumps. A positive result would be no clumps, but a milky white appearance. Riddy repeated the testing two more times with her heart racing fast. OMG. I'm PREGNANT. How??? There had been no symptoms. She still had her cycle like clockwork.

While rotating the slide one more time looking hoping for clumps, Riddy saw a pair of black polished boots. Army boots. She looked up into the face of Steve. Talking about a double whammy. Riddy looked stunned. Thank God, she thought. She had gotten away from the full uniform and just wore lab coats.

Riddy stood at 5'2", 120 pounds and a size nine dress. Sometimes she could squeeze in a seven, and a shoe size of seven and a half. She wore a rust color v neck dress, and matching color shoes. Riddy's hair hung down beyond her shoulders.

Not now, she thought—about both situations.

Riddy did notice the thickening of her waistline, but she rationalized and attributed it to her not exercising, lately. She did start complaining to Erle about how every time they left work to return home together, and once they walked out of the elevator, she would become nauseous. It turned out that the hallway would have heavy aromas of garlic and other strong spices, emanating from their East Indian neighbors cooking down the hall. The smell would hit the pit of her stomach and would not let go. She did not know that her hormones had shifted.

After being rattled she now stared into the eyes of the man whom she still loved. But her morals and respect for God and marriage would not allow her to be a mistress.

He stood at the lab's threshold, and their eyes met. He looked handsome in his uniform. Steve was 5'6", mulatto skin, medium built, and weighed in about 170 pounds. She still loved him. Erle was a rebound love. Subconsciously, perhaps, Riddy felt that he knew that.

The marriage was doomed. What was done to her, she now did to Breen. A cycle developed. Steve was stolen from her. Erle was stolen from Breen, and later Rolanda would steal Erle from Riddy. The beat would go on.

Steve finally spoke telling her that he was back in Chicago and that he had been searching for her. He told her how he was very sorry for his actions—what he had done to her. Riddy did not answer. *What was there to say*, she thought. He then swallowed hard, turned on his heels and left. Riddy had to sit down and close the lab door to weep. A few questions would surface in her mind like *when will this torment and stalking end? How will the stalking end?*

Well, then it was time to go home and tell Erle that she was PREGNANT.

"You can't be pregnant. You kidding. I'm too old. Erle Jr. is twelve. I haven't fathered a child since. How did this happened?"

"How did this happened?" Riddy repeated.

Did he really want her to explain the anatomy and physiology of conception? Did he want her to explain the notion of no condoms, not used in September, and that a man no matter the age, could always father a child, but women stopped having children at a certain age due to menopause and she was a young fertile woman. He was almost ten years her senior.

Erle finally calmed down and got over the shock of embracing fatherhood again. Riddy knew it was the girl child that she asked for although the baby's back was turned during the ultrasound and the gender of the child could not be determined. She knew within her heart the baby was a girl, and she was right.

Riddy felt a strange sensation that was never, ever felt before. On June 21, 1979 her daughter was born. She weighed in at seven pounds, nine ounces, twenty-one inches at 5:59 a.m. She was born in Rush Presbyterian St. Luke Hospital.

A few weeks prior there was a false alarm. The water bag had begun to leak, but no baby. The two of them attended Lamaze classes. Erle fixed all Riddy's favorite foods fried chicken, cream style corn, broccoli, and biscuits with lots of butter. Erle took over the cooking because Riddy stopped eating when she got pregnant. Her thought was that she did not want to lose her shape. Erle would have to cook the food and watch Riddy eat every morsel with a declaration that she was not going to starve his baby.

Months later, after that Sweetie was born, Steve called while Kat was visiting. The phone rang and a familiar voice was at the end. "Steve?"

"I heard you had a daughter," Steve said, adding, "I hope that you will be happy."

Riddy hung the phone up, and Kat would have an inquisitive look on her face.

* * *

Months later Erle, this good man would be beckoned from his home into the arms of a sister from Mount Orgy Missionary Baptist Church. Riddy got tired of the yelling and throwing, and the breaking of things.

She no longer knew this man and the baby was becoming nervous. In a fit of rage he threw a dinner plate set up into the ceiling of the kitchen. The set scattered onto the floor in pieces. In another rage as she sat on the couch clutching their baby, he threw the bassinet. It was time to exit. Riddy left with the clothes on her back, diaper bag and Sweetie.

In a few weeks, she would be served a petition of dissolution of marriage proceedings. "He is divorcing me?" Well, Riddy did leave while he was at work.

She called his job and asked to speak to him. Erle took the phone, but both of them held the phone waiting for the other to say their final goodbyes.

Erle had to get back to work. He is a definite workaholic, but great provider—and yeller. He told Riddy she did not have to work. She could keep her money and she would have one bill. The phone bill because he would not be calling anyone on it.

Riddy used the money for groceries and to fix the place up. She even tried to set up romantic getaways and quiet dinners. He never wanted to go anywhere just work and home, and on the weekends, he wanted to hang out in the bars to get drunk. He was a master at holding his liquor. Riddy could never make him happy. One day she asked him if he loved her. Erle's answer was always the same, "I married you didn't I?" Riddy's heart was ripped and the rest as they say is history.

One day Riddy decided to give the apartment one last look. She still had the key. Erle rushed to the door. Riddy wondered what he was doing home during the day. He would not let Riddy inside the apartment. So she left and got on the elevator. She took it from the seventeenth floor to the sixteenth floor, and stood in the stairwell. Well. Well. Well. Rolanda, her sister in the Lord, met her eye-to-eye, and dropped her head down in shame. Riddy froze while blood ran down her legs—and it was not time for her cycle. Blood was running down Riddy's legs due to shock, because the shock of her friend screwing her husband was devastating, *the two-faced heifer*.

It was hard facing people at the church the next Sunday. Riddy had continued to go especially during holidays, so their daughter could see her father. It was so hard being there. The sister in the Lord was a married friend with two children. They had visited each other's homes. And they had even discussed their husbands. A minister's wife. A tempest. A Jezebel. A Delilah. A two-faced wrench. A church *HOE*. And the kicker, Riddy found out that the Reverend had a girlfriend, who was in the same choir of the church as the wife.

There were love triangles and orgies throughout the congregation. Riddy discovered that wife-swamping happened as well. Riddy left Erle, never to return. And their fifteen-month-old Sweetie would cry herself to sleep at night, hugging her daddy's picture. It was a picture of mom and dad taken at their reception.

The baby would rock herself to sleep, while Riddy cried herself to sleep. If that was not enough, the bold hussy would be in the car when Erle would pick up Sweetie for visitations. *A double slap in the face. Okay*, thought Riddy.

Rolanda Johnson and her husband divorced, and now Erle is divorcing me. Hmmm. Riddy found out that Rolanda left her husband, the church, and she and their children moved back in with her parents. She now attended her family's church.

Rolanda's dad was a head deacon, and her mother was a missionary. They appeared to be angelic. So if Rolanda can sit in the car in front of where I live, I can sit every Sunday at her church and glare at her with my baby, planned Riddy. It was on.

Every Sunday Riddy made her way to St. John's, faithfully sharp as a tack, burden-free with her baby. Rolanda would be in the choir loft. The organist would crank up the keyboard and run the notes when Reverend John preached. Everyone, and I do mean everyone, would do the holy rock shuffle. Folks would fall out, and others would roll up and down the aisles.

Riddy would start her own jig from her seat. She'd dance her way toward the altar in front of the choir loft and do a spin, touch down, and then glare at Rolanda who would squirm in her seat. Rolanda's mother and father would look at Riddy in confusion then look at their daughter's weird response. Eventually, after several months of this Rolanda disappeared.

Rolanda stopped riding in the car on pick-up days and she left the church. After several months, the thrill was gone, and Riddy moved on with a smirk.

The day before the divorce, after visiting Sweetie, Erle asked if they could try again. Riddy heard God say, "No." She could only say what God had said. "NO."

She had to watch him walk down the stairs, heartbroken, yet obedient. The marriage had been built on lies, deception, abuse, rebound, suffering and pain along with lack of communication, and wham-bam–thank-you-ma'am sex. It was an unfulfilled, godless marriage. So what was the point? Pointless.

The only good that came out of the marriage was Sweetie. She remembered praying six years prior for a daughter. Riddy was not saved nor had a relationship with God, yet he heard her.

Big Mama, told her that whenever she wanted something or had a problem to talk to God. Sweetie was a present from God. Riddy conceived Sweetie around her birthday in early September, 1978. It was a month after Big Mama died that Sweetie would enter the world. She conceived a month before her marriage in October of that year, but would not discover the pregnancy till the end of the Indian summer.

She remembered a few friends, biological brother, her brother-in-law Will, and Erle moving in the new furniture. Everything fitted in the elevator except the gigantic couch that had to be carried up seventeen flights of winding staircases with Riddy giggling on every landing as she gleefully watched. There was a lot of colorful swearing going on with Erle asking, "Why, the heck did you pick this thing?"

"Well," Riddy would say, every time he said it. He had set Riddy free in the furniture store, and told her she could have whatever she wanted, and he was going to enjoy it, whatever she picked. She recalled Erle saying, "That's gonna take a while. So I'll sit right here." He planted himself on a soft showroom recliner, "Come get me when you finish."

To that, she laughingly said, "Then I'll take everything."

The lugging-the-couch-up seventeen-flights-of-stairs was hilarious. After everyone reached the apartment, there were lots of food and drinks to behold. That was the least that the grateful couple could do. One of the items brought into the apartment was a black fake fur recliner that the couple experimented on resulting in Riddy getting pregnant with Sweetie.

Riddy worked at Rush a/k/a Russell Medical Center and returned to school to obtain two advanced degrees. While attending school close to graduation, she sought out a promotion into the position of laboratory supervisor. After obtaining the degree, she did not get the position. God had other plans.

She filled out an application at Rush Hospital. She interviewed for the position, and Riddy felt the head of HR was prejudice because she declined her a second interview with the pathologist.

Several months would pass when she felt an urgency to try again. This time she would receive the coveted lab position only through default, and guilt, by Dr. Jay Roberts. Dr. Roberts' secretary had booked the appointment during clinic. He gave Riddy the option to reschedule. She would attempt to interview Riddy between patients. Two and a half hours passed, and when the tired nephrology doctor finally got to interview her, it turned into a swift ten minutes. All that she asked was, "Could you start in two weeks?"

A brand new life for Riddy and her baby abounded. After four years, the atmosphere became toxic among the women in the lab. Riddy wanted out. Dissension was so thick that it could be sliced with a dull knife. After a successful interview, Riddy left the main hospital to the professional building laboratory, unfortunately not far away from the demonic activity that would meet her at the door in the form of Raynell.

Several weeks later, Riddy was in the parking lot at work pacing back and forth saying to herself, "Raynell, I hate you. Every time you are around there's drama. You are always stirring something up like the witch that you are. I hate you. I wish that you would drop dead. I could slap you right about now. You do not know how to talk to or treat people. You are a pain in my butt." *Now to go find the old heifer*, thought Riddy as she paced back and forth in the parking lot thinking, *Raynell is a racist Hill Billy*.

The end of the work week did not end well. Raynell made a flippant comment to Riddy passing by her to go to the rest room. Riddy chose to ignore it, smile, and show class to that red-neck hillbilly. Over the weekend, Riddy allowed the comment to fester and could not let it go.

It's butt-kicking time as Riddy turned the doorknob to the laboratory at 7:00 am. Riddy's eyes panned the room and there was no Raynell in sight. She placed her belongings under her assigned workstation of the week and took her seat at the platelet machine. She took a deep breath. The work flow was heavy as usual for a Monday morning. After several hours it is now 3:00 p.m. and here comes Raynell, entering the lab. She is working the second shift, unknown to Riddy.

Akewowo, the lab supervisor, charged into the lab from his adjoining office and asked, "BORN AGAIN! What is this BORN AGAIN? Someone, please tell me what it means to be born again?" He spoke in a heavy, thick Nigerian accent, in broken English.

The whole lab went into a hush as Raynell walked forward and assured him that Riddy knew all about it, and she is so sweet and kind. Riddy's jaws dropped open as Akewowo approached the platelet machine with an inquisitive look and hand gestures awaiting an answer.

"I will meet you in your office," offered Riddy as she high-tailed it to the bathroom. He briskly turned on his heel and returned to his office. Riddy repented in the bathroom stall. "Lord Jesus, forgive me," then she went back into the lab and headed for Akewowo's office.

Akewowo begin to tell Riddy what happened during his lunch with a guy friend. The guy friend called him a heathen which was very upsetting and told him he needed to get saved. Akewowo admitted that in Africa he was a part of a church network called Four Squares while growing up and he had slipped away. He explained that he was ready to recommit his life back to Christ.

Raynell burst through the door catching the two of them, Riddy and Akewowo. Riddy sat at the lab supervisor's desk, bent over an opened Bible. They both looked up, simultaneously, and stared at Raynell who turned beet red, and vomited. Riddy left the office after praying for her supervisor and advising him the type of church to look for to attend. Whew!!! A soul saved Riddy felt great. Raynell could not take the excitement and left the lab for home.

Riddy had done a bilateral transfer to the professional building lab from the nephrology laboratory. She had left Cook County Hospital after Sweetie's birth because she could no longer handle swing shifts, unpredictable lab staffing schedules, and she could no longer work in her high heels.

* * *

Now, Riddy is sitting with the women at the POW WOW meeting scheduled days later. The women still wanted to keep meeting although Big Mama was no longer here.

The verdict was in at the women's weekly POW WOW meeting. He got another woman all the women would nod in agreement in the kitchen after asking a series of questions like, "So y'all doing anything?"

"No."

"Is he coming home late?"

"Yes."

"When was the last time y'all did it?"

"Up 'til Sweetie was born."

"What?"

Then someone yelled, "Somebody's a freak." Everyone would burst out in laughter.

"He said it will make the baby look pretty."

"Now nothing?"

"Nope."

"Is he eating your food?"

"No? He is always yelling at me. He wants me to put curtains up in the window. Nobody in the building have curtains. We all have blinds."

"He wants me to clean the corners of the floors in the apartment with a tooth brush like his Mama."

"You have got to be kidding me!" Yelled one of the POW WOW women, Deb who burst out laughing and snickering. Ms. Ann was Riddy's nickname from Deb.

"We are not down south in the back woods," protested Riddy.

"Well honey, he got somebody."

Riddy left with her baby in her arms and headed home. The marriage was doomed. The courtship was heavenly, but the marriage was hell.

After Riddy and Erle divorced, Riddy started working at Rush St. Luke Hospital in Chicago in the Nephrology Department then she did a lateral transfer to the professional building.

Chapter Seventeen

December 1982 rolled around. Riddy could not see herself going into a new year with pain, sorrow, or disappointment. Riddy contemplated suicide. She thought about using poison from the lab.

Later that evening, she went to a disco with a friend that she met in high school. Riddy sat at a table with many people. She was dressed in a cowgirl corduroy outfit with boots and her long black hair flowing. A guy asked her to dance. She had no pleasure and felt out of place.

Riddy's favorite pastime had always been dancing. She took modern dance, and it was nothing for her to exercise four times a day! But lately, Riddy found pleasure in nothing, or anybody. Madea took more and more care of Sweetie. Riddy even went back to school for another degree.

Earlier that year, Riddy experienced back-to-back problems. She had to have her gall bladder removed after a trip overseas to Egypt, France, Italy, and Israel in the month of June.

She was now officially divorced. In addition to that, her car broke down, and she needed another car. She had begun to experience severe money problems.

Riddy's world was getting darker and darker. She was sinking further and further into the dark hole. She felt so alone.

After leaving the dance floor and returning to the table with newfound seekers of pleasures. Riddy had barely sat down before she heard a voice out of nowhere saying with great force and emphasis, "GO TO CHURCH"! Every hair on her back stood up, as Riddy swung around looking for this powerful voice.

* * *

It's a hot summer day as Riddy sat with Mary, Junior and Serena as she began to mutter over and over repeating what Sammy Davis Jr.'s character said on stage. *Stop the world, I want to get off.* It finally made sense now. *Just get off the world! Get out of here.* It makes sense. The huge globe on the stage suddenly stopped rotating. *How do I end this madness,*

Riddy pondered. There have been many sleepless nights filled with salty tears and a wet pillow. Riddy had done everything, yet ended with nothing. Yes. Degrees, careers, traveled most of the United States, and to foreign soil.

In retrospect, Riddy had traveled to Europe to places like France, and Italy. Jamaica and the Bahamas. She even visited Egypt and Israel. As an adult she traveled to California, Indiana, Louisiana, Missouri, Nebraska, New York City, Philadelphia, Washington DC, Virginia, Nevada, and passed through Tennessee, and the Carolinas. In growing up in her younger years she traveled to Canada, Michigan, Wisconsin, Ohio, Florida, and Georgia.

She had, had at one time or another, a sports car, a husband, and a house. Riddy had enjoyed a life of fine dining, great theater, bougie friends, shop-'til-you drop excursions. Yet her heart ached. She even had a baby girl that she could nurture and look after, but yet and still her heart wreaked with pain.

The pain in the depth of her soul, she could not explain. Her pain lingered day after day; night after night; and year in and year out. It was a void that could not be filled by any temporal means.

GO TO CHURCH!! The Creator had spoken, and it sent an electrifying chill down Riddy's spine.

"Did you hear that? Riddy shouted over the music, asking the man whose arms she was wrapped in on the dance floor. "I heard a voice."

"What?" Asked the dancer with a bewildered look on his face.

The voice returned with more force GO TO CHURCH!!!

Riddy broke away and left the man right there on the dance floor. She ran and sat with her friends. The voice returned again, and Riddy asked her friends, "Did you hear that?"

Everyone at the table, in a drunken stupor, yelled in unison, "Hear what?" And they continued to drink. Riddy never drank in her life.

She was the lookout girl for her friends when they went out. Her head was clear on the night she heard the voice. *WHO IS THIS?* Thought Riddy.

It is time. The who, what, where, when, and why is not the problem. The who is Riddy. The what is suicide. The when is now. The where is the bedroom. How? She thought, *I'm left with the how. How do I end this life? The how.*

"Where are you God?" Well, its December 31, 1982 at 11:30 p.m. and Riddy left the disco holding on to the reasoning.

I've got to get off this world before 12:01 a.m. A new day. A new year and I will have to repeat this vicious cycle again. Got to go. Got to go. Got to get out of here, thought Riddy. She can hear the clock ticking. TICK Tock. It's now 11:45 p.m.

Four minutes later, it's 11:59 p.m., one minute before midnight. Riddy thought. *Should I jump off a building, slit my wrist, overdose, stand in the middle of traffic, or drink poison? How will it end?*

I can watch TV before I go. She grabs the remote control. Click. Click. Click. Click. She stopped on channel 38. Swaggert. Jimmy, an old country preacher starts preaching, "Jesus the son of God died for your sins." He explained Adam and Eve's fall in the garden, and God's plan for redemption. "Repeat after me, 'Lord Jesus come into my life. I believe that you are the son of God. Forgive me for my sins.'" Simple. Riddy falls on her knees. PAUSE. Riddy's natural man dies.

The search is over going from man to man. The search is over driving up one way streets. The search is over driving down the exit ramps of expressways. The search is over walking the streets at night club hopping. The door of Riddy's heart had been kicked open. A spirit possessed, yet it's holy. The Holy Spirit.

The voice speaks out. I need a spiritual awakening. The voice of God entered Riddy's soul. The church is now inside of Riddy which is a building not made by earthen hands.

I am the church. She thought to herself.

Riddy had a Saul conversion experience. She was arrested by Jesus. She accepted Him, and He had accepted her long ago. She remembered the depression that plummeted her into the dark hole; a very dark hole.

A few months prior Riddy had remembered and tried to follow that voice. She ventured out to a church that Kat's sister, her aunt Ms. J, had told her about.

The pastor was a lady. While preaching, the pastor encouraged fornication. She told a member of her congregation, "You'd better put some rubbers on your son's sticks." Riddy was shocked. "Is it okay to fornicate," Riddy asked herself? Riddy chose to hang in there, because after all, God did say, go to church.

Well, there were times she visited the pastor with other members at the pastor's house. But one day the pastor was hosting a special event at her house, for the life of Riddy she could not go. Unknown to Riddy, God had placed a barrier in the way.

On the next day, which was Sunday, Riddy was greeted by the church's nurse with a "Girl, you missed it." It was out of curiosity that Riddy wanted to know what had happened.

"What do you mean, I missed it," Riddy asked? "We went under. You went under," Riddy inquired??

Pastor transported our spirits to a hypnotic realm. She had George clucking and strutting like a rooster after putting him under a trance."

It was under that notion that Riddy turned on her heels with her baby and ran out of the church with no intention of returning, ever.

Another Sunday rolled around and Riddy chose to visit the church that was her old stomping ground. Riddy went to visit, although Marshall, everyone, and the majority of the people she knew were gone.

Riddy had settled into the church. She was faithful in attendance, and paying her tithes. She joined a committee, and the war was on.

In the first meeting, it broke out into a fistfight. So, she resigned from the committee, and decided to just be a part of the congregation.

Riddy had started making friends when a short, large bosomed woman with a close cut hairdo and a black mole on the right side of her face approached her. After the pastor had preached his finest sermon, it was while everyone was fellowshipping at the end of the service that this woman leaned forward, and tried to kiss Riddy in the mouth. Riddy jerked back, and with her baby in her arms, she ran out of the church, never to return. She later found a medium sized Baptist church congregation that was pastored by a renowned recording artist in the eighties.

The choir could SANG, and it felt comfortable to be there. Then one Sunday Riddy was sitting in the congregation, the pastor was preaching, and she experienced a phenomenon that she had never felt before. Suddenly everyone was moving in slow motion. A mist had floated through the air. People were jumping up and down in slow motion. People were clapping in slow motion. Riddy sat with her mouth wide open. After looking around Riddy looked up at the pulpit, and the pastor's countenance had changed. His eyes were red as fire. He used scriptures out of the Bible from the book of James, John and a portion of the Apostle Paul's teachings. He ended his sermon by saying that, "A man has a plug, a woman has a plug, and at night they plug up together." Riddy was appalled and once again she picked up her baby, and ran.

Riddy sought this voice from church to church but only found confusion, strife, womanizing, manizing, racism, sexism, and all other isms, and chisms. She could not find God in the church. Realizing church was inside of her, she begin making the necessary steps to have a personal relationship with God.

Madea knew that there was something different about Riddy. Riddy stopped going to discos. Riddy stopped dating, and talking to men on the telephone. Madea really knew that Riddy had changed when one day, Riddy picked up every forty-five record and her albums, and she threw them away in the garbage. Madea could take all her changes except one. She pleaded with

Riddy not to give up men. Madea proclaimed, "If you don't have a man, you are going to crack up."

Madea had one of her friends who was a minister to speak to Riddy. She told Riddy that one day she would be a minister. Riddy shrugged. Madea confirmed the announcement one Thanksgiving Day when all were gathered at the family table. Madea was staring at Riddy who looked up and said, "What?" Madea then announced that Riddy would be a minister.

"What?"

"I see it on your forehead."

"Forehead! You see what?"

Madea repeated herself with great pride, and it was at that moment that Riddy loss her appetite and rushed to Big Mama's mirror that was attached to her old dresser. Riddy screamed, "I DON'T SEE NOTHING."

Madea screamed back, "It don't matter, you still gonna be a minister."

Shortly afterwards, one of Madea's minister friends asked to speak to Riddy, and she shared her experience at the disco, attempted suicide, God's bedroom visitation, and the various churches she visited.

Riddy also told Bee about how she felt forced to stay home and watched church on television where it was safe. Bee recommended a safe haven of a church that she could attend. The church was interracial. The congregation walked in the spirit and demonstrated God's power in signs and wonders. So, after six months of fearfully being glued to her television, Riddy ventured out again to a church.

Chapter Eighteen

During this time, God blessed Riddy with a church home for five years. It felt like heaven on earth. It was there that Riddy received the baptismal of the Holy Spirit while wearing a pair of slacks, silk top, hair in rollers and tied up with a scarf. Riddy had one dress in her closet; she eventually gave away all her pants to her sister Serena.

Madea decided to go to church with Riddy because she wanted to see what type of church this was that her friend had recommended. Riddy and Madea were sitting together when the preacher asked if anyone would like to receive the Holy Ghost. Riddy turned and looked at Madea, and said, "I am going up there to receive the Holy Ghost."

When Riddy went to the altar, she did indeed receive the Holy Ghost. Madea was astonished that Riddy received the overflow of the Spirit of God. It was an awesome experience. However, Riddy was still in the dark hole, and had not yet escaped to freedom.

Riddy began to meet all kinds of people, including Chinese, Indian, Jamaican, Bohemian, Mexican, Asian and Whites. The new church was a melting pot indeed. Riddy's horizon was broadening.

Pastor Joe was miniature in stature with a thick black glossy mustache, and had twinkling eyes. It was from time-to-time that he would go into a trance-like state. It would be at this moment that the ushers would line up people in front of him. After Joe snapped out of it, he would prophesy to people.

He had about fifteen hundred members, and the church was rapidly growing. Soon there would be a need for an additional service, or a larger building.

It was Riddy's turn to stand in front of the preacher. He reminded her of a Wild Wild West cowboy. He stared deep into Riddy's eyes, and told her that, "Someone is doing witchcraft on you."

"Wow!" Riddy left from his presence, numb. "Witchcraft? Do people actually do that?" She asked. She had only seen witchcraft being practiced in movies.

Her mind went back to one night she was lying down in bed when she had a vision. She saw the father of her baby standing in front of the door at waist length in height. He was walking with a stuffed teddy bear that was clothed with an engineer's suit and cap. Riddy saw herself go to the door to open it.

After the dream passed, there was a knock on the door. Sure enough, Riddy went to the door to find her baby's daddy with the teddy bear. After he left, she felt pressed to throw the stuffed animal away with all the other toys that he had brought. Riddy started thinking and putting things together. She had begun to recall that every time he would visit, strife and contention would be left in the house.

Everything was fine at Tabernacle Society and Riddy made a lot of friends, Pat, in particular. The two were inseparable as sisters, or even twins. You would not see one without the other.

They both had things in common, one child, ministry, and enjoying life. Pat had a son while Riddy had a daughter. They attended new member's class where they sat together to learn how to be members of the church. After every service, Pat and Riddy would go to IHOP to eat, and even traveled out of town to Missouri to visit some cousins of Pat's. They both were lay ministers at the church, and there were times, they would visit one another.

* * *

Sweetie, Riddy's baby, was growing and developing. She began to have fevers. Riddy took her baby to Dr. Chung who prescribed phenol barbital. However, the preschool informed Riddy that Sweetie's motor skills were underdeveloped for her age. This was devastating news to hear.

Riddy and Madea took her baby to Dr. Kaye, her former pediatrician. She called and expressed concerns. Dr. Kaye shared his suspicion of mental retardation. He told Riddy that all that he had to do was look at her. Dr. Kaye stared into Riddy's eyes, shook his head, and looked away. A sharp pain pierced Riddy's heart and soul.

Riddy ran out of the examining room into the women's bathroom. Madea ran after her. Riddy cried, "What am I going to do?"

Madea shot back, "Believe in God."

It was from that point that Sweetie no longer had to take phenol barbital, and was put on every prayer line at church. Riddy and Madea saw immediate improvement.

One particular day, Riddy stopped at an elementary school to meet with a Mrs. Elson, the school principal. Sweetie would soon be emancipated from pre-school and into grammar school. Riddy was unhappy with the meeting because she needed a year-round program. The school had a summer program, but it was for low-income families. The principal, however, stated while leaning over the desk, "If you tell me that you have more children, I can get your daughter into the program."

Riddy said with conviction, "I cannot lie." She instructed the woman to sign up her daughter for the school year. She exclaimed loudly, "God will work something out for us." Riddy marched to her car and pressed her head against the steering wheel, and prayed out loud, "God did you see that she wanted me to lie? This is a Christian school. I wish I could take care of my own daughter during the summer."

Suddenly Riddy had an overwhelming desire to see one of her favorite high school teachers, Ms. Barto. Riddy drove to her old stomping ground, Flower High School. She had begun to experience flashes as she walked toward the school of the great times she had at school.

Riddy walked to the office and requested a pass to see Ms. Barto. A silver-headed woman in a red jacket walked away from the counter to retrieve a pass from the desk to give to her. It was then that the voice who spoke to her about going to CHURCH returned and said, "Ms. Barto is quitting, and I am giving you her job."

She shivered and hairs began to stand up on her back. She shook her head. The voice of God repeated. As Riddy was trying to get herself together, the voice returned with more force, "I am giving you Ms. Barto's job."

At that point the silver-headed clerk gave Riddy the pass to go see her beloved teacher. She climbed up to the fourth floor, and knocked on the door of classroom, four eleven. Ms. Barto came to the door, and she had a weird look on her face. Riddy thought that she was not happy to see her.

Ms. Barto requested Riddy to return within fifteen minutes. She slowly walked down from the fourth floor with the intention of not returning. She got ready to leave the building before a lunchroom lady called her by name. The two of them spoke for fifteen minutes. Since fifteen minutes expired, Riddy decided to go back upstairs to see Ms. Barto. The classroom was empty and they began to chat about old times.

Riddy shared with Ms. Barto about how much she appreciated her, and how that there was something about her that made her stand, head-and-shoulders above all the other teachers. Ms. Barto smiled and said that she was simply doing her job. Riddy then asked her if she was a Christian. Ms. Barto said, "I love Jesus."

It was at this point that Ms. Barto began to glow and said, "I am retiring. I prayed on Friday that a Christian would take my place, and you, my successor, arrived on the following Tuesday."

Ms. Barto really cared about the students and wanted them to be in good hands. So, the two of them met with both the assistant principal, and the principal. Riddy was instructed to get in contact with the Board of Education right away to begin her paperwork. In the meantime, Riddy kept her employment at Rush until she received a telephone call to start working for the Board of Education.

Riddy's mind went back, at Rush Hospital, although very prestigious, and renowned for its medical services, the University, behind closed doors, was no picnic. It was very stressful, especially in an all-female environment. Some were hormonally imbalanced and a pain in the rear. Although, there were only four women, they were stacked on top of each other. The area where they worked was very small.

There was Vonte who was confined to a wheelchair due to an illness. Then there was Rachel who was Vonte's sidekick. Raynell was the nosey one, and Claudia was the quiet one.

Raynell was responsible for training Riddy, and it was an instant dislike on Raynell's part. Riddy looked at life through rose-colored glasses. She thought everyone loved her. Well, from the start Raynell had it in for Riddy. She always had nasty comments or a negative backlash. She would time Riddy whenever she left the lab.

Raynell even began to check Riddy's work, and she was not even the supervisor. She would always look for something to accuse Riddy of, like one or two extra white blood cells counted. One time after checking Riddy's work, Raynell found one extra red blood cell and reported her to the lab supervisor.

Raynell was always unhappy and vented her frustration out on happy-go-lucky Riddy, who always had a smile on her face, and a kind word for a soul.

One Saturday, Riddy attended a prayer breakfast downtown at a hotel that Tabernacle was hosting. She was sitting at a table with friends, when a prayer line was called, and God spoke and said to Riddy, "Get into the line." Riddy did not even know why she had to get on the line. It was a healing line.

It was not until she stood in front of Pastor Joe that she heard God say, "Eyes."

Pastor Joe asked Riddy, "What do you want God to do?"

Riddy spoke, saying, "I want God to heal my eyes." Pastor Joe prayed for Riddy.

Riddy returned to the table where she was sitting previously and laid her head on the Bible. She looked at the Bible and saw that it went from a black color to a navy blue. Riddy thought her Bible was black, and she remembered arguing with someone about the color of her Bible. It then occurred to Riddy that she was color-blind.

When Riddy walked into the lab on the following Monday morning, a strange eerie feeling fell upon her. She also noticed that Vonte, Rachel, and the others were acting so strange. Riddy saw Raynell and the lab supervisor whispering in the back of the room. Riddy's stomach began to turn.

Riddy immediately got up and went into the bathroom to pray. When she returned to the lab and sat down, Raynell and the lab supervisor surrounded her. The supervisor wanted Riddy to take a color-blind test. Riddy passed with flying colors, and so did everyone else in the lab.

Riddy remembered two weeks prior, she had asked Raynell about a test color to ensure that she knew the right color for the test results. Riddy looked up from the platelet machine to see the red face of the supervisor, and to hear her stern voice snap at Raynell.

It was a few months later that Akewowo replaced the supervisor. Riddy wondered how long he would last, and would survive the persecution of Raynell who quickly fastened her eyes on a new victim. It did not matter that he was a man or her supervisor, Raynell knew no boundaries.

The lab was quieted down and the chief was able to seize control of the lab, and the workers. Raynell was unsuccessful in jabbing the African supervisor because he was always in his office from sun up to sun down. He would enter the lab with a good morning mutter under his breath and headed straight to his office, and shut the door. Raynell was disgruntled and returned to persecuting Riddy.

The next week Riddy got a phone call to report for work at the high school. Riddy gave her resignation, and Akewowo made the announcement in a lab meeting beaming with pride. Another announcement would be forthcoming from him. He announced that he and his family were moving to New York. He was accepting a position at the United Nations. He had told Riddy the week prior to the staff meeting when she submitted her resignation. Raynell was floored and so were the others. Raynell dropped her head.

It was after the meeting that Raynell went to Riddy to apologize for all the ill treatment, and to ask if it was her fault. Riddy assured Raynell that her new move was the result of a divine order. God wanted Riddy to move on.

The lab gave her a send-off party, and Raynell gave Riddy flowers, and a hug. However, before the departure a Bible study was set up six-months to Riddy leaving where Toni another saint and Riddy would ask each other what the word for the day was every morning, and one of them would quote and expound on a scripture while working at their stations. It would always be quiet. Then one day, Toni and Riddy got very busy. The afternoon seemed to rush by. Suddenly, Raynell yelled out, "What is the word for the day?" The lab froze, so Riddy spit out a scripture and it was on. God moved.

Riddy had a one-month vacation before she reported to Flowers High as a teacher, or in professional language, an Educator. God had created this job for her. She would be the first laboratory technician to work for the Chicago Public School System. She marveled at the power of God.

Chapter Nineteen

Previously, of receiving the position at Flowers High, during a youth counseling training session at Tabernacle, a young woman named Julia walked toward Riddy and began to prophesy and said, "Teach, teach, teach my people." Several months passed when Riddy would find herself out of the health care system and into the field of education.

At the time, she had a prayer partner name Rosy, and the two of them prayed every day. Rosy told Riddy that she saw changes coming her way. Well, the night before, the two of them prayed for Angels to be released to guide Riddy before Riddy met with Angela, the interviewer. God gave Riddy favor to the point that no questions were asked, although she was to be interviewed.

Riddy drove 5.1 miles and parked the car in the parking lot close to the security guard. She was a half an hour early for her interview. The place looked like ghost town on Pershing Road. She approached the security guard and asked him what building she should enter. He got up from the counter and left his walkie-talkie. Riddy startled him as she drew near. He was not too happy to steer away from his favorite television program. Once he instructed Riddy which entrance to go through, the guard returned to his post and returned his feet up on the counter to resume watching television.

Riddy enters the building, and a man in a two-piece suit told her, "You are going to use this elevator to see Angela." Riddy got on the elevator and so did he, but he stood behind her. While in the course of the conversation, Riddy noticed there was a cafeteria and told the man, "I'm going to get some breakfast before I see Angela since I am early. Do you want to come along?" Before he could give her an answer, the elevator door opened. Riddy noticed that when she got off the elevator, so did he.

Riddy went into the cafeteria; he stood along the wall watching her every move. After Riddy retrieved her breakfast, she took a seat, and he sat behind her. When Riddy stood up, so did he. As Riddy walked out of the cafeteria, he stopped her and told her to go up a set of stairs that would lead her to her destination. Riddy politely thanked him for his assistance. As she grabs hold of the doorknob, she looked back to thank him again, but he had vanished. Riddy just shrugged her shoulders and began to walk to Angela's office. Unknown to her, the angelic being was in human form.

Riddy was given good instructions, and she found Angela with no problem. Angela sat behind the desk with thick-horned eyeglasses. A petite woman that looked trimmed and fit would later die from kidney-failure. Riddy gave her the resume that Rosy had typed.

Angela's face lift and she asks Riddy to approach the desk. Angela showed Riddy a pay scale and asked, "Would this be enough money?" Riddy almost fell over because it was double what she made at Rush Hospital. Angela never asked any questions. Riddy could not wait to tell Rosy about her day.

As soon as Riddy and Rosy re-connected, it was Rosy with a great thrill that pointed out what Riddy did not notice because she was excited about the new job. God had answered every aspect of the prayer. The man that led Riddy, and guided her to Angela, was indeed an angel, Riddy shivered at that divine revelation.

A few months later after going through the process of physicals and completing HR documents, she returned to Flower High School to start her new job. She was back to her second home where she spent the majority of her life, and it felt good. As Riddy walked through the Hall of Ivy, although she was on the other side of the desk, she noticed the time had moved forward. The Hall of Ivy was the graduation song and expresses walking through the halls of the school.

Back in the day, Flowers High was an all girls' school. Although, there were no boys in the classroom, they were not missed. Boys surrounded the school in the morning, during lunchroom breaks, and after school hours. It was nothing to hear, "Hey baby!" So, it did not feel like boys were not around.

Flowers High was not cohabited by boys and girls. A young man in the early eighties bucks the system. This young man protested about having to leave the neighborhood for an education, and petitioned for the rights to attend a school located across the street from his home.

The little militant won his argument, and fought to enroll as the first boy. Afterwards, the school began to be bombarded by boys who now had the opportunity to get inside instead of hanging outside. Although Riddy was not against the little militant, it took something away from the school.

Riddy took a deep sigh as she walked pass the school auditorium. Then she paused there and began to remember a woman who courageously taught her and the core Bible studies while jeopardizing her job. Riddy reflected on the day that the girls went wild when an all boy band played, and they charged the stage and ignorantly tore up their equipment, which caused the administration to not only have to pay for their performance, but their equipment too. She looked at the stage and remembers the dances that the core group performed during the talent shows.

Riddy walked passed the main office where she was a messenger during her freshman year. She walked pass the counselor's office and wondered how Ms. Butler was doing in life. Ms. Butler was the first African-American school counselor.

Riddy went to the lunchroom on the teacher's side. She looked at the hamburgers and French fries. They looked the same. Riddy walked through the student's lunchroom, and stopped at the snack bar. She tried some butter cookies, and noticed that they had not changed either.

Riddy stood amongst students who were dressed very casually in their jeans and fitted tops, and with pierced eyebrows. Back in the day, slacks were not allowed while school was in session; jeans were only worn during the weekend to do household tasks. You only wore gym shoes to gym. Riddy's generation wore skirts, dresses, flats or heels. It was by the junior year that they were allowed to wear pantsuits, and that was after much public debate.

Riddy looked back and remembered a riot that occurred because they were not allowed to wear mini-skirts. A new principal came on the scene and saw the girls in minis, but that was the sign of the times.

Ms. Clara issued a proclamation in the school's bulletin, over the intercom, and even during a general assembly. We were not to wear mini-skirts. However, that was all that the fashion designers had selling in the stores. We had no control over the designers. We tried to explain that to her, but she would not listen so we rioted the school. She could not restore order and the board removed her from being principal and appointed another woman who took another approach.

It was during the general assembly that there were not enough security guards present. A majority of the girls began to boo and tear up the auditorium. Then, they stormed out and headed for the lunchroom and began breaking out windows, and throwing chairs. On the next week, Ms. Clara was gone, and a new principal, Ms. Ward was on the scene. She was able to bring order back into the school.

All the girls loved Ms. Ward. It was most unfortunate that during Riddy's senior year, Ms. Ward died when she lost her battle with breast cancer. It was a very teary day. The assistant principal Ms. Stewart remembered her during the seniors' graduation. It was a bittersweet day.

Riddy finally made her way to the teacher's lunchroom where she was congratulated by some of her former teachers who were still teaching! She was gracious and thankful to them for being role models, and mentors during her formative years.

After lunch, it was time to face her first class. She had been in orientation all morning. Riddy was going to teach in the same class room where she was a science major. She had replaced Ms. Barto. Riddy would call her mentor from time to time.

Riddy felt that Ms. Barto had found the fountain of youth. Except for the gray hair, Ms. Barto looked like she did when Riddy was a student. She was a very plain woman who wore glasses and a short boyish haircut. She wore loose fitting long sleeve tops, long skirts and tarnished orthopedic shoes. The only jewelry she wore was a watch.

Although Ms. Barto was up in age, she had no problem chasing after a student down the hallway. She was a riot in every respect. Riddy could count on one hand that she had disciplinary problems with students.

Riddy wondered how she would do as a teacher. After all she had no degree in education, coursework, or experience in teaching. Riddy's job was a miracle from God, the Divine. Riddy came into the system as a vocational education teacher, and she was also responsible for teaching biology, and general science.

Riddy took the mentality of it's either you or me, and she entered room 411. She stood in the doorway once the bell rung, and welcomed her first class into the room. Riddy's heart raced, for she was only seventeen years older than her students. Riddy wondered if they would listen to her.

On the first day, a gal named Rochelle tried to challenge her and the two of them locked horns. "Why are you so mean?" she asked Riddy.

In return, Riddy told her, "It's either going to be you or me, and it's not going to be me."

Between the break, Riddy called Angela and informed her about the student Rochelle who acted like a butt. Angela came to Riddy's rescue and informed Rochelle that she would have to behave, but explained to Riddy that she was going to have to maintain her class.

Riddy turned to prayer. God began to give her favor with the students. Riddy worked for six years at Flowers High School. Some of her students spent weekends with her and her daughter Sweetie and a few of them even lived with her.

A new principal came on the scene. The power hungry principal who did not have a life and who was obsessed with Flowers High School became difficult. She had it in for Riddy. God began to warn Riddy in a dream.

Riddy did lose her job as a teacher, but the Board sent Riddy back as a substitute, and she would be bounced between the classroom, office, and hallway. The administration pitied her, and some laughed and asked her, "Where is your God now?"

The students were stunned. Riddy refused to change and held her composure in the midst of the humiliating situation.

Riddy had experienced a severe salary decrease. She wondered how she would keep her household going because she and her daughter had just moved into a condo and Sweetie was attending private school. Then there was the car note, and credit card bills. She also had to keep food on the table. Riddy had to believe God to provide.

Unexpected checks arrived in the mail box, then after praying, bill statements came paid in full. She and Sweetie received invitations out to dinner. Riddy was staring at the television when a red lobster commercial came on and said Lord I wish I could go to Red Lobster. Ten minutes later the phone rang and one of the missionaries from the church said she received a settlement and wanted to celebrate and Riddy could pick the place and she picked, Red Lobster.

Then there was another time when Riddy and Sweetie ate for weeks only rice and string beans and Riddy cried out, "Lord can we have some meat?" Then she went to church that evening and a member asked to be dropped off. She wanted to offer gas money but she turned and told Riddy that God told her to give her a pack of pork chops and then she reached in her bag and gave her a package of ten count pork chops. God provided time and time again. Supernatural provision.

Riddy still attended Tabernacle until one Sunday she walked through the church doors and the church shrunk. Riddy asked people if they saw what she saw. People looked at her like she was crazy.

Riddy went home and got on her knees and she saw in a vision a man dressed in a robe standing at a podium. Riddy prayed and asked, "Is this my next pastor? How will I find him?" A few weeks passed and a friend named Barbara asked Riddy to visit a church. Riddy really was not interested. She felt comfortable and at home with Pastor Joe and the others. However, Barbara just would not quit.

Riddy finally gave in to Barb, and they went to CFA Plantation Center on a Wednesday. It was unknown to Riddy that they had just moved into the church building. The two of them along with others sat for over two hours before it was announced that there would be no service. Riddy was burned about it, and vowed that she would not return. Barb begged her to return on another Sunday. Riddy said, "I don't think so." A few more weeks passed and Barb begged each week. Finally, Riddy gave in again.

It was after the praise service when a familiar face came out from a side door. It was the man in her dream. Riddy felt God tugging at her heart. No, I love Tabernacle, Riddy felt within herself. A war had started. Riddy prayed a quiet prayer. She said, "Lord, if you want me to join this church, let the pastor stop midway from his sermon, walk out of the pulpit and down the aisle and prophesy to me." It was but a second later that the request manifested.

Riddy submitted herself and joined the new gang of believers. Although the congregation was one race, they were very kind and friendly. A strange thing occurred, Riddy lost contact with Barb—the very person who convinced her to attend.

Riddy attended many Bible studies, services, retreats, and shut-ins. God was changing Riddy's character, disposition, and attitude. Riddy was encouraged, and her baby Sweetie was growing and flourishing in their new place of worship.

Riddy was dumbfounded as to why she had to leave Tabernacle. It would be ten years before Riddy found out. The work of the flesh and the love of money entered Pastor Joe's heart. Riddy would bow her head in silence and shame for Pastor Joe whose ministry came to ruin. The board of the ministry threw him out due to adultery, alcoholism, and the promoting and the condoning of pre-marital sex with the children.

The spirit of God had lifted off Pastor Joe. It became quite evident when he traveled to Haiti one year. A group of natives got a hold of him and fractured his pelvic bone, and he was in a wheelchair for a whole year. After Pastor Joe was released from the hospital, Tabernacle went through a split, and many devoted believers left, and joined other ministries. Yes, Tabernacle did shrink. Eventually the whole chain folded. No more Tabernacle. At the time, Riddy wondered what her future would be at CFA Plantation Center.

It was about three weeks after joining the new church that a prophet visited CFA Plantation Center name Prophet Hilly. He was not the traditional minister. He was not even five feet tall. The minister had curly hair and wore western clothes. He had a team of ministers that traveled with him, and they also wore western outfits. The whole team wore black and red. They had a spooky persona about them.

An announcement during the service was made to come to the camp meetings. Riddy still did not have a car and had to walk to CFA Plantation Center and back home with her daughter. During this time, her money was funny and she had just recovered from surgery. Riddy went to the first meeting to hear Prophet Hilly. He was from Texas, and famous, too.

Riddy had to have her gall bladder removed after a series of vomiting and pain on her left side of her body that radiated to her midsections. It was during her travel to Egypt that she experienced an episode that convinced her to have the surgery.

Prophet Hilly had a diamond ring on his pinky on his left hand. Riddy was so impressed with the way he preached with fire and gusto. Finally, it was offering time and Riddy had no money. But she looked on her wrist and had a thin fourteen-carat gold bracelet. She said within herself, *I will offer this to God.*

Prophet Hilly wanted to know who had put the bracelet into the basket. Riddy trembled as her knees knocked while she walked forward. He took the diamond ring off his finger and placed it on Riddy's hand, and prophesied, "God had just made a covenant with you. God promised to always take care of you. He will even give you diamonds and gold. You will suffer many things, and people will be jealous of you, but remember God."

Before the week was out, people who Riddy knew and did not know gave unto her gold and silver jewelry. She would just give a compliment, and the next thing she knew, they would take it off and give it to her. God was faithful to His word.

The first lady of CFA Plantation Center was very happy for her. She was such a genuine person. Riddy would have conversations with her and noticed that there was a difference between the two of them. There was such a purity about her and a holiness that Riddy did not possess. Riddy did not have the fruit of the spirit which is the divine nature of God and Christ. A lot of Christians are lacking this because preachers seldom teach the fruits of the Spirit. The focus is on money, healing, and miracles.

God used CFA Plantation Center to root out spirits that were lodged deeply inside Riddy's heart. The church would be very instrumental in her spiritual development, and change of character. Little did she know a lot of painful experiences would surface. Riddy would spend nineteen years of her life in attendance at CFA Plantation Center.

The church came into existence after a very courageous man name Pastor Patrick "Pat" decided to leave after a sharp disagreement with his spiritual leader, Pastor Freddie.

Pastor Pat was serious in serving the God of his salvation; however, Pastor Freddie was no longer committed to God as before. The love of money began to usher in evil spirits in the congregation. Fair-weather Freddie was constantly out of town, and the burden of the people fell on faithful Pat.

The church was appropriately named Raiders because that is what eventually occurred later on. Back in the 80s Pastor Freddie led a select few members to raid luggage at O'Hare airport and eventually had to serve time in prison because of it.

Riddy had a girl in her class who complained every day about the Raiders. She mentioned how the pastor was trying to get underneath her dress, wife swapping was prevalent, and how people were actually having sex in the church although they were married to other people. Riddy believed in God, and that each person is responsible for his or her own soul. Every day, Riddy encouraged Mizzy by saying, "You have to know God for yourself."

Riddy also told Mizzy, "You ought to inform your mother of the preacher's advances toward you and you might want to stay out of his range. Nevertheless, what you are experiencing does not justify you from disobeying the Word of God." Eventually, Riddy's persistent affirmations to Mizzy silenced her.

In the back of Riddy's mind, she did wonder who in the world are these people? Riddy would actually meet the offspring of fair-weather Freddie also known as Ready Freddie whose spiritual off-spring is Pastor Pat.

Why is it that man never learns not to repeat a negative history? Why is it that those who are oppressed oppress others? Why is it that those who are abused abuse others?

Chapter Twenty

Riddy's life was now full and somewhat peaceful, even though at times, she would think about Steve. She now had two college degrees, and was about to obtain a graduate degree in social work. Riddy did have one profession as a Medical Laboratory Technician, but now has moved onward to become an Educator with the Chicago Public School System. She drove a nice car, wore nice clothes, and although her marriage to Erle failed, she had a beautiful daughter who was a pearl. Yet, Riddy felt so alone and empty, but not depressed or suicidal like a few years ago. Steve would pursue her for the next twenty years, even though he was a married man with a child.

The daughter that Riddy has could have been Steve's. It would be seventeen years later when she would hear from him one last time before he settled into the life that he chose.

The last time Steve contacted Riddy would occur upon her moving into a townhouse. After returning home from an errand, Riddy's seventeen-year-old daughter said to her, "A man named Steve called asking for you. He didn't leave a number. Who's Steve?"

Riddy still loved Steve, but in spite of all her sins, flaws, and failures, she loved God more. She respected the institution of marriage. Would this respect payoff one day?

In the future, Riddy had a vision of Steve lying on a couch. As Riddy stood at the foot of the couch, she told him, "You must forget me." Riddy disappeared in the vision. Several times, Riddy would have visions of Steve.

She was also bound in her character of bitterness, hatred, anger, unforgiveness, jealousy, and envy. She was really upset with Steve. Nonetheless, God delivered her from all those evil spirits.

After the intense deliverance by the Holy Ghost from heartache and heartbreak, Riddy would one day phone Steve's mother on a bright sunshiny day to tell her, "I'm free, and no longer feel hurt and sad." Riddy finished it off with, "Let Steve know that I forgive him." A few months had passed and she would wonder if her request was honored. Steve's mother was still alive at the age of eighty-two.

In a vision God showed Riddy that Steve's mom was standing at a stove. Steve's mom turned slightly, and she began to utter the words that Riddy had forgiven him. Steve was sitting at a table, and bent over with peace and relief. Riddy would never hear from Steve again. The twenty years of seeking forgiveness would finally be given, and he then moved on.

* * *

Riddy had her career, her daughter and was involved in church. She reflects back at the age of twelve that she prophesied to herself that she would become a career woman. Riddy did not know at the time the meaning of the term. She did not know what a career woman was because she never heard of that term until she almost burned the house down after being forced to cook a meal. Big mama was animate about Riddy learning how to cook. She believed a woman should learn how to be domesticated.

Riddy became deeply embedded into CFA Plantation Center. She still yearned for a husband. From time to time Riddy would meet men, but they were not Steve. Riddy also noticed that the quality of men was becoming slim as she aged. The men Riddy's age were either gay, dead, jailed, mental, blind, crippled, and in many cases crazy or lazy, after white women, or marrying sistahs from Africa. The men Riddy met were at the bottom of the barrel. This was where Riddy was emotionally and mentally in life? She also noticed that many men were unemployed, underemployed, or were in search of a sugar Mama.

Riddy began to spend more time with God and getting closer to Him. And there were times when she had out of body experiences. Riddy was even getting closer to Madea now that Big Mama was gone. Well, time quickly went by and everyone called Madea, Granny. She was so sweet. God did a work on this woman. Yes, she was now a work of art. A masterpiece.

Although Madea walked slower, she was kinder these days and more loving, too. Madea no longer went upside anyone's head because she had a closer relationship to her God. Madea told Riddy numerous times, "Childe you need to write a book." Madea saw a lot of things that Riddy went through and would go through in life. Thank God Big Mama's death was a blessing in that aspect.

Big Mama could not bear to see her baby in the many afflictions and hardships that would soon come, but Madea, also known as mother dear, could stomach anything and anybody.

It was because of mother dear, that Riddy had her driver's license. After crashing into a fence with a group of girls in the car at the driving range, Riddy was thrown out of class indefinitely. Madea came to pick up Riddy earlier than what was expected, and the driving instructor had some tall explaining to do. After Madea had her hands on her hip and yelled, "Isn't that why she is here?" Riddy was admitted back into class, and she was glad.

It was also because of Madea that she learned to type. One day, after getting off work as a crossing guard, Madea came home with a flyer. The flyer read Sears Social Center, and it showed different classes that would be offered as well as fun activities. Madea insisted that Riddy sign up for the typing class. Riddy wanted to partake in fun activities, but Madea told her that if she learned how to type, she would never be out of a job. Riddy would find out how right Madea would be. Riddy was never without a job. While she was in college, she typed all of her own papers unlike some other students who had to pay for the service. Riddy saved a lot of money.

The day came when Riddy was laid off, and due to cutbacks, she would lose her job at Flowers. Nevertheless, God opened a door for her to work at Morton, an upper grade center on the West Side of Chicago.

After sitting patiently in the main office at Morton, and waiting for a classroom a whole week, the principal would need a letter typed, and all the clerks would be gone. The principal would ask Riddy, "Could you type this letter? It needs to be faxed to the board immediately." An hour later, the principal offered Riddy a position as a school counselor, and gave her an office with a telephone in addition, Riddy's salary would increase from $25,000 to $42,000 a year. Madea was right.

Madea was also right, making Riddy take piano lessons every Saturday from age ten until thirteen. Every Saturday Riddy had to go with Madea to a house where sweet Thelma taught lessons. Thelma was a very thin petite woman who smoked all the time, but she was kind. She also was the choir director of Riddy's childhood church. Thelma's husband was mean. They had one daughter named Beverly and a son who in turn had one daughter named Connie.

The matriarch of the family was Thelma. Riddy attended the lessons, and in her final year there was a recital. Riddy was crowned Queen after playing her solo, and participating in a play titled, A Hole in the Bucket.

The scene was as if they were on a plantation while dressed in cotton picking clothes. It was a comedy about a husband and wife whom had a dispute over a pail of water. The teacher renamed the woman to be Delilah from a play originally written in the 1700s.

Delilah's husband who is lying under a tree and too lazy to go fetch some water would come up with hair-brained excuses for not getting the water. His laziness was irritating so she would eventually leave him alone.

Riddy portrayed the role as Delilah in "A Hole in the Bucket," and she recited the following:

"Henry. Oh Henry."

"Yes, Delilah says, "Go fetch some water."

"There is a hole in the bucket, Delilah."

"Well fix it, dear Henry."

"With what shall I fix it, Delilah?"

"With a straw, dear Henry."

"But the straw is too long, Delilah."

"Well cut it, dear Henry."

"With what shall I cut it, Delilah?"

"With an axe, dear Henry."

"Well the axe is too dull Delilah."

"Well sharpen it, dear Henry."

"With what shall I sharpen it, Delilah?"

"With a stone, dear Henry."

"But the stone is too dry Delilah."

"Well wet it, dear Henry."

Then Henry grins and says, "But there's a hole in the bucket Delilah."

Ms. Thelma had cancer and became very sick. She eventually died the day after the cotillion that Riddy and Steve attended. Riddy would always remember Thelma because she was kind toward her. Riddy did not believe that Thelma died from cancer; she believed Thelma died from a broken and tired heart. She had a mean husband, a meddling mother, and a daughter who was mentally ill.

Thelma's daughter was on some strong medication after losing her mind over a man. One day, the daughter snapped and attacked Thelma and her little brother. The tragedy was that she stabbed her beautiful five-year-old daughter to death. Riddy cried right along with the family sitting next to sweet Thelma. It would be a few months later when Thelma would get tired and just leave.

Chapter Twenty-One

Madea enrolled into night school because she dropped out when she was younger so she could help her sharecropping family bring in the harvest. Riddy reflects back to when she was eleven, Madea told Kat, "I got to go back to school to help this girl with her school work."

Both Madea and Riddy graduated the same year, one out of high school and the other out of grammar school. Madea had bought Riddy a little ring from the Dells. Riddy did not really like it, but she did not complain.

She asked Madea one day, "Can I have your ring and bracelet?"

Madea told Riddy, "Before I die, I will give it to you."

When the time came, Madea kept her covenant. Riddy kept Madea's class ring as a memorabilia along with the Indian bracelet and ring that Madea bought from Wisconsin Dells.

Madea passed at eighty years old before her husband of fifty-six years. The family had Madea done up right. She was gorgeous. Madea had a lot of gumption and get-up-and-go about herself.

The doctor would tell Madea to get her house in order, and that there was nothing else that could be done regarding the return of cancer. She had only a week or two left. The first time Madea experienced cancer, she had a malignant tumor removed from her brain, and was able to resume household duties. This time it was different.

One day, Riddy went to see Madea upon hearing this dire news. Madea was sitting in the living room in her favorite chair with her feet resting on top of an ottoman. Riddy entered the room and asked Madea, "Are you ready to be with Jesus?" You are going home to be with the Lord? Let's worship and praise him together." Riddy prayed for Madea, and after a kiss, she proceeded to leave out the door.

Riddy took one last glance at her Grandmother and she saw a bright light on her face. Madea told Riddy to follow her to her room. She placed in Riddy's hands the Indian bracelet and ring. Riddy knew that she would not see her grandmother alive anymore. Her heart began to pound and ache. She hugged Madea for the last time and left.

The next day Madea went into the hospital. Erle visited Madea, and she asked, "How is Sweetie doing?" That night, Madea went into a comma and never came out. Following that night, Riddy went to revisit Madea, but she had left the world that was known to her.

* * *

CFA Plantation Center was the place to be on the West Side of Chicago. It was there that Pastor Pat helped Riddy get a house. Riddy had dreamt about an office, and saw Pastor Pat talking to a lady in the dream. Days later, Riddy had a meeting and told Pastor Pat that it was time to move. Pastor Pat encouraged Riddy to meet with a realtor.

Riddy walked into the office and of course it was the lady in the dream. Riddy's mouth dropped open. Riddy was not working nor had any money in the bank. The school was closed during the summer and Riddy was not going back to work until the fall.

They saw the house and Riddy really loved it. The realtor requested ten thousand dollars, and Riddy almost got strangled on her own saliva.

A mist came between the two of them, and the lady said, "Well bring in five thousand." Riddy thought *you just don't know*. Pastor Pat had coached her, "Whatever you do, do not say you ain't got no money."

The mist returned again and this time the realtor asked Riddy what would she bring. Riddy's mouth fell out with hearing the answer. "I will bring back one thousand dollars in one week," Riddy said, not having a clue as to where the money was going to come from. Riddy could just kick herself because a few years earlier, she had the $10,000, but blew it on clothes and good times. Now, she needed the money and there was no money. Only God could prevail on her behalf.

God had miraculously began to send unexpected money. People freely gave money to Riddy, and others began to pay her back. She even received a position and did consultant work to earn additional money. She had acquired exactly one thousand dollars to give as earnest money. Riddy turned the money in to the realtor who then informed her that in three months, she would need forty-five hundred dollars. She had to believe God again, and he moved by His Spirit.

On the day of the closing, Riddy was lacking five hundred dollars, and God told her who to ask for the amount. That individual gave it to her and told her that she did not have to repay. On November 14, 1986, Riddy and Sweetie had owned their first of many houses. It was a two-bedroom condo with a wraparound balcony, storage area, laundry room, secured building, and a parking space.

A few years later, Riddy's niece would come and live with her after accusing her mother, Jeanne of physically abusing her. Wendell, her father, was doing drugs. The police would get involved as well as a social service agency in helping Riddy to acquire custody of Kenya. It was a very stressful moment, but Riddy was used to young ladies living with her and her daughter.

It was nothing for students to spend weekends, attend church, plays, and dinners with them. Kenya lived four years with her and Sweetie. God blessed Kenya to finish high school, and have a major exhibit at the Museum of Science and Industry. The year before that, Sweetie had a major citywide exhibit at the Illinois Institute of Technology. Sweetie and Kenya both were high achievers.

Kenya came to live with Riddy and Sweetie in her sophomore year in high school. It was a real challenge to keep the boy-crazy girl from getting pregnant. There was a time when the radio channel was off the gospel music station. There was also a time when Riddy answered the phone, and there was a guy on the other end. Riddy had remembered the time when Big Mama told her, "Boys and books do no mix."

So, Riddy plainly told Kenya that, "You have to choose between books or guys. If you're interest is in guys, you will have to move back with your mother." Kenya was told to use her energy to make better grades and to plan her future. This was the opportunity to break the cycle of welfare and poverty.

Riddy's good advice fell on deaf ears. You can take a person out of the projects, but could you take the projects out of the person? Just like Moses through God took the children of Israel out of Egypt, but Egypt remained in them. A few years after high school she would blow the golden opportunity of acquiring a job that she could earn thirty-five thousand dollars in the field of horticulture. In addition, Kenya's horticulture teacher had contacts, but she wanted to live a gutter lifestyle. There's a saying, *you can take the kid out the country, but can you get the country out of the kid.*

Sweetie had a dream. In the dream, they were standing outside of their new home wearing new clothes. Kenya was nowhere to be found. Kenya asked, "Where am I?" She was nowhere to be found in the dream. Later toward the end of her living with them, she left one early morning to move in with a guy who was married and wanted her to be the mistress.

Riddy had boasted that Sweetie had nothing to worry about during her senior year in 1997. It was at that time that Riddy had five sources of incomes. The child support stopped since Sweetie's father fell off the roof of his house and had no income. Riddy had two jobs, and she lost one job. Then the job she had cut her salary. Then she did not get an income tax return. Money was fleeing left and right. God wanted to show Riddy who was in charge. Riddy, Sweetie, and Kenya had to believe God for everything. God performed a lot of miracles.

The school had pardoned Sweetie's graduation fees. Sweetie's school debt should have been three hundred dollars since she lost her ROTC uniform and some books, but the school clerk had quoted a fee of seven dollars. Riddy tried to be honest, but no one listened and Sweetie told her, "Mama, all you owe is seven dollars."

A teacher had paid Sweetie's prom fees. Sweetie wanted to know where to get her prom dress. God said, "Sears." Riddy told her what God said. Sweetie went to the Sears in Forest Park,

Illinois. Our credit was too bad to get a charge card, and Sears did not have a layaway plan. So, every day Sweetie would ask for the dress to be held. That went on for two weeks. Sweetie always knew the spot where the dress would be returned. One day Sweetie went to the store and the dress was gone. Sweetie almost panicked. Nevertheless, she found the dress in another area. This went on for two more weeks, and finally God blessed Riddy with eight hundred dollars.

Two days before the prom, Sweetie, Riddy, and Kenya went separate ways in the shopping center to get what Sweetie needed. Kenya went to buy material to make a shawl for Sweetie's dress. Sweetie went to get the dress, shoes and a handbag for the prom. God had moved just in time. On graduation day, Erle took everyone out for dinner at no cost to Sweetie. It was an awesome event to see God's power on the move. Riddy was humble that God's favor was upon Sweetie.

In 1998, the following year, God provided for Kenya as he did for Sweetie. One of the guys from CFA Plantation Center took Kenya to the prom. That night, Kenya and her date got into an accident and totaled Riddy's car. It would end up on her credit report and would be taken off after seven years. The insurance company refused to pay for the accident. After Kenya left, it was Sweetie, Riddy, and God again.

It was great living in the complex rent-free in a townhouse due to a subsidy program. Sweetie had lost her job, and God told her to sell icy cups. Riddy and Sweetie appointed two little kids to walk through the complex while sucking icy cups. Bang! The business began to bloom and they were selling icy cups from 6:00 a.m. until 12:00 midnight. Sweetie's sales reached over two thousand dollars, and held her over until she got a job. This was the second business that they had together. The first business that they had along with Kenya was in Forest Park, which was a hair business, and the focus was on finger waves.

A national movement is happening where the working class and poor people are being priced out of their neighborhoods because another race want the prime property, but God has always made provisions for Riddy and Sweetie. An opportunity had come for them to move to a nice apartment on the West

Side of Chicago, and it was not too far from 3165 West Monroe, which was the area where Riddy grew up. Big Mama, Madea, and Sidney had bought the building for fifty thousand dollars. Big Mama's granddaughter Dorothy lost the family building due to taxes. The building was now worth two hundred eighty-two thousand dollars.

When Big Dot moved out from the second floor apartment, Madea asked Big Mama on her deathbed if Ms. J could have the upstairs apartment. Big Mama told Madea, "You can do whatever you like. I am getting ready to leave out of here."

"But before I depart this earth," Big Mama said, "Let me tell you one thing. If you let that gal, Ms. J, Madea's daughter, in this building, there will never be a moment of peace." And sure enough, that prophecy was fulfilled—quick fast and in a hurry.

Ms. J's children and grandchildren would not help with the bills. The taxes fell behind, and the building had to be sold. Not only did it have to be sold, Ms. J and Howard conspired to cheat Kat, and Big Mama only heir Big Dot out of their shares.

Riddy had a vision three months before the deal went down. An angel spoke to Riddy face to face and said, "You need to leave." Then he said, "Let me talk to Ms. J." A phone call came between them, and he told her that she was about to lose the building. Riddy then called Big Dot to tell her the dream. Three months later, a realtor contacted Big Dot and told her about the conspiracy, and fraud that was trying to take place.

Big Dot asked Riddy what should be done. Riddy told Big Dot to get a lawyer because God's judgment was about to fall. A lawyer did advise her and they got to the bottom of what was planned. The two of them could have done jail time, but Big Dot just wanted her and Kat to get their share of the money.

It was out of Kat's share that Riddy was given a sliver of money. Riddy felt it should have been more and told Prophet Hilly when he returned to do another revival at the church. Prophet Hilly blessed the amount, and told Riddy to be like Abraham and walk into her destiny.

Chapter Twenty-Two

In Riddy's sixteenth year at CFA Plantation Center, she began to become stressful. People started being mean to her. Riddy helped CFA Plantation Center acquire thousands of dollars into the church. She saw people began to change. The family atmosphere vanished, and she was treated like a mindless slave.

Riddy had left her job at the Board of Education to enter into the ministry, full time; after all, Pastor Pat said she was called. Riddy knew that God wanted her to do something on earth for Him. She was not exactly sure what that something would be.

People always talked about physical, emotional, and verbal abuse. There is also what was known as spiritual abuse, where people exalt themselves above God. Spiritual abusers decide whom you may or may not marry; how much you can and cannot have, whether or not you can or cannot have a car, or go on vacation. They are the ones who decide if you are deserving of anything.

The spirit of corruption came through CFA Plantation Center. They had become just like Raiders as Mizzy described. Riddy started having terrible dreams about CFA Plantation Center. There were times that she visited other churches where people did not know her, and they would prophesy and tell her to leave. One minister said, "You have always gone above and beyond. It is never appreciated. God said He is going to cut people out of your life."

Riddy even went to the beauty shop and a woman got caught up in the spirit of God and told her, "In three months you will be leaving your place of worship and enter into your God given destiny. Then you will return to the original plan that God had for your life."

Everywhere Riddy turned, there were a *thus saith the Lord*. Riddy loved CFA Plantation Center, but CFA Plantation Center no longer loved her.

The final event that led Riddy to her Exodus was when she was operating a food pantry. Two of the volunteers who were filled with jealousy and envy began to undermine her authority, and they would even spread lies about her. The killing part was that the lies were not investigated but believed. The dark shadow that was following her, returned.

Riddy was called on the first Friday in January. She found out that two envious volunteers announced through flyers that the food pantry would close. Pastor Pat did not have the decency after nineteen years of loyal service and dedication with pledges, tithes, and offerings to say, "You are no longer needed or wanted here." But God spoke to Riddy before this awful event.

At one time Riddy had two jobs at CFA Plantation Center, one was the food pantry and the other was a community organizer. However; after the unexpected notice of the shutting down of the food pantry, she began to experience tremendous persecution, but she kept her hope in God.

Riddy was being punished and mistreated. She barely had any money while people were being paid for several positions. There would be a time that Pastor Pat would want Riddy to work on special projects with an assurance that she would be given a nice substantial position. All positions would go to other people. She could only have a low paying part- time position. She was hated.

Riddy continued to trust in her God. There was a time that she would want to go out to dinner, and people would invite her out. There was another time that she had no food in the refrigerator, and someone would drop by with a dish. God would lead her to a thrift store where she would get designer perfumes for a dollar, and nice soaps. One day, she had gotten an ostrich purse that sold at retail for three hundred dollars. It became hers for only two dollars. The cashier was shocked that no one caught that mistake. People would drop by and give Riddy new outfits. One of Riddy's aunts bought her a summer wardrobe that consisted of silk dresses. She used to wonder why people would stare her down at CFA Plantation Center. Perhaps, they were perplexed as to how she prospered in the midst of adversity.

God even gave Riddy three doctoral degrees. The first doctoral degree, Riddy's aunt paid for. The other two doctoral degrees, she earned as the Dean of a Bible college. The more that people would try to destroy, harm or hurt Riddy, the more God blessed her. The doctoral degrees were from Midwest Theological Institute which is not in existence now. The degrees are in theology, biblical studies, and pastoral counseling.

An Apostle friend of Riddy's noted that certain individuals were now practicing witchcraft. Riddy refused to comment on such an unbelievable statement. She chose not to focus on that. She did know that God is sovereign and in control of everything and everybody. God would somehow and someway take care of Riddy and Sweetie.

Riddy never told Sweetie about the persecution that she was facing. She had just enough money to pay the rent at CFA Apartment Complex, and bus fare to return to work. CFA Plantation Center saw to her only having the bare necessities. After a period of time when Pastor Pat's character changed, the church really did began to operate like a plantation. The members were enslaved. You had the ruling class and they were even called overseers. That term "overseers" was used during slavery. You had members doing all the work and bringing in tons of money and benefiting while everyone else is in subsidy housing and receiving food stamps.

Riddy began to have bad dreams about the leadership of CFA Plantation Center. The last dream was about a giant dragon that had taken over the center. One of Riddy's friend daughter's named Edie had bad dreams about the center also. She saw four huge spirits that took over the center, but an angel spoke to Edie and told her that she would be protected.

To make matters worse, Pastor Pat told Riddy that he wanted her to go to Jamaica. However; at that time, Riddy had just started a doctoral program at Emoore University, yet she was willing to go. The school's administrator was willing to set up a correspondence program from Jamaica.

Every Sunday during church service, it was announced that Riddy would be serving as a missionary in Jamaica, but it seemed to depress people. It was a queer feeling. Although

Riddy was willing to go, God stepped in and would not let her go.

Riddy later found out that over a million dollars had come the week that she was supposed to go, yet Pastor Pat did not want her to have a penny of it. Pastor Pat wanted the wisdom, and knowledge that God gave Riddy, but he did not want her to have anything because of his hatred for her.

Pastor Pat was known for cheating his own son out of money that they made jointly for a play. Pastor Pat's son had produced a successful play, and he refused to pay him.

Only the elite of the center had homes, cars, and nice salaries, while others worked as slaves on the plantation.

When Riddy walked out and resigned from organizing at CFA Plantation Center, no one called or came by, not even Pastor Pat. There was no farewell party or anything after nineteen years of service. The people at Rush Hospital, where she used to work, did not believe in God, and they at least gave her a going away party.

Riddy walked out with her God. She still loved the people whom she knew for years. She felt like Abraham. Although she knew not where she was going or where the road was going to lead her, she was determined to find a new path.

Six months prior to the food pantry closing down, Riddy met a gal name Vonnie. She was very kind, and always treated Riddy nice and with gifts. The meaner they treated Riddy the nicer God had Vonnie to treat her. She was treated so well that it buffeted the inhumane blows that were thrown her way.

Sweetie had left CFA Plantation Center peacefully the year before. She saw and felt what her mom was going through and decided she no longer wanted to be there. God opened a door miraculously to receive a four-year scholarship. A minister made an announcement at CFA Plantation Center about the scholarship program. Riddy prayed that Sweetie would get an opportunity. The minister approached Sweetie and signed her up.

He and Riddy were told that Sweetie was accepted. However, the day before Sweetie was supposed to actually leave, she received no letter of confirmation or phone call. The coordinator of the college program and Riddy tried to reach an administrator at the Ohio location, but no calls were returned. So, as the final day drew closer, Riddy spoke in faith and told the minister, "You know that I am crazy. I am going to put her on the bus."

On that same day, Sweetie was calling from her job at the Southside Parents and Friends Center every hour on the hour asking when she should leave her job. When Riddy called Sweetie to quit, she had already left. So, she prayed that Sweetie would not do anything irrational. Riddy prayed that Sweetie would come to the office, and she did come to get the information she needed to take advantage of the scholarship.

They went home to pick up her luggage and then to the bus station. Sweetie left a message on her job's answering service that she would no longer be able to continue working there.

Riddy laid hands on Sweetie and told her that she was Moses, the bus would be her ark, prayer would be the slime pit, and the route would be the Nile, and when she got to Central State in Ohio, she would see Pharaoh's daughter. Riddy committed Sweetie into the hands of the Lord, and then off to the bus stop they went. Riddy fought back the tears and returned home after seeing her daughter off.

There was no reason to be in Chicago anymore. Her future was a mystery. She had no inclination of what was ahead of her. She did not even want to be in Chicago. She once had a dream about the foundation cracking under her feet, and four major pillars falling from under the ceiling. Instead, the foundation had crumbled, and the very thing and people she loved had turned on her.

Vonnie had managed to get a job at a school and talked the administrator into hiring Riddy. Riddy began to work on a part-time basis.

One beautiful March day, Riddy walked into the office with a smile and sat at the typewriter to write her resignation and resign from CFA Plantation Center. She submitted it, left, and never looked back. After a while, Sweetie called because she wanted to come home; Riddy would console her and let her know that there was nothing to come home to.

Every time Sweetie would call, complaining about her roommate, Riddy would say, "I wish I was in your place. You have no idea how blessed you are. Do not even dream about coming home because there is nothing here."

Riddy eventually visited Sweetie on campus. She had hotel money but the nearest hotel was so far from the college campus. God fixed it that Riddy was able to stay with Sweetie in the dorm for an entire week. Sweetie's roommate had not arrived for the second quarter.

It broke Sweetie's heart to see her mother because she knew that something was wrong, although she did not know what. Eventually, Riddy told her that Pastor Pat became cruel and treacherous. Riddy encouraged Sweetie to keep her mind on the Lord, and her studies. Riddy's joy was when Sweetie was consistently on the honor roll. Riddy cried with tears of joy.

Chapter Twenty-Three

The last time Riddy heard Prophet Hilly preach, he preached about the sovereignty of God. The message went so deep down on the inside of her. She remembers one other time that in the middle of Prophet Hilly's sermon, she grabbed him by his ankles while huge drops of sweat fell from her face.

Riddy felt like her soul was being ripped into pieces. Once again Riddy's heart ached. God woke Riddy one early spring morning and showed her a vision of the university's president at Emoore pacing back and forth perspiring nervously. Riddy heard the Holy Ghost say, "Paperwork." It was when she came out of the trance that she realized that there was a problem at Emoore.

In two weeks, rumors broke out that the people who had graduated the year before did not receive their degrees. They had paid thousands of dollars and the school was not accredited. All Riddy knew was that she had to get out, but she did not have other plans.

After seeing the vision, Riddy broke out in a cold sweat because God told her to get out. Riddy found out that the administrator and his staff was doing drugs and the administrator had committed adultery and stolen students' money. At the time, Riddy was operating the food pantry and the room was rented for church services from time to time and she found a program at another school with a doctorate program. She was able to get into school just in time.

Riddy was scheduled to graduate from Emoore with a doctorate's degree because of the corruption of the school, she had to look for another.

Unknown to Riddy, the graduation of the new school was supposed to be on the next Saturday, but the graduation had to be postponed. Riddy called the school on that following Monday. The school administrator was familiar with what Emoore's students were experiencing, and even enrolled some of those students.

Riddy was told that she could graduate in two weeks if she could produce certain documents, lessons, and a portfolio, along with five hundred dollars.

God told Riddy to explain everything to her aunt. Years ago Big Dot had prophesied that Riddy would receive a PhD, one day. Riddy was sick of school. She was at a point in her life where she wanted to get married and settle down, but every time she looked up, it was time for school over and over again.

It was after the graduation that a meeting was held where Riddy told Pastor Pat about Emoore. Riddy had told Pastor Pat just in time because the administrator of Emoore was about to rip off Pastor Hilly. Riddy was sure that it was not mentioned, but at least she tried.

Pastor Hilly and Pastor Pat were friends in the ministry. Pastor Pat would invite Pastor Hilly to do revivals. One day that same administrator from Emoore contacted Pastor Hilly out of the blue to do business. Riddy found out and went and told Pastor Pat about what God showed her in a dream and that she found out about the drugs and adultery. She told Pastor Pat so Pastor Hilly would not be a victim. Only God knows if they listened.

Riddy hoped that one day Pastor Hilly would see through CFA Plantation Center. She hoped that he will see that the passion for Christ was now gone, and that flesh now ruled and reigned.

On March 29, 2005, Riddy was dressed in a black short sleeved dress; adorned with pearl earrings and a necklace, and she walked out of the center of chaos.

Riddy later found out that her mother sent a very interesting letter exposing their lusts, especially the lusts of the head of the church, Pastor Pat. Yes, Riddy was bewildered when the first lady gave her a beautiful hand bag and was trembling while doing so. Riddy was now leaving Egypt and the hand bag was a green designer bag trimmed in gold which was symbolic of when God told the children of Israel to go and borrow from the Egyptians.

God had been showing Riddy visions for three years before she actually left CFA Plantation Center. God had also shown her a group of people with white robes and how heaven opened up and a wind weaved through the rows, and some people's heads turned into wolves' heads. Then there was another vision where heaven opened and wind came through, and some people's white robes were blown off them, while others still had their white shiny robes on.

Riddy's last experience that prompt her to leave the Center was when Prophet Hilly visited, and prayed over an offering that she gave. It was after putting her offering in the basket that he turned suddenly and whispered, "Abraham walk into your destiny, and as you walk into your destiny you shall walk into your blessings." It was after that when Hilly winked at her as though he was giving Riddy a secret code. The resignation was submitted, and the escape was planned.

Riddy began to work full time at the Bible college after receiving her doctorate degree and for a while it was peaches and cream. Riddy fell for the administrator who claimed to be not just a born again Christian, but a minister. She found out that he was a womanizer. A whore.

Riddy thought that perhaps he was her husband for the ninety-ninth time. Every time Riddy would meet a guy, she would think *maybe he is the one*. Then the guys would go for others. Little did she realize that God was shielding her, and that those guys were wolves and were not sent from God.

They would only tear and rip her soul to pieces, so after many disappointments, Riddy finally gave up, and learned to be content with herself in God, God's Word, Sweetie and the life that He had allowed her to have. Now, she can discover the wealth that was placed in her from the beginning.

God also continued to deliver her from a spirit of lust, depression, and other evil spirits. God was peeling her like an onion, and was removing layers of evil spirits out of her personality. God was building her character.

After having thirty-five years in the workforce of education, social work, community development, and theology, one day before the dawning of the new day, God woke Riddy up and said, "I want you to teach my people everything that you Know."

Riddy had to figure out what she knew after years of schooling. She knew that she could train and develop people in opening their own agencies and how to operate them and obtain funding for their programs through grants and private contributions.

After completing her doctorate's degree, Vonnie talked to her boss Emery, at Midwest Theological Institute, the school that she escaped to after leaving Emoore University to help Riddy get a job. Riddy was offered a position as a dean at the bible college.

Several months later, upon going to work in her deanship, someone from the outside called the owner with a lie that she did not offer him the right information. Riddy was thrown off the premises despite the many people who fought for her to keep her job.

A distraught Riddy returned home in the midday, but God reminded her of the new task that He ordained for her. So, Riddy dusted herself off, and with only a cell phone, kitchen table, pen, legal pad and a few business cards, the door was open for a not-for-profit business. As money came in, She set up her paperwork, and the structure of her establishment.

Chapter Twenty-Four

In 1996, Riddy had five streams of income coming into the house. One income was the child support payed monthly by Sweetie's father, consultant work, salary as a teacher, income tax refund, and one other source that totaled a nice figure. God blew on the money.

When January 1997 rolled around there was no MONEY. NADA. God wanted to show up and show out and let Riddy know that He is God. God wanted to show her who was in charge. God performed a lot of miracles from reducing a $300 school debt to $7.00, payment of graduation fees were eliminated, down to paying for Sweetie's prom dress two days before the prom after repeatedly putting the dress on hold every week at a store. Riddy's Grand Am during this time was totaled by her niece's prom date; however, the insurance company refused to pay the cost of the vehicle.

One day Riddy went to the mailbox and there was a check for an accident paid to her and her siblings from an accident her father was involved in. Riddy got on an elevator and went straight to 307 their condo excited about money finally coming in. She opened the letter to a check written out to her for five thousand dollars. God was always on time.

Riddy's mind went back. The phone rang.

Riddy picked up. "Yes."

"It's me," Ed said.

The voice sounds familiar yet different. "It's me, daughter. My life has changed," Ed explained. "I don't drink anymore."

"Wow."

"I am doing good. I witness on the bus, and at work I do a Bible study about Jesus. I talk to people about God."

Riddy could hear the change because beforehand, Ed had started back drinking after his third wife, Mary passed. She had been his rock, and now she was gone. The last time Sweetie and Riddy saw him, it was when they had attended the Barner family's reunion, and he was drunk as a skunk.

Riddy did a modern dance to a gospel song and shared her suicidal testimony, which Ed did not take well. It was an embarrassment to him. Ed had missed the whole point and got angry when he heard that she wanted to end her life.

They sat in front of her house in his car. She remembered staring at him saying within herself if he got saved it would be a miracle, and then jumping out of the car and slamming the car door in disgust hoping to never see or hear from him again. Well, miracles do happen.

The two of them had a mini-reunion on the phone and agreed to re-establish their relationship. It had been over ten years since hearing from him.

You got to forgive, a voice bellowed from the podium of the pulpit. It was at those words that Riddy felt something move in a serpentine pattern through her body. She was harboring unforgiveness and had to receive deliverance in order to want a relationship with her father.

Riddy began to spend time weekly with her dad and would bring her seventeen-year-old Sweetie along. They all took a road trip to Nebraska to visit relatives, she knew nothing about.

She would see Hiawatha her father's father for the first and last time. He looked harmless and did not look like the hell-raiser that had been described to her from several decades ago. Sweetie resembled the man who was over six feet, and who now lie helpless in a hospital bed in the living room.

A few weeks after the trip, Ed disappeared. Here we go again. Riddy called and called and there was no answer. She went to his address and knocked on the door and there was still no answer. Riddy went to his job where he worked as a security guard at a senior citizen building, and no one had heard from him. They were good at giving him messages, though.

She remembered stopping by one hot summer day and they could not remember her name. Ed was told that his daughter came by and he explained that he had two daughters. So, he asked if the woman that they saw asked a lot of questions and they replied, "Yes." He then chuckled and said, "That was

Riddy." Serena never ask questions. The less she knew, the less she is responsible for, she felt.

Riddy found out that Ed was in the Veteran's Hospital. The next day Riddy visited Ed and the nurse was glad to see her. She sent for the doctor who gave her the grave news. Ed had cancer of the bladder. Riddy walked down a long hallway to the room at the end and there was Ed. He was skin and bones. Riddy could not believe her eyes. It was just in the month of June for Father's Day that she jetted out of the pulpit and ran to the first row where she grabbed Ed's hand and they did the holy dance and praised God together. Afterwards, they had dinner at Red Lobster. This would be their first and last Father's Day together.

The surgery was successful, but Ed's immune system was weak and he caught an infection that did not respond to any antibiotics. Ed was dying, and he knew it. Sweetie and Riddy stood by his bedside on each side. They were silent. Then Riddy asked Ed to forgive her for not being a daughter to him. She also told him that she forgave him for all the times that he had not been there for her, and she kissed him goodbye.

As Riddy and Sweetie left the room, Sweetie told Riddy that she had a vision and saw Riddy born, and she saw Riddy's different stages of her life. In between there were long lines that represented the long periods of her not seeing her dad. Sweetie then said, "You then spoke those words of forgiveness to him, mom."

As they reached the first floor heading toward the parking lot they saw Riddy's cousin, Thurman. The three of them greeted each other. Then Riddy began to prophesy that heaven was for her homosexual cousin. He broke down in tears and was unable to fathom that God could possibly love and want him.

She tried to get him to go over the repentance prayer, but he refused. Riddy and Sweetie walked away and was about to go through the double doors and Riddy felt that Sweetie should pray him through. She obeyed the assignment unknown to both, Thurman was dying of AIDS, and that would be the last time that either of them would see him alive.

It was at a distance that she saw Sweetie leading Thurman over the sinner's prayer with thanksgiving and gratitude. Thurman accepted Christ with a bowed head and eyes closed with lips moving. Riddy sighed with relief. Another one bites the dust. Yes Lord!

It would be the last time she would see the black sheep of the family who was an outcast, vagabond, thief and homeless. Everyone hid their purses, and stuffed their money in their bras when Thurman came around. Everyone. Big Mama, would shelter him, but after her death there was no advocate because he was band from Big Dot's house by his step-father Ern. It was because of his thieving ways, and the final straw was when he caused the death of Ern's beloved German Shepherd Woody.

Several months later, Thurman would be separated from his lover, diagnosed with full blown AIDS; however, God would bless him to finish his final days in a new facility built from the ground up. He would have unusual favor with the administrator who would periodically visit Thurman to play chess and checkers with him. There was one time Thurman snuck out the facility, and other times he would disappear, as sick as he was, and the administrator had a built in inner GPS system in her heart. She was always able to track Thurman down and return him to the facility. Thurman later got weaker as the end approached. He embraced his death, and Christ.

Riddy had a dream of seeing a roof raise off a house three times, and then the house collapsed and slid down a hill into mud. The sky would open and the sun would shine then the hand of God would reach into the mud and pull out this gold bar and pull it into heaven and the sky would close.

The gold bar was Thurman. This dream would bring solace to Big Dot who had wondered about her son's final resting place. The son whom she loved above all, who was conceived, while Ern was in the military. It was on a lonely night that impregnated her.

Upon Ern finishing his duty he returned to an eight months pregnant fiancée, and confessed his infidelity to Big Dot as well. Big Dot now had to choose. Ern chose to leave the child and mother overseas because of his love for Big Dot. Big Dot chose Ern and although she chose Ern, she lived with Rodger every day because Thurman was his splitting image. Ern felt the distance between him and Big Dot a many of the cold sleepless nights, and he would hate the sight of Thurman because Big Dot would love the sight of Rodger through Thurman. She would live tormented for the rest of her life as to whether she made the right decision due to Ern womanizing ways.

Riddy sighed as she sat on the couch fanning the check from the car accident that Ed was in prior to his hospitalization and surgery. It was a bittersweet moment because he did not live to see that the judge ruled in his favor. He was able to leave an inheritance after the hospital bills were covered to his three children.

Riddy now looked at the black leather couch, loveseat, dining room set that was mingle amongst the country style furniture set in Ed's apartment.

She remembered the furniture people calling while she stayed in Ed's apartment looking high and low for an insurance policy in order to bury him. The one she found was less than two years old and was contested, and all others had lapsed.

She remembered Ed begging her to take insurance out on him before finding out his condition, but she was filled with unforgiveness and resentment especially with him disappearing for ten years and then later intruding into her life. He was AWOL an army term for missing in action without intentions. She told the people about Ed's death, but they got crazy and started to do back-to-back phone calls after promising that they would close the account and charge it off. After all, people do DIE. So, she told them to go to the funeral home and to see Ed for themselves. The next morning they tried to break down the entrance door to the second floor to retrieve the property, but the landlord chewed them out.

Now it is time to move again. God spoke to Riddy about moving back into the city. She then began to dream about a White House, but she rebelled and concluded that she would remain in Forest Park, Illinois. Then Sweetie told her mom about dreaming of a new house. Then Riddy's niece had a similar dream of moving into a new house. Riddy then sat everyone down and let them know that they were of age and could leave, but she was staying in Forest Park. It was that night that Riddy dreamed about a bunch of dots in midair and the word mice was written above it. It would be two weeks later when mice would invade the building.

The condo association members got into a bona fide fistfight, and extermination contracts went un-sign for months. Riddy and Sweetie would be held hostage in the master bedroom. While Kenyatta was there, Riddy would throw her out to scout for food due to the fact she was from Cabrini Green. She was used to seeing rats.

Riddy slammed the door in her face and Kenyatta screamed, "Auntie that's not right."

Riddy and Sweetie heard a concession of screams as Kenyatta managed to navigate the hallway that led to the kitchen, and ran back with food. The next week Riddy beat everyone packing. She was the first and the others followed her lead. The house was on the west side of Chicago at Jackson and Western.

Riddy thought back to CFA Plantation Center and everyone was happy that Prophet Hilly and his team were back. *It's gonna be hot tonight*, thought Riddy. Hilly's assistants who constituted a preaching machine told Riddy that God was going to restore the job that she had lost, and when she returned she would get a promotion. It was true, Riddy had gotten laid off from the Chicago Public School. It was during the break that Riddy entered into the bathroom and a white lady who had not seen her in service told her everything that she was told by Hilly's assistant. While listening to the prophecy, a slim black lady latched hold onto Riddy's cheeks and squeezed the heck out of them, while saying that her cheeks were like a baby's. She was even talking in baby language. "Coochie Coochie."

Really? Riddy did not know whether to smack the woman or allow her to continue to coochie-coochie her while continuing to hold her large baby fat jaws. So, Riddy froze and realized that

God was doing something peculiar. The lady then gave her a real estate card and said that if she ever needed a place to stay feel free to contact her. *Hmmm,* Riddy thought.

Days later, Riddy called the lady about the house, and she recalled giving her the business card regarding a house. The lady then gave Riddy a house for her and her family to live in. It was rent-free, and she would only be responsible for the utilities.

The prophecy was fulfilled and Riddy returned to the Chicago Public School system with a promotion that came with a whopping salary increase! God is awesome.

About five years later, Riddy and Sweetie found a brand new renovated upscale apartment. During this time, Sweetie graduated with her degree from her dream school. The complex was ten minutes away from the United Center and fifteen minutes away from the lake. An awesome location.

The front door led to the spacious kitchen that was filled with pine cabinets, new stove, and new refrigerator. The left was this humongous living room in a circular pattern, with three huge windows overlooking a garden and the main street. The building was attached to two other buildings, and they lived in the middle section on the first floor. The building was a secure building with a buzzing system.

A so-called friend who lived in the complex wanted her to live in the west building on the third floor, across the hall from her. However, Riddy was not feeling it. She had the opportunity to tour the entire complex before apartments were leased. Riddy kept coming back to this apartment and felt led to settle in apartment 101. It was a great choice even though the apartments on the second and third floors of the building were larger.

Riddy plowed ahead with her new assignment from God, with Sweetie by her side. Riddy was doing incorporations, 501c3s, bylaws' workshops and seminars through a not-for-profit that God instructed her to formulate. She even had a radio program and later added a television series through her not-for-profit organization. Donations were flooding in and she had started the business with a pen, a tablet, a cell phone, and sitting at her kitchen table. Now, three years later, she had a home office with office furniture, equipment and supplies in the living room. She had questioned God why she could not be downtown or in the market district. The creator spoke, and said, "Use what you have."

Riddy felt she had nothing until God told her to look at her pen, phone, etc. The Creator spoke, "As you walk forward, I will make you a magnetic force, and you will attract everything you need. Just obey Me." Sweetie enrolled in Roosevelt University, helped out in the office, and with the chores.

Chapter Twenty-Five

Riddy began to have a series of dreams with the same theme. She saw a hotel, hotel lobby, front desk, and rooms. And then one day while out driving, as she passed a hotel, it was as though it was highlighted. Riddy parked and went inside, and it was the hotel in the dream. God spoke to her about doing a conference. Riddy was stunned because there was only twelve dollars in the bank. How would she afford to pay for the conference? But the Spirit of God kept moving upon her and she could not shake Him. So finally, Riddy made an appointment with an event planner of the hotel. The staff gave her a tour and went over prices and interviewed her. The cost would be $5,600, and she would need $500 deposit, ASAP, to hold the date of September 10, 2006.

Riddy swallowed hard. Very hard. She informed the young woman that she had to meet with the board. The thought of the board consisting of *God the Father, the Son, and the Holy Ghost*—and there was still only $12 in the bank account.

After getting on her knees, the next day, a client needed services and she received exactly the $500 she needed for her deposit. Now she needed $5,100 more before September, 2006. Cool.

Riddy relaxed after she and God went back and forth about her signing the contract. Riddy reminded God that on Earth, they needed and used money. She needed money before she signed the contract. God shot back, "Sign the contract, and I will give you the money." Riddy humbled herself and signed the contract. Whew!!! God will take care of everything, she assured herself, while pressing forward.

Riddy and Sweetie would pray and put together a to do list for the conference and upcoming planning sessions. They sat at their desks that were at opposite sides of the room. After putting the program together, workshop topics and made contact with speakers to confirm, Sweetie asked how they were going to get the people to attend the conference. "It's just us scheduled to be there." Sweetie said. God gave the ideas of emailing, phone calls, faxes, and the posting of flyers because there was no money to purchase or mail invitations. In addition to that, God would not allow Riddy to charge admission.

Sweetie prophesied that in one week, people would begin to hunt her mom down. Soon the phone began to ring off the hook. People were calling, wanting to reserve their spots for the conference.

Before the people started calling, in the back of Riddy's mind she wondered how the conference was going to get paid for especially since God wanted it to be free because he wanted to bless His people.

It was now August, 2006 and the balance was not paid. Riddy received a call from a new event planner from the hotel requesting her to come and finalize everything. "Lord, please don't let them ask for any money," was Riddy's prayer of the hour.

The previous event planner had been fired and someone was snatched from the front desk to serve. No questions were asked for Riddy's part. Wiping her forehead with relief thinking, *Phew*!!! Riddy was about to celebrate her 50th birthday as well.

She had checked out a gold leather suit that cost $300. Sweetie, two weeks later got the suit from the same company for $99! She picked up a pair of stilettos for $15, regularly priced for $125. God was putting things together. A lot of donated items came through the door to be raffled off at the conference. They ranged from dinner vouchers, gift cards, printers and gift certificate services. Banks and companies had agreed to be sponsors, but unknown to Riddy, checks would not be released until after the event.

An unknown protocol. The stress of this thing was mounting up now it was count down. It's now one week before the event. Riddy was in prayer with an apostle friend. She tried to reach out to people to help her especially family members, but she was ignored and was on her own. Riddy's van had been stolen a couple of years prior and Sweetie wanted to know how they would get to the event with the one hundred workshop folders, packages, and items needed. Riddy's response was, "We will get on the bus if necessary."

"Oh no, mother," was Sweetie's response. God led Sweetie to contact a brand new limousine service that agreed to provide service for $50.00. A miraculous movement of God indeed. Unheard of. Limousine service for $50.00. Everything was falling into place, except the balance for the event. A woman even donated a free two-night stay at the same hotel chain at the Marriott on the south side because she was a stockholder. Free of charge. Riddy's apostle friend informed Riddy that God was going to move another way.

The Friday before the event, Riddy could not take the pressure any more or the mounting uncertainties. She began to go downtown and knock on bank doors. She even called leading renowned pastors of the City of Chicago. One particular church collected $500,000 every Sunday and kept it locked in a church vault. The church would not give her a dime. Surely, $4,600 was nothing to sneeze at. She was declined. So, it was off to the banks, and Riddy could only find one Vice President to hear her appeal, and who was willing to bring it up at the board meeting that was about to happen in fifteen minutes.

As Riddy stood in front of the lady, the Shekinah Glory, a cloudy mist stood between the two women. The mist lifted and the banker then said, "No." Riddy tucked her tail between her legs, so-to-speak, and went home on the Al—mean-mugging God all the way. The Al doors then swung open and an artist sat across from Riddy, and began to draw her in charcoal. He gave her the picture and it was not a pretty sight. It was as though God was saying look how you're looking. Riddy turned and looked in the opposite direction. She remembered an earlier conversation with God about approaching fifty, and it was time to retire and stop. She reminded God that she was turning fifty. God shot back, "Moses was eighty when I called him."

Well hush my mouth, Riddy thought.

Riddy and Sweetie would be driven to the hotel on the south side because there were no rooms left at the hotel on the west side in order to check in the day before the event. They were dropped off by her step-father who assured her that the cake was ordered and would be ready for the event, and that he would pick it up. After checking into the elegant hotel, the two had a quiet dinner, and then retired early for the night.

Sunday morning, September 10, 2006, Riddy asked again what was she to do. No answer. Riddy turned and looked at Sweetie, saying that, "We are truly in the hands of God."

The limousine pulls up to the building and God still not saying anything. NADA. Zip. While on the elevator, no voice, approaching the limousine, still no voice of God. The limousine drives to the hotel on the west side cruising down the highway and approaching the driveway to the hotel. The manager and event planner were standing outside of the hotel waiting for Riddy. Riddy became unnerved and her heart palpitated, and God was still not saying what to do with this large balance. She stepped out of the limo, and Sweetie did the same from the opposite side. Each step taken, her heart did a thud, thud that sounded like ringing in her ears. God still was not answering.

Finally, upon reaching the staff and as Riddy tripped but managed to steady herself to regain her footing, she heard, "Go with the flow." No money was asked for, and Riddy was whisked off to do a final check of the registration area, workshop area, lobby, restaurant setup, and patio setting, and all was well. She was left alone and used the time to call her apostle friend, and together they praised their God, and gave thanks.

Riddy had a team besides herself and Sweetie. Mom, Stepfather, Sherry, Robert, and Vonnie were nowhere to be found. Riddy made the mistake of introducing the new convert to a so-called friend who, out of envy, and unknown to Riddy, ousted her out of Vonnie's life.

Karon was covetous, and everything Vonnie did for Riddy she expected likewise. Before the conference, Vonnie and Karon visited Riddy at her home to inform her that Vonnie would now be under her leadership. *Hmmm.* Riddy had the conference and did not have time for pettiness or a tug of war.

Then there was Sherry that volunteered for everything and it was with caution that Riddy warned and told her that she did not want anybody to overload themselves. Sherry's duties were to work on name tags, dinner passes, and workshop questionnaires.

Robert was supposed to contact radio stations for PR and do security with a friend. He did neither and decided to have a BBQ outreach the weekend before Riddy's event and browbeat everyone to come to his event to help with his pastoral anointing. Riddy gladly helped. But later found out that he did not do assignments nor would he do security, but sulk through the whole event wrenching with jealousy like someone had did him an injustice.

The day of the event, one speaker had flown out of town and did not show up but God had a ram in the bush. Another speaker showed up in the morning stating that she did not have any material for the afternoon session even though she had received a one month notification. Riddy calmly gave some simple tips to get her started.

One day when Sweetie was going to purchase folders at a penny store, Riddy felt that she should also pick up some name tags, and that together they would work on the dinner passes and the questionnaires.

Sherry told Riddy at the last minute that she could not do the registration table, but God provided another ram in the bush. And then she came super late without the name tags, and dinner passes, but she had the questionnaires. She had even promised to bring a camera.

Sherry's husband innocently informed Riddy with Sherry standing there that his wife told him to put it back, and then Sherry turned beet red. During Riddy's workshop, Sherry passed out questionnaires by slamming them on the participants' table arrangement in anger. Anger and the spirit of sabotage was subdued by the Holy Ghost.

Riddy wore a pinstripe suit for the first workshop session, *Proposal Letter Writing* which was done at the lower level of the hotel. There were four other workshops titled *Department of Human Service, Banking, Housing,* and *Financial Literacy*.

After the workshop, Riddy, Sherry, and Robert was in the elevator headed for dinner. Robert's eyes scanned the dinner passes and commented to Sherry about the great job done by her. Sherry looked shame-faced, hung her head, and answered that Riddy had did the dinner passes for everyone. Robert looked up with a questioning expression on his face, but no sound came out because he knew that was one of many assignments that Sherry did not handle because of the spirit of pride. It was revealed that Sherry was just showboating.

The restaurant would be closed and only open for Riddy and the guests where they would feast off of Italian cuisine. Then there was the patio to enjoy the downtown view. Riddy's event had the whole hotel. Rather God's event. The hotel lobby was to be filled with vendors. After dinner, then Riddy and the guests would return back to the lower level to a theater – style setting for a 50th birthday celebration which was part of the conference. Riddy thought, celebrating her birthday while at the conference was an excellent idea. The birthday cake was free due to a mix up.

Anyway, the keynote speaker addressed the crowd, and the raffling off of prizes were done and excitement was in the air. One of the winners pitched in and helped out where needed for the remaining part of the evening of the event.

Vonnie surprisingly came with Karon trailing behind looking back because she was a no-show for the committee meetings, and she looked sheepishly. What in the world had Karon been pumping into Vonnie?

Riddy really did not have the time so she moved forward. After the keynote speaker the spirit of prophesy burst forth through Riddy talking about the upcoming collapse in the banking industry and the housing market plundering.

After dinner a waiter gave Riddy the long awaited bill. The bill was marked down to $3,500. Riddy knew it should have been $4600. The waiter would not listen, so they all went down to the theater seating after Riddy changed into her leather suit and was escorted into the service. Apostle Jim and his wife were co-laborers and God used them to usher in deliverance.

Hotel workers stood in the threshold of the door and beheld the glory of God. Riddy expected nothing but was showered with gifts, and even money that was used to pay the speaker and sound man. Still no money to pay the hotel balance. The next two days Riddy called because a check for $1,500 came through to go toward the bill. Upon arrival to the hotel she was informed that the balance of the bill was $2,500 instead of $3,500. No one would listen when Riddy tried to explain otherwise. The debt had been reduced by God to $1,000. A few weeks later a check for $300 appeared and Riddy turned it in to the hotel and the balance was $700. Finally there was no balance. God paid for everything. The event ended up costing $2,300 instead of $5,600 to teach and feed 100 people. God is awesome. He moved.

After the service guest mingled in the hallway where various hors d'oeuvres, sweets, and non-alcoholic drinks were served until Riddy asked them to leave the area.

The conference and the stress during and leading up to it was well worth it. People left very informed and free to incorporate the classes into their everyday lives.

Chapter Twenty-Six

A few months later it would be time to prepare for Sweetie's graduation from Roosevelt after transferring from Central State of Ohio; however, the climax of the house changed. Sweetie wanted to work a job, but Riddy advised against it and encouraged her to complete her studies and do chores. The evil one that followed Riddy during her most difficult times invaded Sweetie's mind and convinced her that Riddy was using her. Sweetie thought, *Riddy was sitting on her tail, and had it easy making appointments and meetings with clients which required no blood, sweat or tears while I would be cooking, cleaning, and doing the laundry.*

Riddy had to believe God for the rent, electric, bills, food and transportation and surely Sweetie could manage and free her up to do so. Conflict arose. There would be times Sweetie promised to cook dinner then changed her mind, and when Riddy finished working there would be nothing prepared. Riddy always had breakfast, usually cold cereal or a granola bar, and fixed a full breakfast on the weekends. Sometimes she would skip lunch. If she ate lunch, it would be a light salad or a sandwich. She just asked Sweetie to fix one meal a day, and that was dinner. Sweetie could have cooked a few meals a day, which could have resulted in Sweetie only having to cook just twice a week then Riddy could have warmed up the meals.

Laundry was done two times a month, and Dad helped by transporting Sweetie to the laundry. Sweetie became very disrespectful and unkind. Riddy would call her and she would not answer or she asked a question and she would not respond and just ignored her.

Riddy remembered how one time, Sweetie was in the bathroom taking a bath, and Riddy was talking through the door, asking her questions. She was non-responsive, and Riddy opened the door and Sweetie still did not open her mouth. The mother-daughter relationship had deteriorated at an alarming rate. Riddy cried many nights.

She had a great pregnancy, labor, and delivery. She had no behavior problems with Sweetie as a toddler, adolescent or young adult. She rarely got a whooping because she was obedient and if she did anything wrong, all Riddy ever had to do was to talk to her—and Sweetie would straighten up right away.

The question arose—how does one parent discipline an adult child? There was no text book, method that covered that subject matter. Should Riddy become barbaric like the ancestors before her and just go upside Sweetie's head. Should she jump on her—so late in life? Sweetie had turned on Riddy.

Well, strange things started happening, clients would come and do business and upon completion they would begin to ask if she had a daughter and to send for her. Sweetie would be home and they would all prophesy the same thing. Respect your mother. Honor your mother. One particular prophet had her on her knees before Riddy, apologizing, but it was all to no avail, the misbehavior continued until one day Riddy told her that if she continued her behavior, God was going to separate them. And she was not going to like how He did it. Sweetie did not take heed, so the pending doom was just around the corner.

The phone rang and Riddy answered, "He is going to put her on the street." Cherise said, a woman who knew what was going on with Sweetie outside their home.

"What? Proclaim Riddy," in shock.

"Yes ma'am. Please do not let Sweetie know that I told you that he is an ex-con who used to do drugs and was a pimp. Sweetie has been hanging out with these three girls, and ma'am they are not her friends. Ma'am, I had to call you because the week before graduation, she plans to run off with this guy to marry him," Cherise explained.

Riddy sat down.

"The only reason why I called was because I was not going to say anything but then I had a bad dream and in the dream, Sweetie died.

"No. I won't say anything. I will let God lead me into what to do. Thanks," Riddy said.

Later in the evening, Sweetie came home, and Riddy decided to share Cherise's dream as though it came from her.

Riddy opened up with, "I want to tell you about a dream."

She did not mention Cherise at all. After sharing the dream, Sweetie broke down and confessed. Sweetie had started coming home late, and missing classes and she even talked about the guy on her own and about him being a pimp and once did drugs, but Sweetie wanted to give him a chance because he had paid his dues to society. But lately she had been feeling pressured by him because he had become demanding and she needed to get away, but did not know how to get away from him.

Riddy answered with, "Give me your cell phone." Simple.

The confiscation of the cellphone broke the bondage and Sweetie went on to graduate. Riddy had also explained that if the man had loved her he would not have wanted her to miss her graduation from college.

Riddy was able to barter with a client for limousine service and Erle rode in the limousine along with Riddy and Sweetie. Although, Riddy and Erle was no longer together, they put on an united front—the two people who dearly loved Sweetie.

Riddy had planned to visit Junior for the summer in Florida after Sweetie's graduation. She had reunited with her brother after many years of silence. Riddy told him about the dream she had of an apartment building and Sweetie getting a place.

Before heading to Florida, Sweetie and Riddy went to Vegas to celebrate her graduation. Afterwards, Riddy continued traveling to Florida while Sweetie went back to Chicago.

Riddy specifically told her not to have anyone in the apartment while she was gone because that would be a lease violation. Well, a next door neighbor would later reveal that Sweetie had moved a girl into the apartment. Riddy had left Sweetie in charge of the business. Riddy had outlined the tasks and she called biweekly to make sure everything stayed afloat. Riddy would call, but there would be no answer, then she had the dream. God was showing Riddy that while she was on vacation, Sweetie had planned to move into an apartment and wipe out the savings, therefore, rendering Riddy unprepared and ended up homeless. Sweetie's plan blew up in her face and she ended up homeless.

She contacted the police department in Chicago to do a well-being check. They told Sweetie to call her mom.

Sweetie called that afternoon, and her behavior was questionable. She was told by Riddy that the trip was being cut short, and that she would be returning home. Sweetie offered her mother a nasty response, saying, "You can do whatever you want to." It was a stab in Riddy's heart.

Riddy spoke with Junior about Sweetie's behavior. He said, "Well, sis based on what you told me. I think you'd better go back to Chicago. You will be missed."

Riddy boarded the plane that Friday to return to Chicago. The weather was lousy and a rainstorm had created an outpour. Welcome back. Dad was supposed to pick up Riddy, but after several hours of waiting and calling, she had to proceed without him and an umbrella. Riddy had several stops before making it home. She had cleared out the checking account to pay the rent, electric and other bills.

When Riddy arrived, Sweetie's head was in the window, and the house was dark from the outside. Sweetie dashed out the door and hugged her mother, but there was something odd. Strange. Off.

Upon entering, there was a young lady. Riddy smiled and greeted her, and then asked her to leave. The young lady had given up her apartment. What God showed Riddy, all fell into place. Sweetie and the young lady, Sandra, were saving up money to get an apartment, they had planned to move out and to leave Riddy high and dry without a goodbye. Riddy would be homeless because she had no preparation for such a move.

Sweetie wanted to be on her own, and that was not a problem, but Sweetie wanted to leave abruptly with no warning. Riddy would have welcomed Sweetie's move for independence and would have been willing to help Sweetie plan the transition. However, God threw a brick in her plan. After the young lady left, Sweetie went into her room. Riddy went to the bathroom and overheard a conversation, but it was not clear. She returned to the living room.

Sweetie was visibly upset and began to pace back and forth and told her mother that the money in the bank was gone. Then Sweetie had a lightbulb moment. It dawned on her that Riddy had removed the funds. Sweetie lost it and became violent. The police had to be called. The police was forced to remove Sweetie from the home. Riddy felt distraught.

The next morning, Riddy arose to clean the apartment. It was in shambles. She had left it neat and clean, prior to her vacation. What a gruesome mess. It was late in the evening when Riddy searched through the suitcases of Sandra, and sure enough there was an application for an apartment. The Holy Ghost do not lie. Well. What was planned had backfired. "Oooh Sweetie. My precious Sweetie." Riddy exclaimed.

A few days later with a police escort, Sweetie picked up some of her personal items, while Riddy stood by helpless. Sweetie wanted out. Nothing is wrong with a young woman wanting to be on her own. That was not the issue. The problem is the way it all happened.

Several years passed before they reconciled.

Sweetie was on her own prematurely and unprepared for a cruel harsh dose of reality. She has just enrolled into the school of hard knocks and knee-ology.

Chapter Twenty-Seven

Riddy was a guest on Mary's TV show and a call came in. "Okay caller, you are on the line." Mary listened intensively as the voice stated that she had a building to donate. Riddy squealed with delight and had previously dreamt about the TV station and saw a building. Mary also was in need of a building. Before Riddy arrived at the TV set, God had spoken through a vision of a TV with static and assured Riddy that everything would be all right—just trust Him.

Pain hit Riddy in the stomach as the caller hung up and Mary did not offer instructions for the caller to on hold in order to get the number. Riddy said, "Oh my God, this is going to be like a needle in the haystack. How are we going to find this caller amongst millions of people?"

Three months later the caller would call the station again, and ask for Riddy's information, which started her transition from the apartment complex that CFA Plantation Center owned, and the Exodus will now be completed. Riddy had no more obligations to CFA. Thank God.

The persecution at CFA Plantation Center now had become more intense. In order to remain in the building, and not on a curb, she had to be assigned a case manager. It was the very position she was supposed to have had talking about insult to injury. However, Pastor Pat and his followers, the upper crust notorious for promising you something then snatching it away and giving it to someone else, then put you face to face with the person who has the position. All because Riddy would not falsify records nor send food across state lines or violate a contractual agreement with a local food bank. Riddy was not inhumane.

The First Lady would send Riddy to delivery vicious messages to others, and soon she would not have to deliver any more messages because she would have no more connection to CFA. When the minister's wife gleefully sat on her throne and asked Riddy, "Well, what did she say? How did she look?" Riddy would always answer that she just delivered the message and left without getting a response. That comment always seemed to knock the wind out of the pastor's wife. How could anyone so beautiful, talented, and accomplished be so mean?

Yeah, Riddy had to have a case manager from CFA now to meet with her in her home and not the office. This tactic was to get inside of the apartment and to see what was happening. So, Riddy put up decorative screens in the living room to hide the desks and file cabinets. She never required any services nor put in any requests. Riddy's response was pretty much yes or no or cut and dry. The case manager eventually vanished after nothing could be uncovered.

A few months later another incident would occur when she was invited to get dental services for free, but there was a stipulation and that she would have to travel to Indiana on a service night. She declined because she knew of people that needed dental work that was shipped to Indiana the sister church that did not make it back to Chicago. Riddy believed their plan was to do her the same way.

Then the folks at CFA Plantation Center declared a meet and greet, and held it across the hall from Riddy after a neighbor moved out. These meetings were mandatory. Riddy declined explaining to them that she was aware that they wanted their rent and in order to give them their rent she had to work. Then they wanted to use some of her chairs and Riddy politely allowed them to. She cleaned them all off with bleach, and they even brought her food that she threw away in the garbage outside. These people just would not quit, and they even held a prayer meeting to pray her back into the fold. If they were spiritual, then they would have known that God had another plan for Riddy. However, the dirtiest hard blow was yet to come.

* * *

Riddy's mind thought back when Kat was approaching forty years of age. My *mother is a beautiful woman*. Life had been good to Kat. She had just started using and experimenting with different wigs.

Madea and Kat at the time were in deep conversation as Riddy saw her baby brother, Sean, lying in Kat's arms — a very thin and long baby. Kinda skinny. He looked different from the others in Kat's litter because he was by a man named Mr. Cooper that Kat had an affair with. Most times she would get with someone outside of her marriage. This time she ended up pregnant. He left her and she had to return home.

The older two siblings behind Riddy only saw a baby picture of the older boy in a little navy and white sailor suit, and he was dubbed the nickname, Billy because Kat deemed the elder unworthy of having a son named after his father.

Another thought of a sibling crossed Riddy's mind back when she was five years old. She remembered the singing baby, another sibling named Jeanne.

Riddy tiptoed in the bedroom after Kat had emerged to go into the kitchen to warm the baby's bottle. This was after moving back home from Kat's second marriage. Riddy recalled hearing Lala Lala Lala that's how Jeanne cried.

Now, for Riddy's other siblings she remembers a recollection of the trio's drunken stupor during her parents' card game when they crawled under the kitchen table and stacked themselves with Serena being the lightest to reach the bottle of liquor on top of the refrigerator.

* * *

It would be years later that Riddy would seek a relationship with Kat. When she called, Kat said, "Look. You can call me, but I do not want to hear nothing about no God, Jesus or anybody. Let's keep religion out of it." This was Kat's condition in getting to know her now twenty-five year-old eldest daughter.

The last time, Riddy spoke to her mom was right before she slammed the phone in her ear after demanding a high school graduation ticket. She felt entitlement after long absences, dismissed from the phone, and walking past her without a glance or any form of acknowledgement in her formative years. She did come to her eighth grade graduation and said nothing to her. Now it was the high school graduation and she sent a stereo system for a ticket to the graduation.

Now Riddy accepted the guidelines to have a relationship that would expand over the course of thirty years. It was exciting to get to know this woman. Big Mama was Mama. Kat was her birth mother. Riddy started thinking, *Who is she? What is her favorite color? Flower? Meal? Will this relationship amount to anything or lead to a dead end?*

Kat would always make the mistake of asking her eldest child how her week went, and that would give her the opportunity to witness and share testimonies about God doing some astonishing. That always left Kat with her mouth open and questioning, "When is something good going to happen for me?"

Kat was brought up in the Christian faith in the Baptist denomination. She walked out because of the hypocrisies and no one in her church home was taking God's Word seriously. She ventured into holiness, Pentecostalism, church of God but settled for Singh Sang an eastern Hindu religion. A funny thing is, people failed to realize that Christianity is also an eastern religion.

Kat was the middle child of Madea's. She was known to be the most difficult child in the whole family. Kat's little fanny got worn out often.

At one time, Kat did secretarial work and even worked for the Internal Revenue Service.

Riddy tried to piecemeal her mother's life. She married young at nineteen and was pregnant three months afterwards. She married to get out of the house, and from Big Mama and Madea because they were determine to keep her on the straight and narrow path.

She received her final beating that led to an exodus a little after her high school graduation and eighteenth birthday. It would be right after she came home from a midnight date. A definite NO. She disgraced the family's good name. Well it was time to go, so she married Ed, Riddy's father.

Johnnie Mae called Kat a heifer. A hussy plus she was nasty and left her drawers sitting stiffly in the middle of the bathroom floor and refused to move them. Ed and Kat lived with Johnnie Mae and Nate after the wedding when Ed failed to secure the promised apartment. It was very humiliating to move in with Ed's folks.

Johnnie Mae never had a daughter and would try to lavish gifts and affections onto Kat, but Kat found her to be of a smothering and mothering nature and it was unwanted. Even after Ed and Kat moved into their newly built apartment in the projects, Johnnie sent a cocktail table set as a gift only to have the resentful daughter-in-law send them back to the store from where it was purchased. The two, Kat and Johnnie Mae, would constantly lock horns throughout their marriage.

All Riddy knew was that Johnnie Mae said Kat never showed up in court during the divorce proceedings to claim the three eldest children. Kat walked out of the marriage and motherhood. Midway through the marriage, she got involved with a guy with the same first name, Ed. He would be her eternal love and they had planned to kill the other Ed, Riddy's father.

Kat would have the second Ed in the apartment while Ed was at work. One day Ed came home and the other Ed hid in the closet of the bedroom. Ed was facing a mirror brushing his hair while talking to a nervous Kat, when the reflection from the cracked closet door showed the other Ed with a loaded gun in his hand.

Ed abruptly fled to his mom's by leaving the apartment to never return. A few weeks later the second Ed returned to service. Kat got sick of both Eds and moved back home to 3165 West Monroe, pregnant and later gave birth. Riddy had to move out of her little bedroom temporarily, and slept with Big Mama in order for Kat to have a place to stay. What a mess.

The judge awarded Ed with full custody of all three children through default. Johnnie Mae called Big Mama and Madea to ask why Kat was not in court. It was to Madea's horror that she busted into the little bedroom to demand to see the letter that Kat hid by beating everyone to the mailbox. Madea snatched the letter that had the court date for the divorce and custody hearing and let out a scream, "How could you!!!" And she turned and walked away.

Riddy was left with Big Mama, and the other two siblings were to be reared by Ed, Johnnie Mae and Nate. Kat later would marry the other Ed and moved out of town into an apartment on a military base. The family rarely saw her and the newborn singing baby. Eventually, the womanizer and Kat broke up, and she had to work. Her dream of being a house wife, actress, rich and famous and white was not going to take place. She began to have numerous affairs in spite of her disdain of others from the Baptist childhood church she grew up in.

Kat moved far away from her family. She would occasionally call to speak to Madea after rushing Riddy off the phone. Riddy would recognize her voice and just offer a hello. She would be so happy to talk to her mother and when she would try to make small talk, she was dismissed by her queenly mother. But now here is an opportunity to get to know her.

* * *

Here is the final blow from CFA Plantation Center. "Sorry. We did not get the check."

"I mailed it," swore Riddy. "I got a copy of the money order."

"That do not mean a thing!!!" yelled Nellie through the phone receiver.

"If we do not get that payment by tomorrow you will receive a five day notice and afterwards, eviction proceedings will begin against you." And then the phone went dead.

Riddy then went hurrying to the nearby currency exchange and explained the dilemma.

"Well. We usually wait thirty days before investigating, and then there is a fee to do so." But Mr. Calloway looked into the frightful eyes of Riddy and smiled and said that he would help. Riddy sighed with relief.

"Come back late tomorrow," Riddy heard Mr. Calloway say as she exited the place.

"Sure."

Riddy returned to find out that the rental payment had been cashed by CFA Plantation Center. Riddy appeared at the leasing office and slammed a copy onto Nellie's desk. She informed her that if she and CFA Plantation Center did not stop with the persecution that she would consult a lawyer. Well. The enemies were held at bay for at least a while.

Now, thirty-two years later Riddy is now operating a business and being dean at a Bible College where Vonnie is the school president.

Kat just followed Riddy to the Bible College and was a tremendous help and she even helped with the not-for-profit organization. Kat started sharing dreams with Riddy. She would have two dreams that would be repeated over and over again.

The first dream, Kat saw that it was the end of the world and that people were all running toward this huge white boulder. And when she got to the boulder, an angel told her that she had to go back because she was not a Christian.

Then she had another dream about a lot of people just standing and waiting. Then airplanes came around and began to drop suitcases into people's hands. Some suitcases contained golden shower caps, and some people received them, but then there were others who received nothing. Kat knew that somehow that when a plane came to her that there would be no golden shower caps for her. And sure enough a plane came, a suitcase fell into her hand, and there was no golden shower cap. Then a huge angel came and called for those with the golden shower caps to follow him. And Kat could not go.

Riddy sat with her jaw dropped while Kat asked the meaning of the dreams. The dreams were self-explanatory. Kat's heart was hard, and she was not about to give up Singh Sang for anyone not even for God, himself.

All of this happened right before Riddy got a call from someone at the TV station who wanted to donate the building. Riddy was now totally freed from CFA Plantation Center. She moved out. The irony was that she stayed on the same street, but three blocks down facing east closer to the United Center and the downtown area. The Center did not want to give her the security deposit. She had to contact a lawyer and then they released the deposit. The building was a turn-of-the-century building with exquisite designs.

It was a two story house once owned by an Italian family, but it needed a lot of work. There was no mortgage. The taxes were low. The furnace worked and next door was a neighbor, Tom with a pit bull. Riddy had hoped to convert the once-boarding house into single-room occupancy units. She had many contractors to give bids. She wrote many grants, but could not get anyone to help her.

Funds began to dry up and she could only keep the electricity running. Eventually the water and gas got cut off and things begin to go downhill. Well, at least she was not at the center any more. Riddy got fired from the Bible College over a lie and she had people to speak up for her and assured the owner that she was lied on.

Frank, the supervisor, chose to believe a lie over the truth. It was time to leave. It was getting dangerous to work at the Christian Bible College. A few months earlier Frank had gotten obnoxious and refused to pay his staff particularly Riddy. So to avoid a five day-notice, Riddy would have to advance her pay unknown to Frank to stay afloat.

It was easy to slip money by collecting money from students and not recording payments. It was not the right thing to do, but the rent needed to get paid and Frank was taking his sweet time with paying Riddy her salary. She cried to God apologetically for her thievery. The rent was coming up due again and she just pleaded for her pay to a stony heart.

One day, Riddy met with a potential client for her business and was going to go home and not into the office. She was going to call Vonnie to say she would not be in the office but an overwhelming feeling seized her, giving her an urgency to go into the office.

Sweetie had told Riddy about a dream in which she was pushing a shopping cart and it was taken and thrown into a safe. She had to call the authorities to open the safe so she could retrieve the precious shopping cart. This dream is symbolic to what is going to happen next.

Riddy went to her appointment. The Bible College was located in a yellow three-story brick building on Damen Avenue across a busy street. The first floor was a chapel and then there were three sets of stairs to bounce up before entering the college.

Riddy swung opened the door and Vonnie was on her way out to do errands. She asked Riddy to manage the reception area.

Riddy threw her coat and briefcase in a chair in her office and Vonnie proceeded to leave out. Then she heard God say, "Put your things up where you usually do." She did a U-turn and placed her purse in the third drawer of her desk, and hung her expensive leather coat across the room on a coat hanger. Then she left the door partially closed. Vonnie returned forty-five minutes later. She threw her purse on top of a file cabinet. Riddy suggested that she put the purse up out of public view. Riddy had a queer feeling. Vonnie said the purse would be okay.

Fifteen minutes later the door burst opened and four guys entered. They were dressed in all black with black hoods with guns drawn. Riddy was seated at the desk with a window behind her with nowhere to run. Vonnie stood frozen at the cabinet. The owner, Frank, was in the conference room on the phone and saw the men and closed the door. The coward left the women to fend for themselves.

Riddy' eyes bucked as she slid under the desk while Vonnie talked to them. Two of them yanked Frank out of the conference room. Riddy was on her knees in a cold sweat speaking in some sure-nuff tongues, clucking, with her hands in a prayer position. Suddenly a voice yelled out, "We missing one. We missing one. Where she'd go?"

A hooded face appeared saying, "Come out, ma'am. Nothing is going to happen to anybody. We just here to rob you all that's all."

Riddy obeyed nervously. Two of the guys were walking Frank back into the room where we were, and he tried to run and was hit upside the head with a forty-five caliber automatic. Riddy thought, *Fat head.*

The guys took Vonnie's designer purse, designer wallet, designer sun glasses, $400 in cash, her check book and credit cards. Frank's school was robbed of $450, and he was robbed of a thick gold chain, diamond class ring, leather wallet that contained $500, and they wanted the gold out his mouth.

Frank lean over a cabinet, and said to the man, "This ain't coming out. The dentist put this gold in. You got everything. Leave us alone."

They also took his designer 2004 air gymmies. They told everybody to lay, face down. Everybody loudly protested and said that they would sit down on the floor. It was customary during this time to shoot people in the head that were faced down, and flee the scene.

Frank said, "If you gonna shoot us then do so face to face."

The lead gunman yanked the phone lines out of the wall and told everyone to start counting to 100. After the men left, a queer thing happened, Frank looked into Riddy's eyes and said that he had money stashed elsewhere, and that he would make sure that she would get her rent paid, promptly. And all the while Frank was being stripped he was looking Riddy in the eyes, and he knew why he was being robbed.

He robbed Riddy so now he was being robbed. Riddy had prayed the day before and now Frank was being robbed because he had defrauded Riddy, and was about to cause her to be kicked out of her apartment.

God showed Sweetie a shopping cart that was precious to her in the dream. The shopping cart represented her mother, Riddy. In the office on the third floor while the robbers were there, she was in a tight spot with her back against a window. There was nowhere to go and that is symbolic to the cart being put in a vault. Where the authorities were called in the dream was when Riddy began to speak to God in tongues. She was calling on the only authority that could save and protect them.

Frank immediately hired a security team and then relocated the school. Later Frank would call, telling Riddy how afraid he was and asked if she was afraid.

"No," would be Riddy's response.

Frank did not believe her. Well shortly afterwards strange phone calls would come through the office. People would call and hang up. Riddy would gleefully inform Frank who would become a nervous wreck. *Gotcha* Riddy revengefully thought. She'd repent, later.

Frank had several business locations and had fired the west side staff, but kept Riddy to straighten out records at that location.

Frank then hired a new receptionist named Janice. Riddy and Janice hit it off and from time to time they would treat each other to a lunch or breakfast. Janice would share her hopes and dreams. Riddy offered to incorporate and assist Janice to get into her own business.

Riddy invited her on an off day to help Janice understand the way to get clients, and she showed her how to earn money. Riddy was not charging Janice anything for all that valuable information. She informed Janice that when a paying client comes through, she would have to work on meeting their needs and then get back to Janice.

Janice twisted mind from that point began a series of setting Riddy up all because she would stop working on her paperwork to tend to PAYING clients, yet she was getting her stuff done for free.

Frank began to ride Riddy's back until Janice boldly stated that it was a payback. "Wow," was Riddy's response. Haman was about to get hung on the gallows that she built for Riddy. A few weeks later Frank stripped Riddy of dean duties and transferred a great deal of responsibilities to Janice.

No sweat. Riddy continued to work on her business and future plans. Frank told Janice in no term in front of Riddy to let Riddy have keys to open or close the business doors anymore.

Riddy had even helped Janice when Frank withheld her pay with the new payroll system. Janice snitched on Riddy because one day Frank came bursting through the door all wild eyes and could not say anything without implicating that Janice told.

Well. Janice was living high off the hog. Frank gave Janice a pay raise and she would flaunt it in Riddy's face. However, one day Janice overplayed her card. Janice announced that she was leaving early and would not be in the next day and shoved Riddy the key.

Whenever someone was off Frank would let them inside of the satellite college offices. Janice knew the protocol but gave Riddy the key anyway. It was ten minutes later that Frank would call asking for Janice. She left early without Frank's permission. Frank was pissed. He blew up and said that he would be there in the morning to let Riddy into the school. Riddy swallowed hard and informed Frank that Janice had given her the keys. Frank hit the ceiling, and when Janice returned to the office, an office meeting was held and it was announced that someone had to go and it was not going to be him.

Frank began to interrogate the heck out of Janice over those keys, and expose her back stabbing ways out in the open. Frank had turned on Janice. Then the unthinkable happened. Janice then reached out to Riddy asking her to help her. Judgment fell on Janice for her double dealings. Frank fired Janice and restored Riddy back to her deanship.

Several hours later Janice got kicked out of her apartment and ended up in a shelter. Riddy was speechless. Then several weeks later a student would lie and Frank would fall for it and, puff, Riddy was gone. Frank seemed impressionable and can be persuaded easily.

Chapter Twenty-Eight

Riddy had settled into her new home, totally free in the building that was donated. The first floor was her office, along with an art gallery and computer lab. The back area had a bedroom and a kitchen. The basement and second floor would be converted into single room occupancy units. Also, a built-in wall aquarium would be on the first floor. The antique furniture left would be integrated throughout the house.

Riddy was excited to own a home once again. No mortgage. Yes, she would have to pay taxes until the processing of the application for tax exemption was approved.

She started having regrets when she thought about connecting to CFA Plantation Center. She had kissed her condo in Forest Park goodbye and wished that she had remained there, but it was time to go. She left Forest Park to own a townhouse, then onward from there to an apartment complex, now ownership of a building to use for God's glory.

One morning the phone rang and Riddy was awakened out of her sleep by another sibling named Terry who was the baby. Riddy instantly knew that Kat had a stroke from a dream she had. In the dream Riddy saw Serena. There was a dark diagonal shadow that radiated from the shoulder down toward her legs. Instead of Serena it was Kat. Serena is the splitting image of Kat in her heydays just a shade darker. Riddy had an eerie feeling. The doctor would inform the family that Kat would need twenty-four hour care and would not be returning home. Wow. Kat was shipped off to a rehab center in downtown Chicago.

Riddy waited several hours before meeting everyone at the hospital. It felt awkward after being dismissed from Queen Kat's life abruptly. Riddy thought their relationship was improving. She even helped with a conference and seemed to enjoy it. But one day Kat was late coming to the board meeting and she entered with downcast eyes. Riddy felt a cold chill emanating from her mother.

After the board meeting, Kat hurried home. A few days passed before Riddy tried to reach her. The phone just rang and rang until finally Riddy's step-father, Eli, Kat's fourth marriage with her third husband, answered. Riddy was considering calling the police to do a well-being check.

Dad began to apologize and to inform Riddy that Kat was changing her phone number. She did not want to hear from Riddy anymore. No explanation. Dumped again. Wow. So, after several months, Riddy wrote a chronicle outlining Kat's life and pointing out that she was in the valley of decision. Kat had made her decision after reading the chronicle.

She was going to have to choose between God or Singh Sang. Kat only wanted to hear about Christ when there was a problem or an ache or pain. However, she wanted to hold on to Hinduism. Riddy shared with Kat about the Old Testament Prophet Elijah who asked the children of Israel how long would they be halted between two opinions? If God be God, serve Him; if Baal be God, serve him. Riddy also shared how the false stone image, Dargon's, hands were cut off, and the image was thrown to the ground. It was then that Riddy told Kat that she would begin to have a series of dreams.

Kat was getting older, and it was time to either choose God or leave Him alone. Riddy also reminded Kat how God, during their time together manifested Himself to Kat. Riddy wanted to buy Kat a gift and she was going to buy some vanilla field perfume, but God told her to buy White Diamonds.

During the time of serving in the food pantry Riddy called Kat into her office and handed the gift to her. Kat unwrapped the gift and sat down, astonished. She said no one knew that she wanted White Diamonds by Elizabeth Taylor. No one. She said that every time she went to buy some the store either did not have it in stock or she did not have the money.

Riddy assured Kat that God knew and that He had His eyes on her. Then on a Saturday, Riddy received a package that Kat told her to look out for. Well at 1:00 p.m. Riddy called thanking Kat for the package. Kat was like, "What package?" Then Riddy began to explain what Kat had promised in the mail. The phone went silent. Then Kat spoke and said that it was impossible because she mailed the package at 10:00 a.m. the same day.

How was that possible? Riddy explained that an angel must have brought it to her.

Riddy invited her step-dad Eli to help with the building to keep him busy and not worry about Kat. Once a week Dad would come by to pull weeds, cut grass, and do other chores. During the winter he would help shovel snow and take her on errands and appointments in between visits with mom at the rehab center.

Financial doors began to close, left and right, and no grant money was available to pay for rehab, and a second winter was approaching fast and it would be fierce. The house was becoming really cold because it was not insulated.

The previous owners just milked the building dry and did not replenish it now the old girl was dying and in need of a burial.

During the day, Riddy would make appointments with non-paying clients, attended business training sessions and did research and concluded the day eating at a local restaurant for heat and warmth. She would get home very late, warm up her bedroom with an electric space heater and prepare her bed. She would put seventeen covers on it and slipped into a set of long johns, tights, jogging pants with a hoodie, and gloves. She would turn the heater off to prevent a fire because the wiring in the building was not the best. Then she would wriggle herself underneath the covers, talk to God and then fall asleep and repeat her day and evening all over again.

In her living quarters she had a TV and a few pieces of furniture. One particular night in early December she heard the frightening weather forecast. The next week would be single digits with a wind chill factor of negative 20 below zero. Riddy had nowhere to go.

Riddy's childhood home was sold. She no longer was a part of CFA Plantation Center, and she had no friends. Sweetie was at the YMCA downtown Chicago in a one room and no guest could stay overnight. Riddy knew of no local shelters.

The city did have warming centers near her home. If the cold weather continued, Riddy would have to stay at a warming center to keep from freezing to death. This chill factor would begin Monday and it was now Friday. Riddy prayed and cried for God to help her.

Sunday morning Riddy girded her loins and attended another service at a new church that she had been attending since leaving CFA Plantation Center for the past three years. The service was awesome although Riddy's heart was heavy and the pending danger was near.

There was a prophetic guest speaker with her team. The pastor picked out people to receive a prophetic word and instead of letting the prophets flow and go forth to minister. Pastor Steven had a disagreement against Riddy. When she first came to help and tried to fit in where she could, she was rejected which was nothing new. Riddy had the ability to see through people's pernicious ways. She saw what others could not or would not.

Riddy did not fight because she had her own personal battle and that was to survive the winter. She retreated and relied upon God to help her. Service was over and Riddy always made it her business to be the last to leave in order to get as much heat as possible, than on to Edie's Soul Food Café to have a cup of coffee until 7 p.m., closing time.

A few people were lined up after service to hear from God from a member of the prophetic team. Riddy stood in line for what felt like an eternity. The lights were being flicked on and off for people to leave the building, so Riddy decided to leave out when suddenly a voice called out after her.

"Do you need a word from God?"

"Yes," with tear-filled eyes, answered Riddy.

The young woman, several years Riddy's junior, told her, "I don't understand what God is saying. Well it's not for me to understand, so I'll just say it. I heard the Spirit of the Lord saying that you will not be cold or hungry this winter."

Riddy broke down and cried like a baby, uncontrollably. She was so choked up yet at ease. She had attended the service heavy-hearted, out of sorts, and dismayed yet hopeful. God had spoken. Riddy dried her tears and squared her shoulders, and her little shoulders braved the alarming cold weather that was approaching.

Onward to Edie's for a hot cup of coffee before forging home, she thought. Edie was just a block west of the church. It was a cozy establishment even after now being under new management.

Riddy remembered when Edie's used to be a little store that Big Mama sent her to buy her first Kotex belt. The joint had only counters and barstools.

She would manage from, time to time, to break out the old neighborhood, but a force always drew her back. She was always drawn back to her roots. Riddy's childhood happiness seemed distant. Another world. Everyone was now gone: Big Mama, Madea, Sid, Debra, Ms. J, Ed, Johnnie Mae, Thurman, Penny, Lester Sr., Lester Jr. Everyone that she loved was now gone. Riddy would from time to time, stand in front of 3165 West Monroe and just stared at the place that for many years served as a refuge for various family members.

Now 3165 West Monroe was gone to another owner. The three-flat Greystone was now painted all white. Big Mama would have had a stroke.

Riddy sat at her usual booth and waved at the workers who were now her second family. She was estranged from her siblings. Riddy sighed and looked at the new location, which was a quantum leap from around the corner. Edie's has been here at the new location for the past twenty years and the décor had become worn.

Riddy remembered the pink and maroon color scene with floral designs. A small counter with six barstools. There were additional booths and a few tables and chairs settings for groups of fours. Behind the counter would be the usual choice of German chocolate cake, chocolate cake, pineapple coconut cake, and patrons had a choice between peach cobbler or a slice of sweet potato pie.

The menu consisted of beef, chicken, steak, fish and sides. Then there would be the daily special of either oxtail stew, chicken & dumpling, northern great beans with neck bones, and other delicacies.

When money was a surplus Riddy would order and eat high off the hog. She even ordered a porterhouse steak at one point. Everything at Edie's was delicious.

Riddy reflects on Edie's place being the go-to for all who migrated from the South. Edie's hard work paid off with visits from chief civil right leaders, city officials, the mayors of Chicago, dignitaries paid a visit to Edie's. Anybody who was anybody ate at Edie's.

Riddy remembered meeting Edie, once. They exchanged business cards.

"You're doctor who???" Edie asked.

Riddy would laugh; however, her notoriety to Edie was short lived, when Riddy had to walk home and Edie's eyes followed her.

She recalls her next visit would be met with what kind of a doctor are you??? You ain't got nothing. She would berate Riddy. Riddy would smile and choke back tears and take her usual seat and ordered whatever her current prosperity would allow.

The booths were brown leather and across from the counter was a passage that led to the kitchen. In the back of the restaurant was a coat rack, juke box, and a table to leave flyers and business cards. Around the corner would be both the women and men's bathrooms. Then there were a large room for rental for events from receptions, meetings, book signings, and church services. It was hard to believe that the restaurant was in trouble. The restaurant was dying and Riddy was witnessing a slow death.

Edie used to always be packed with people standing willing to wait an hour or more to be seated. But a storm was brewing underneath. All glitter is not gold. Edie had not filed taxes for over ten years. She showed Riddy tons of documents. Edie did not take advice well and refused to acknowledge that times and trends had changed and perhaps she should retire. But the restaurant was all she had. The restaurant put a wedge between Edie and her only child, a daughter to the point when she got grown she moved out of state far away and did not want to have anything to do with Edie or the restaurant. The heir of her legacy was bitter.

Edie claimed to keep the restaurant going afloat so that those who had been with her forty, thirty and even twenty-five years would have a place of employment. The employees had become Edie's family, while her only child became a stranger.

Before Riddy fell from grace in Edie's eye, the restaurant was sold to a vendor named Captain and his wife. Edie still came around to help with the transition and to show her face to keep customers coming.

Not very long, Riddy did not see Edie. Then months would roll pass and no Edie. Finally Riddy asked a waitress about Edie's whereabouts. She was dying at the West Suburban hospital in a western suburb of Chicago. She was losing her battle against ovarian cancer. Riddy was wondering why Edie was on such a health kick and promoting and selling a wonder juice that fought cancer.

Now she knew and felt pressed to visit Edie. Riddy asked if she could go with the cousin for a hospital visit. A few weeks later they embarked on a visit. Edie was delirious and in a lot of pain. The doctor informed the cousin that it would be a matter of time. All they could do was to keep her as comfortable as possible. Riddy dropped her head in a moment of silence to pray. Then a strange thing happened. Edie came out of her stupor and recognized them. Riddy aggressively yet tenderly led Edie over the repentance prayer. The next morning she died.

Now the Captain and his wife managed the restaurant until his wife died. Then the Captain and his son tried to make a go, but the restaurant folded. Riddy had no idea that, that Sunday would be her last day of seeing her adopted family.

Back to the arctic blast which was fast approaching, Riddy would be home and was so well insulated with clothing that she felt nothing. Eli came over fifteen minutes later. "What is going on?" He asked. Riddy played dumb, but Eli would not let the subject change. Riddy had to fess up that the water was shut off as well as the gas therefore she could not get any heat, but she was fine. Eli put his foot down and demanded that she was to pack a bag and go home with him. Riddy accepted the exodus cheerfully.

At nightfall the arctic blast had reached Chicago and Riddy was in a warm bed in a warm house. Thank God. In the morning, Riddy was on her way to the bathroom when she was greeted with a warm pleasant good morning from Eli, but Riddy discerned a strange unidentifiable look on his face as he called after her from the gray plush sofa that he sat upon with legs crossed while the top leg rocking in a back and forth motion.

Eli was medium built. He was eighty-one years of age, and had been married to Riddy's mom for over forty years. She remembered the day they entered the house and announced their civil nuptials to the women at their scheduled POW WOW meeting. Big Mama would yell it's about time and congratulations would ring out. Riddy was a senior in high school. Eli had fathered Riddy's seven-year-old sister, Terry. Kat and Eli dated fourteen years prior to getting married. Big Mama nudged him into holy matrimony asking him, "Why don't you give the baby a name." So the rest is history.

While living with dad she joined a prayer call group and was a member for four years. During this time, Riddy and dad would attend to the house donated building where Riddy used to live. People started breaking in and the neighbors were complaining. Eli had given Riddy her mother's key card and a set of car keys. She just had to be back in time for him to visit mom. Kat was still in a nursing home.

Sweetie and Riddy's relationship was rekindled and Sweetie would visit. The three of them from time to time visited a timeshare that was family owned. Eli started to want to have Bible studies. Riddy thought that was a good thing. She was particularly happy because Eli and Kat were practicing Hinduism.

Terry was allowed to choose her religious preference and would attend various church services with her eldest sister then she drifted away due to her obsession with boys and sex. Eventually, Terry married Derrick against the prophetic warning from God not to. Riddy remembered meeting him and could see demonic forces dwelling inside of him. Terry later asked what she thought. Riddy let her know it was not what she thought, but what God is saying. She wanted to marry Derrick.

God said, "No."

Terry said, "I do."

It was from that moment he made her life a living hell and beat the stank off her. Terry chose hell over heaven. God would speak again and she would answer, "I do," again for an abortion of a prophet that God was birthing into the earth realm. Then for a year judgment fell and Terry would end up in a life and death aneurism situation that would require a team of intercessors to reach God which included her sister to turn her captivity over to God.

Three months would pass before the unthinkable occurred during a Bible study. Eli wanted to study a scripture from the book of James about confession of one's fault one to another. Eli had a confession. He would begin talking and Riddy had a sickening feeling on the inside. Eli told Riddy that he had noticed that she was chosen by God, and he had taken notice of that since 2004. Now nine years later, he wanted Riddy to know that he was in love with her and desired to have sex with her. Riddy was appalled and her mouth dropped open and her mind raced. She felt ensnared. She felt helpless. Riddy wanted to run, but there was nowhere to go. There was nowhere to run to and it was dead smack in the middle of the arctic blast.

"Oh my God!" Riddy's response was that he was married to her mother. She would know him for over forty years as her step-father, only, and he was the father she never had. She rarely saw her father. Riddy assured him that he did not fall into love, but into lust. Eli slowly got out of his seat, weeping for a forbidden lust that Riddy was not going to entertain. The two of them would later eat dinner in silence, and Riddy would go into the bedroom and lock the door. She did not feel safe anymore. She felt warm, full, but not safe.

Riddy sat on the side of the bed, her mind racing wondering *where were the clues, red flags*. She remembered a small clue that she overlooked that brewed in her mind. Eli had dropped her off at a reunion of the prayer group at a downtown hotel. She gave him a hug and this strange look came upon his face. Then when they were in the elevator she spoke of a renowned married movie director that divorced his wife and married his step-daughter that rocked Hollywood. Riddy spoke against it, but Eli had a somber look on his face. Then the two of them were in the elevator, one morning and a male neighbor angrily asked Eli where his wife was?

Then there was a strange look on his face the following morning when Riddy stayed at the apartment. He looked like the cat that swallowed the canary. And Riddy had a strange feeling. Now the truth has unfolding in regards to all his helpfulness, kindness, and availability.

He had been stalking and grooming her like so many predators do their victims before they ascend on their prey. In his eyes, it was time for her to drop her drawers. He was not the protective father. Lord Jesus, what a mess. Riddy made sure she wore jogging suits, she also kept her distance. She made sure that she ate her meals separate from him, and required less of his time to assist her with any errands, but dad was persistent and was determined to wear her down.

Every three months he asked for sex after Bible studies. Riddy discontinued Bible studies. But she would share the Mosaic Law about how a man could not have his father's wife and explained to dad that was for both the goose and gander.

She shared Paul's teachings that spoke against sexual impurities, and the crisis at the Corinthian church where a son had his father's wife and they were all members of the church, and no one had spoken against the forbidden incestuous relationship.

She shared the works of the flesh and the fruit of the spirit with him. He acknowledged that the thought had developed in 2004. Riddy explained to him that it was a stronghold of an imagination that needed to be cast down, and not entertained.

After six months it appeared all was well, but his hot pursuit would restart. And Riddy would tell him no and he would mention it again how the Bible stated that one is supposed to confess their faults and he wanted to share his sordid details of how he wanted to make love to her—correction—make lust with her.

Riddy knew that every good and perfect gift came from God without shadows, variables and turning, and she knew that God was not giving her mother's husband to her, and that this was not a gift from God. When God gives you something or someone it will not be contrary to His Word.

In addition, Riddy could not afford to breach her relationship with God. Every time he pursued her, she quoted and stood on the Word of God for that was all she had. God's Word. Others might have fallen and rationalized being with him. He was a nice guy, had a steady income, nice apartment, nice furniture, and a nice vehicle.

"No," would be her answer, and God would make a way of escape again. Riddy then began to clearly outline to Eli that their relationship is that of a father and daughter and that the affection he felt was meant to help her as a daughter and that he was taking it the wrong way. In the meantime, Riddy had put an application in to the housing authority. It would be four and half years of No's to her dad. He was bent on wearing her down. She was bent on standing her ground of saying, "NO."

Periodically, Riddy would check for her name on the Chicago Housing Authority (CHA) list and it was slowly moving up. She even took the initiative and sought out apartments to no avail.

The rental housing market shortage was a nationwide problem. In the meantime, Riddy kept her distance and the bedroom that she occupied locked. Riddy would attend business training sessions to fill her time as well as drum up business.

Riddy thought that she would be the only one at Eli's for the winter. Sweetie joined them.

Now a fourth winter had come and now Sweetie lived with Eli, too. Sweetie's landlord and her sister ended up in a power of attorney struggle that resulted in Sweetie being illegally evicted. Eli welcomed Sweetie to the apartment. Riddy slept on the couch in the living room and gave up the spare bedroom to Sweetie. However, one day, Sweetie got into it with a security guard who did some checking and found out that Riddy and Sweetie were staying within the building illegally.

"Mr. O'Neal. I understand that you have someone living with you. Either she come to see me or she needs to be gone in seven days."

Eli walked through the door with a strange look on his face. Riddy had a bad cold and was on the couch. He would save the news for the next day. Riddy had a dream that her dad told her that management wanted to see her. The next day the bombshell was dropped. Riddy and Eli went to the office and met with Mrs. Herbert who informed dad about his lease violation. She asked for and deactivated the key card. Due to her age she could not be added to dad's lease. Riddy was too young.

In addition, Eli had begun to show signs of Dementia, and Riddy shared that with Mrs. Herbert. She was given papers to apply to be a home healthcare giver and advised to take Eli for evaluation, but until there was approval Riddy could not occupy the unit. Riddy was instantly homeless again. She then explained her situation. Mrs. Herbert dropped her head and murmured loud enough for Riddy and Eli to hear.

"Just sign in and out," she said.

Security confused Sweetie and Riddy. They did not realize that there were two people instead of one. Whew!! So, the two returned upstairs. The winter hit with a biting cold and bitter wind chill. Wow. God had been true to His Word she had not been hungry or cold for four winters now.

At one point, Riddy's finances had dried up, and dad gave her Kat's debit card that had $550 on it every month. Riddy was able to buy personal hygiene products, food, and take care of bills and personal items. The apartment although small was quaint.

Kat had won building prizes for decorations. There was a huge grandfather clock that met you at the door. A gray plush loveseat. A huge gray plush round chair and in a corner near the kitchen was a black leather recliner and ottoman. The background décor was crème, beige, and gold. There was a fake fireplace and the mantle had family pictures on it. A huge Islamic painting of the mosque in Jerusalem hung above the fireplace. A huge glass aquarium sat in the middle of the living room without fish and water, the inside of the aquarium had a black velvet fabric with fake diamond gems on top, and a glass top that set and sealed the aquarium. The mantle had an Egyptian god and the goddess head, and on the side of the fireplace mantle was a brazen serpent that stood two feet tall. There was nothing special about the kitchen. Kat's bedroom was jammed with a twin bed, office desk, French provincial bedroom dresser and mirror from a set that was thrown out because it was too large for the apartment. Every stitch of furniture was from Kat's third marriage to her second husband, Ed.

Chapter Twenty-Nine

Eli's dream came true to live in this luxurious building that had three towers, and he lived on the twenty-first floor of the south tower. The buildings had a geometrical shape and was surrounded with row houses. The first floor was the place for the mailboxes, offices, doctors' offices, and just recently a grocery store had moved into the building. The second floor housed a computer lab, fitness center, theater, café, vending machines and two laundromats from the third to the twenty-eighth floors of each tower. Eli just knew he would finish his years at the facility. Fate would prove otherwise.

Kat could no longer live here. She had worn out her welcome. The short white coat doctor peered over his glasses speaking Eli and Riddy in the conference room because the facility could no longer afford Kat. The insurance will not cover any more services nor her stay and she was no longer wanted there.

"She bites, kicks, and scratch the staff. She has thrown food trays and items at my staff," the doctor explained.

"She has even thrown medication clear across the room and refused to swallow her pills. And until you find another facility which would take a while, we will be feeding her intravenously."

The meeting was concluded and Riddy and Eli stared at each other and the pile of papers to be completed to qualify Kat for long-term care at a nursing home facility. *Where could she be transferred to?* Thought Riddy.

The next few weeks Eli and Riddy would complete the paperwork and with the assistance of the current facility social worker would help in relocating Kat to Silverville after Eli, Sweetie, and Riddy returned from vacationing from a local resort. During Kat's calmer days the broken slurred speech would lead to her to talk about her life. She spoke of painful situations, hurts and disappointments.

You see, there was no help for women who experienced domestic violence, no talk shows, no shelters, and no hotlines. Whatever happened, happened. Kat began to unload.

As Riddy was listening to Kat's story, Riddy got the gumption to ask Kat why she was given away to Big Mama. A piercing look surfaced on Kat's face and her mouth dropped open, but no sound came out. It then was clear that Kat gave Riddy away to protect her, and upon asking Kat, she nodded, yes.

A pain pierced Riddy's inner soul and she had a series of flashbacks of encounters of sexual abuse of incest. A flashback of drug lords, forced the door open and beat Kat, Serena and Riddy into a beaten stupor leaving them lying in a blood bath. When Ed and Junior came home from a baseball game, Ed refused to call the police on the drug lords because he owed them drug money. Then there was the flashback of being in Ed's bed at the age of nine during a visit to Johnnie Mae.

A sickening feeling swept over Riddy while Kat was talking about it. She now understood why Kat gave her to Big Mama. It was an act of love to protect her firstborn. And through the years, she could not look at her because painful memories would flood her soul. Kat's appearance, rather her lack of appearance was a strategy to break all ties with Ed—and perhaps, in the far away distance, she could redeem the children. The raising of Riddy would be left to Big Mama and the others would be raised by their paternal grandmother Johnnie Mae and her husband Nate.

After the long discussion with her mom, Riddy took Sweetie out of town to their favorite resort where they could breathe the good old country air, rest, and eat well. After about five days they returned to the city and Riddy thought *I will see Kat one day next week*, and then she fell asleep.

Riddy had two dreams about Kat. The first dream she saw a nursery and seven angels each holding a baby and gently lying the babies on their sides. The babies were beautiful, and Riddy began to count and counted only six. Then she heard a voice that said go and count again, and when she recounted the total was seven. Riddy then heard God say that she is a mother of seven. Riddy instantly knew that God was talking about Kat.

Then she had another dream, and in this dream she saw Kat holding a baby in a hospital room and a man that Riddy had never seen before was talking to Kat and then he walked off and left out of a back door. And then she saw Eli walk up some stairs to enter the hospital and entered Kat's room.

Riddy woke up in the morning and prayed and felt led to see Kat that day and not wait till next week.

"Hi mom, I just got back in town and had planned to visit you next week, but I felt that I should come today."

"Glad to see you baby." I had two dreams about you. Let's go out on the terrace."

"I'll help you in the wheelchair." Riddy explained.

"Okay."

"Wow, doesn't it feel good to get fresh air. You've been in your room all day?" Riddy said, as she wheeled Kat to the terrace

"Yea."

"The nurse hasn't taken you out yet?"

"No."

"Well, I am here."

Riddy begin to explain, the first dream, "I saw angels with babies in their arms going into a nursery. One by one the angels lay each baby on their side. I began to count them one, two, three, four, five, and six. I heard God say count again, so, I did and then the count came to seven. Ma. What's wrong? Why you looking like that? Did you have seven children?"

"Yes."

"What happened to the baby?"

"I had an abortion."

"Wow mom."

"Then I saw, in the second dream, you holding a baby in your arm and talking to a man that I never saw before. I then saw him turn and leave the room through a back door. Then I saw Eli come walking up the front door of the hospital and entered your room. What's that about mom? Why are you trembling? What's wrong?"

"I was dating a man before I met your step-father and he left me when I told him that I was pregnant, so I had an abortion then after the abortion, I met your step-father but the guy came back around, and I got pregnant again and he left me again. So, I told your step-father that he is the father of that baby."

"Who? Terry?"

"Yes."

"What??"

"I didn't know what else to do."

"Wow. I want you to tell him that Terry is not his baby."

A cold chill went down Riddy's spine and she knew that Kat was dead serious. Forty-two years have passed and now dad will find out that Terry is not his child, gone now is the era where women could pass a child off on a man. The DNA testing now takes care of that. Eli was branded with a child that was not his. *What will Eli do? What will Eli say?* Riddy thought.

Her mind began to race. A definite hot mess. Geeze. Eli was due a visit to Kat in the next hour. Maybe Riddy can convince Kat to leave the past in the past. Buried. Dead. Gone. But Kat still stood her ground and wanted Eli to now know the truth.

Riddy wheeled Kat back to the room. Dad then walked in the room and Kat looked at Riddy and uttered, "Tell him." Riddy questioned if Kat was sure and she responded, "Yes."

Eli sat and looked inquisitively at Riddy who would be the bearer of bad news. Riddy swallowed hard and felt a lump in her throat and then she broke out in a cold sweat. She proceeded to tell him all that Kat wanted him to know. He sat stunned, and then took a deep breath. His response would allow Riddy to see him in another light. Eli began to explain to Riddy that he was married to another woman prior to her mother and she had a child that was not his own son. However, he loved him as though he was and he had that same love for Terry.

Then Eli got out of his seat and walked over to Kat who was still in her wheelchair. He bent down and touched her hand, and told her that, "The only thing that I want is for you to get well and come home. I want you to focus on getting well. I love you."

Riddy was floored at the magnitude of this man. Who was he? Oh my God. One thing for sure, he was not an average man.

* * *

Riddy's last visit was abruptly ended by a nurse when Kat took a cowardly position to imply that Riddy hit her. Oh what a lie. It was 10:00 p.m. and the CNA had put Kat to bed, but she wanted to get out of bed. Riddy blocked Kat's movement because a roommate had said that Kat had gotten out the bed several nights before and was not found until the next morning on the floor. The facility was short staffed and Kat's roommate had a broken hip. She rang the bell several times, but she was ignored, so Kat spent the night on the floor. Riddy rang for the nurse to explain to her about Kat trying to get out of the bed, but Kat put on a scene. The performance was Oscar worthy, and the nurse threw Riddy out of the room.

In addition, while trying to hold Kat, who was in a fit of rage in the bed, Riddy had experienced Kat kicking and scratching her.

A few days past and Riddy met Eli at the rehab facility and Kat glared at Riddy and shouted for her to GO. "Get out!"

Riddy asked her to think about it because she would not be returning ever. Kat paused then thought and answered, "Go."

Riddy left to wait for Eli in the lobby. Strangely, she had an inner peace and knew that she had done all she could to win Kat for the Lord. She still loved her mother.

"It is well with my soul," Riddy softly whispered.

About a half hour later Eli surfaced and tried to offer comfort and to encourage Riddy to start back visiting Kat.

"All is well," was Riddy's response and they went home together.

In the days and months to come, Eli tried to get Riddy to start back visiting. Riddy did not budge. She politely declined.

A month later, Riddy, and Sweetie went back to the resort for a short vacation. Riddy was taking in the clean air during her morning walk and the phone rang. It was Eli. Then suddenly the phone was quiet, and Kat was on the phone mumbling and Riddy could hear bits and pieces of her saying, "How are you?"

Riddy responded, "fine," and wished her well. The need for approval or love was not there any longer. The love of God was now enough. Riddy released Kat and totally embraced God.

Kat was a tormented soul bound with a gall of bitterness and a bond of iniquity. She confessed her sins that was heavy laden and with her lips accepted Christ. But only God knows if she meant it with her heart. Whatever the case, Riddy was done.

Chapter Thirty

A blizzard hit Chicago and Riddy had a terrible cold. During the day, she spent time with Eli and at night Sweetie would sneak her into a room that she rented in a two-flat building. Sweetie, for a while, had the whole second floor that had three bedrooms. Several months later a lady name, Lula, had the front bedroom and she would sneak her son in as Sweetie did her mom. The landlord did not live on the premises.

The landlord's mother occupied the first floor, a wayward cousin, and a mentally disturbed male relative. Well, eventually Anthony snapped, and the white coats came for him. Bernard got arrested for possession of a controlled substance.

The old lady always went to bed at 7:00 p.m. and her bedroom was in the back of the house, so it was easy to sneak Riddy inside the apartment. Everyone on the second floor became family.

Lula would have something hot on the stove those nights Riddy would come over. Everyone pitched in and brought items. Riddy always left the following morning at 6:00 a.m. One day the landlord came unannounced and Sweetie caught her at the door. Riddy had to use the bathroom, but when Sweetie had motioned that the landlord was there her pee froze and she no longer had to go to the bathroom. Thank God the landlord left fifteen minutes later. Sweetie locked the door behind her and Riddy raced to the bathroom.

Sweetie's room was so hot. Eli's place was suffocating with heat. It was so much so that Riddy had to be hospitalized for dehydration for a few days a saline infusion intravenously. Dehydration was a terrible thing, the room was spinning and Riddy vomited several times. Well at least she had somewhere to be for a few days without sneaking here or sneaking there. Finally, Riddy was released from the hospital.

During the day she went to Eli's apartment. Thank God there was a new security guard present. "Whew!!!" Later Riddy had an overwhelming desire to see Sweetie. Eli tried to talk her out of it. Riddy had to go for the feeling could not be shaken. She assured

Eli that she had on plenty of clothes and she would be driving in a warm car.

Riddy called Sweetie who assured her that it was safe to come because the landlord was now out of town. There was a period where the landlord had started hanging around, but their paths never crossed.

Sweetie unlocked the gate, and door and proceeded to tiptoe up the stairs. Riddy saw mail at the bottom of the stairs that Sweetie forgot to pick up. She whispered that she would bring the mail upstairs. Riddy picked up the mail and a local sales newspaper was still left on the floor, Riddy bent down again to pick that up as well and a letter from the Chicago Housing Authority was behind the advertisement. She quickly ascended to the top, excitedly showing Sweetie the letter. The two quickly went into the bedroom and Riddy opened the news of a brand new twenty-five million dollar facility with seventy-nine units were available and to attend an orientation. Riddy's heart fluttered that she could hardly go to sleep. Riddy finally fell asleep with the letter clutched in her hand.

At 5:00 a.m. Riddy dashed to the car and cleaned the snow off and drove to Eli's house. He rung her into the building. She burst through the opened door, confessing that she now had a place to live. He asked, "Do you have the keys?"

"Yes, I have God."

"Well," answered dad.

Suddenly business began to come in and Riddy perceived that God was giving her the income so that she could move into an apartment.

When Riddy got to the meeting, she was horrified to find out that she was number 138, and it was just at 8:45 a.m., and the orientation would not start until 9:00 a.m. She was told that people had been there since 7:00 a.m. Riddy stood in the middle of the lobby trying to decide whether to leave or stay because there were only seventy-nine units and she was number 138. What was the point?

"Lord, I will trust you. I will ride this out." The orientation was quick and to the point. People had to be registered and then told if they qualified, they would receive a phone call.

Days later, Riddy received a call and would be ushered into phrase II, where tons of paperwork had to be filled out. Tons. Then she got to a part of the application she could not answer. There were lots of people going from table to table assisting people with their applications. God spoke and told her to ask a particular man about the question.

In addition, Riddy told him that she was homeless. He requested from Riddy some information and gave his fax number. The next day Riddy submitted the information and a few days later the man called and congratulated Riddy, and welcomed her to Shepherd Hall. There had been 450 applicants, and God shifted Riddy through the system. Of course the devil would have to show up in the form of Terry.

Back at Eli's, he was walking through the house itching and scratching. One day Riddy went to his room to ask a question. When he swung the door open there was blood everywhere. Riddy focused her eyes and saw little bugs and would find out that they would be bed bugs. Well Ms. Herbert already excused Riddy's unofficial presence there. How would she react to bed bugs?

Sweetie got some spray, mattress covers and other items, and the two had planned to deal with the situation. Sweetie and Riddy set a date. Riddy left dad thinking about all the packing that needed to be done. Well. Terry happened to come by and Sweetie later reported to Riddy how she turned stoned-faced. That following Monday a call from management occurred.

The coward never bothered to ask anything. The next three months would be hell. Terry always had the tendency to shoot first and ask questions later, much later with a guilt ridden conscious. She also had the tendency to think with her vagina that always led to some abuse at the hands of a man.

Terry had a nose problem that was longer than Pinocchio and always seemed to be in everybody's business but her own. There is an old song that says, sweep around your own front door before you come sweeping around mine by The Williams Brothers. Terry would sweep a whole neighborhood and miss her spot. This would set off a series of fueling between the two sisters.

Management hired pest control to deal with the critters. It took three months, then her step-brother, Robert, would come to explore the matter. He was non-bias and rather supportive, the opposite of what Terry expected. He did not come in with drama. He listened, learned, assessed and helped. The whole ordeal would blow up in Terry's face shortly, and Riddy would be vindicated.

Eli asked Riddy after dreaming about her mother in a casket, what God had to say about mom. Riddy had hoped that he would never ask. She had to tell Him that mom would never return and that she would pass on. In all actuality Kat had been officially evicted from the premises, and would soon be evicted from the Earth realm. God was compassionate with her tormented soul.

Sweetie told Riddy that God was making Kat take care of Riddy which she had failed to do. Wow. After standing in the window, Riddy did re-arrange her mother's bedroom and unpacked her things. In the process of being in the room, she had found hidden treasures that would go with her to her new place: tons of perfumes, jewelry, money, nice clothing, coats, and items.

Kat was very materialistic, and a hoarder. She tried to numb her pain with things, but was unsuccessful. She was a very unhappy tormented soul. Riddy never judged her, but knew by the grace of God she could be the image and likeness of her lunatic mother. Kat was mentally deranged.

Ed, Riddy's biological father, was diagnosed with psychotic tendencies. Both of Riddy's parents were insane, and Riddy was hanging on by a thread herself. A thin thread. Kat hated Riddy because she looked like her dad, and seemed to have the life that she never had, and always desired.

Shortly after Kat was transferred to a nursing home, Riddy had a dream about stepping up to a window and reporting that her jewelry was taken. Riddy would find out several months later that Kat would demand that Eli bring all her jewelry to the nursing home and she gave everything to Terry.

Sweetie at that time lived with Terry until a fall out and found out about the giveaway that blatantly and specifically left Riddy out. She gave Sweetie a fake stone ring with hope that Riddy would find out.

One morning, Sweetie and Riddy were together and Riddy shared her dream. Sweetie told her what happened and that she was hopeful that she would never find out about the giveaway. A few years prior to having a stroke, Kat told Riddy, that she wanted her jewelry to be divided amongst her daughters and for her two sons to have her books because nothing would be left from her insurance policy.

Riddy marveled at the love and dedication that Eli had for Kat. She treated him so badly. Riddy remembered riding in the car with him to pick up groceries when suddenly he pulled over and leaned over the steering wheel crying that he did not know why Kat did not love him. She treated him very poorly.

At one time, he ran out of money and Kat refused to share food with him. Then there were other times she would send him out to pick up vegetarian meals, food, veggie pizza and he would be so happy, but then he would be informed that none was for him, and he went to bed hungry. Riddy was shocked and refrained from answering because she did not know, but would later learn of Kat's insanity.

The phone rang and dad was told to come immediately to the hospital, while Riddy slept at Shepherd Hall, the new apartment. A few hours passed and the phone would ring and she would hear Eli's voice.

"Your mother has passed," would be met with dead silence on Riddy's end. There was nothing to say.

Finally, Riddy told him that she was sorry, which was the truth; however, there was no regret for Riddy did not have the strength to go visit one more time even after the urging of Eli, an aunt, and her full-blooded only brother. Riddy's brother eventually turned on her in the midst of the chaos after the bed bug incident.

Junior got caught up with Terry's drama, and he told dad to put Riddy out. Riddy overheard the conversation.

"Just put her out."

Dad rebuffed with, "I can't do that. That's Terry's sister."

Riddy had no one to take solace in, but God. Sweetie and Riddy's relationship was barely restored, then Riddy had an aunt with Alzheimer's. She repeated the same things, over and over, like a parrot and it gave her a headache. Riddy would have to politely excuse herself and get off the phone.

Then there was the nature of a man that would rise in her eighty-four-year-old step-dad, Eli. He was almost like Dr. Jekyll and Mr. Hyde. He was mild mannered during the day, and a potential terrorist at night.

Serena called wanting to know if she was participating in any aspect of the funeral arrangements. Riddy just relayed Kat's wishes for her remains to be cremated and she did not want a service, and that each daughter was to get her jewels, and the sons her books. Those were her final wishes.

The death certificate stated that she died from a lung disease. Riddy and Kat knew that her pending death would be contributed to a broken heart due to the betrayal of the only man she ever loved her second and third husband, Ed. It was all through the marriage that he was a womanizer, and she left him at the Army base to return to Chicago to rebuild her life with her remaining children.

Kat loved Ed, but she was like so many women who loved the bad boys. After their stint of marriage, she moved back to Chicago. Ed would follow on her heels asking for forgiveness of his womanizing. The two became one once again, so Kat thought.

The couple and their children settled in the Roseland community. Roseland was a very profitable piece of real estate located in the far south side of Chicago. Ed appealed to Kat by telling her she did not have to work and that he was the man and would take care of everything.

Finally, Kat would be treated like the queen she deserved to be for at least six months. Riddy and Kat would talk from time to time. One day Riddy called and there was trouble in paradise. Ed walked out on Kat and the children. Abandonment.

He vanished with his clothes. No mail had been opened by Kat because she trusted Ed. Disconnection notices started to appear for the water, electric, and gas. Then no mortgage payments were made, and the house was in foreclosure. Kat had nowhere to turn to, and no job. Riddy prayed for her.

Eli came into her life like a knight in shinny armor and swooped her and the kids up and placed them into an apartment. Several months later he wanted to marry Kat, but Ed would not sign the divorce decree.

Kat had an ace card in her pocket. She blackmailed Ed who would concede and sign the divorce papers. Eli and Kat married. Now Kat was gone.

Eli stood next to the bed, and then called Riddy. A few hours later Eli would shout through the phone with pain, "Did you hear me? Your mother passed."

"I am so sorry." Riddy informed Robert and Serena of Kat's wishes. Well they did the cremation, but a service was held and Kat was knighted and entered into sainthood with a full Christian service.

Riddy chose not to attend in honor of her mother's wishes. Family members would be angry over her decision, but they had always had a problem with her so what would be new? And they did not have a heaven or a hell to put Riddy in so—moving forward.

A few weeks later the phone rang, with dad saying that his left arm was numb, and he was having trouble talking. Riddy told him to go to the ER immediately and she would call and check on him. Sure enough Eli had a stroke. He was transferred to a rehab center. A full recovery was expected. Riddy was glad.

Surprisingly during a visit Eli confessed his love for Riddy again and asked her to marry him. Riddy was very angry. Eli had called her a few weeks after Kat's death to ask her such a thing—how did she feel about getting married again. It was in innocence that she answered that several white guys were after her who was exciting but she was fine, and then Eli popped the question.

Riddy stood her ground and repeated it would be illegal, immoral, and would not be glorified by God at all, but would bring a disdain, anger and confusion. She did comfort him that had he been another man and they met under other circumstances then the answer would have been, yes instead of no.

Eli's character was everything that she ever desired in a man, attributes, protection and provision. He was kind, attentive, supportive, encouraging and he knew that his role as a man was to serve, protect, provide and love a wife.

Eli's first wife cheated and left him for another man. Kat only married him to escape her dilemma of being put out on the street. It was a marriage of convenience. She used and resented him. She always whined, complained and gave him a hard time. Kat was so bound to her past that she could not enjoy her life with Eli. Well, at least she was smart enough to not take the bait when Ed resurfaced and tried to get her back with crocodile tears. But she was not smart enough to know the caliber of man she had in Eli. When you saw the two together, one would never suspect a dysfunctional marriage.

Eli was discharged and his health improved. No wheelchair. No cane. No walker. He did not look like he had a stroke because there were no visible signs. Riddy found out that Eli had an early stage of Dementia, mild heart problems, hypothyroidism, high cholesterol, and an enlarge prostate. The man was eighty-seven.

The pursuit continued. Then finally God himself spoke and told Eli you had the mother you cannot have the daughter. God revealed this to Riddy. She wept. A sigh of relief came to her.

Eli had to move into a long-term facility because he could not live alone anymore. He would miss days of taking powerful medication which his body needed.

In the midst of the hectic move, vast amount of things had to be thrown out intentionally and unintentionally. Kat's ashes landed in the Chicago city dump, accidently. The strange thing is Eli never missed or mentioned the absence of Kat in his new apartment with supportive services. It was with that aspect that Dementia was a blessing in disguise.

Two years would forge forward and there would be no mentioning of the cremated tormented soul of Kat. One semi-cold day in the month of December, Riddy picked up Eli to take him on errands so he could get some air. Riddy pitied him. Eli had been through so much and sacrificed himself and put himself in harm's way to help Riddy and even Sweetie.

Several months before he moved, Sweetie was without an apartment because of the power struggle of two sisters over a family building. Anyway, Riddy picked up Eli and she drove down Lake Shore Drive, southbound from the north side of Chicago on a beautiful snow bound afternoon. Eli had been talking about his upcoming birthday for several months.

Riddy asked him, "Are you really excited about turning eighty-eight?" Because she never heard him even mention his previous birthdays.

Eli then with a sly grin said, "Riddy let me tell you what I want for my birthday. Can I tell you?"

"Yes," Riddy answered not knowing that a trap had been set. Eli's response was that he wanted to be intimate with her for his birthday. Riddy got nauseated and felt like vomiting and was about to lose control of the car. It was then that she informed Eli that she would no longer be his health power of attorney, and that she would remove her name off every stitch of documents pertaining to him, and when asked why such a move took place, she would reveal the sexual harassment and the bullying that she had endured trying to care and serve him as a daughter. She would tell the people at the facility where he lived and his son, Robert, as well.

Eli began to beg, plead and cry, saying he took it back. Riddy was determined to cut all ties because he just would not quit. Eli would let three to six months pass then he would start this mess up again. ENOUGH WAS ENOUGH! Eli thought *Riddy did not want him because of his age*. NO! Riddy did not want him because she has known him for forty-one years as her stepfather. Riddy did not want him because God's law said, NO. Riddy did not want him because this would not bring glory to God but confusion, hatred, reproach and gossip to satisfy his flesh.

Riddy's relationship with God was all she had and she was not giving up God for a moment of pleasure. She felt like Joseph in the Bible when Potiphar's wife who was after him to lie with her. MAN. Riddy has truly in her lifetime living out the scriptures for real. Riddy dropped Eli at home and refused to answer the phone for almost a week.

Riddy's love for Eli was not Eros, but Philo and agape. Plus Eli had sacrificed himself to help her and Sweetie. Then there was the promise to look after him. Riddy also knew that although Kat fussed him out, he missed having a wife. Riddy was not the solution.

She felt so pressured and high strung. She realized that Satan was behind this hot pursuit not Eli and that she would have to reach into the heavenlies and bind up demonic forces.

One day Riddy answered the phone and Eli wept with a sincere recompense apology and they were able to move forward and value the relationship that God intended them to have as father-daughter, and sister-brother in the faith of the Lord Jesus.

Shortly afterwards, Eli would receive the gift of the Holy Ghost and he began to speak in unknown tongues. Eli would tap into heaven. Now it's a matter of time before his departure from this world that had changed greatly before him.

Riddy also had to deal with a lot of doctor's appointments since the new year of 2015 came into being. She had been diagnosed with fourteen medical conditions, which floored her. She had not had a vacation in two to three years. Riddy's life had been stressful dealing with homelessness, living in an abandoned building that she could not get funds to rehab. Then her estranged relationship with Sweetie, her dad in hot pursuit, bed bugs, Terry and her issues, dad's landlord almost putting her out, then Sweetie's homelessness, and now the health issues. Then BAM she got news of an abnormal mammogram. It was repeated and came back abnormal again. Then two other additional tests were ordered and they were also abnormal.

Riddy's jaws dropped when the radiologist had recommended a biopsy. Cancer? Breast Cancer? Madea and Nonnie, her first cousin, had breast cancer. Riddy's biological father, Ed, had bladder cancer. Sweetie was floored and burst out crying and hightailed it to church and tracked down a prayer warrior name, Martha, a member of Living Word.

After Sweetie calmed down, she had to make a decision on who would pray for her mother, Pastor Bill Winston or the prayer warrior, Martha. Martha assured Sweetie that prayer was prayer. Martha later told Riddy that as she prayed she saw a dark shadow move, and she then told Sweetie that her mother did not have cancer. And Riddy also attended a healing clinic in Avalon Park District where a sister in the Lord, Angie, showed her a scar from a breast cancer surgery. She told Riddy that when she returned to the doctor that nothing would be found.

Madea was fifty-nine when she contracted breast cancer and now Riddy was fifty-nine. God was destroying the generational curse that was trying to take hold of Riddy. God had broken the chain.

* * *

Back in the beginning when Kat and Ed found Riddy, Ed screamed, "Noooooo," in anguish as he dropped on his knees in the dark basement while his wife stood in horror with eyes bulging—her mouth open, but unable to utter a sound.

There lied Riddy Ann stripped of clothes, covered with mud, feces and urine with semen spilling from her mouth with eyes bucked and glazed. The babe was covered with dried blood caked on private parts.

Ed takes his coat off in thirty degree weather and covers his three-month-old daughter then rises with Kat following with her mouth cuffed and it is now night fall and all the neighbors were now inside.

The water began cleansing Riddy of the past and present simultaneously. The water pours, pours, and pours. Riddy now becomes one. The dirt and stich of the past and present, and the aftermath of the dark tunnel is now washed away.

Years later after one horrific experience after another while a dark shadow followed her for most of her life, Riddy lifts herself with her right elbow enough to steady herself to get on her knees, and pushes herself up into a standing position on the cobblestone sidewalk. The rain downpours all over her body and she began to turn around and around allowing the rain's healing properties to take place.

The rain suddenly stopped and Riddy looked to her left and then to her right. She sighed, and takes a deep breath then looks ahead and began walking forward into the beaming hot sun that was now out. She is feeling its warmth that clothed her body. Riddy walks away from the INSANITY. IT IS FINISHED. It's time to soar!

From the Author's Desk - Epilogue:

Readers, you have completed a vast number of pages which describe the journey of the character Riddy Ann. If you can overcome personal adversity, then you have the foundation to overcome any business obstacles. Those of you that are embarking or contemplating opening or expanding your business, you can come up with strategies to become successful.

There are some character traits that you will not acquire in a college setting or even by reading a book. You must experience life and how you respond to it will determine if you will be successful or unsuccessful. Universities, colleges, trade schools and training programs can teach you a skill, but they cannot instill inside of you perseverance, stamina, tenacity, resourcefulness, nor innovation.

Adversity, trials, and misfortunes or whatever you want to call them, can also assist you in your growth. The goal is not to be immobilized, beaten down into a stupor, or find oneself as a victim. You must rise and conquer any situation and then overcome whatever situation arises. Difficult circumstances can surround you and come at you from every direction, but you must stay focused on your mission.

In the prior pages, the past was described. Since then, much has been achieved and accomplished. People have been taught to overcome through consultations, workshops, ministry, and through assistance by identifying the problem and then developing a plan of action in order to avoid being stagnant. You may find yourself in a painful situation, but you do not have to stay there. You must OVERCOME.

Everything starts with your personal life which will affect your business life. Whatever is happening in your personal life, will affect your present and bleed into your future. If you quit now, then you will falter and quit later. You must fight to OVERCOME. You must fight to survive in your personal and you must fight to survive in the business arena. You will win if you do not quit.

Lastly, wherever you are, move forward.

I am Eurydice. I am Riddy Ann.

Dr. Eurydice Moore, Business Consultant

Bio Brief

Founder of Eurydice

- Assisted Churches, Schools, and Agencies in acquiring over 3Million in Resource Development Fundings
- An Author of 4 books: Riddy Ann Overcoming the ODDs, How to set up a Not-for-Profit, A-Z guide in for profit set up, Resource Development Going to the Next Level
- Grew up in Chicago's East-Garfield Community and graduated from Lucy Flower H.S. in 1974
- Graduated from Central YMCA in A.S degree in Medical Laboratory Technology 1976
- Graduated from College of St. Francis in B.S. degree in Health Arts 1984
- Graduated from Spertus in M.S. in Human Services Administration 1986
- Graduated from Concordia University in M.A. in Urban Education 1993
- Graduated from Northern Illinois in Advance Certificate in Entrepreneurship Program 1991
- Graduated from Midwest Theological Institute in Indiana in PhD Pastoral Counseling 2004
- Completed City of Chicago's Business Affairs & City College Business Start up 2007
- Completed Mormans Consulting Group's Business Coaching & Business Strategies Trainings 2016
- Medical Laboratory Technician at Rush, Cook County, Mount Sinai, Mary Thompson University of Illinois of Chicago Hospitals 1973-1985
- Educator & Work Study Coordinator at Lucy Flower H.S. 1985-1991
- Guidance Counselor at Morton Career Academy 1991-1995
- Over 30 years of combine Not-for-Profit experiences at Chicago Public School System, Churches, Social Services Center, Safe Haven Community Skill Center & Hannah Community Development Center 1985-2004
- Established Eurydice Moore & Associates 2004 to present, served over 12,000 clients in distribution of free grant and resource development information, incorporation, and 501c3

- Established Eurydice January, 2016 to offer business set up, coaching, trainings & development, incorporation, 501c3 set up, grant writing, and resource development.
- Internet & Radio Personality 2005-2007
- CAN TV program in Not-for-Profit & For Profit Business Resource 2007-2009

In order to contact Eurydice Moore for speaking engagements, consultation, business coaching, incorporation, 501c(3), grant writing, seminars, and other services, please email: eurydicemoore1@gmail.com.

Telephone: (773) 544-5341

More titles by Dr. Eurydice Moore
Coming 2017 – 2018

For more information, contact

McClure Publishing, Inc.
at <u>WWW.MCCLUREPUBLISHING.COM</u>
800-659-4908

Eddie, Sr. and Kat

Kat's High School Graduation

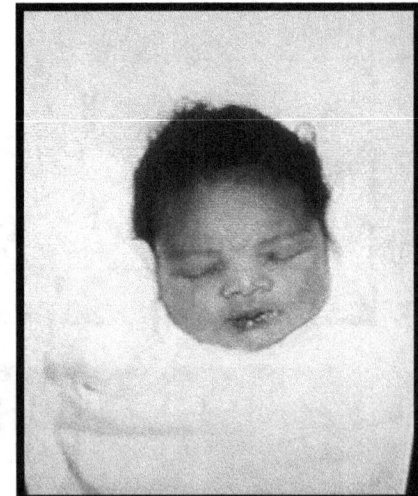

Rita a/k/a Sweetie

Rita a/k/a Sweetie

Riddy and Steve

Riddy and Steve

Riddy and Steve

Riddy and Steve

Riddy Prom and Steve

Riddy at Steve's prom

Riddy in the Office

Kat as a Bride

Madea Norwood and Big Mama

Sidney and Madea Norwood

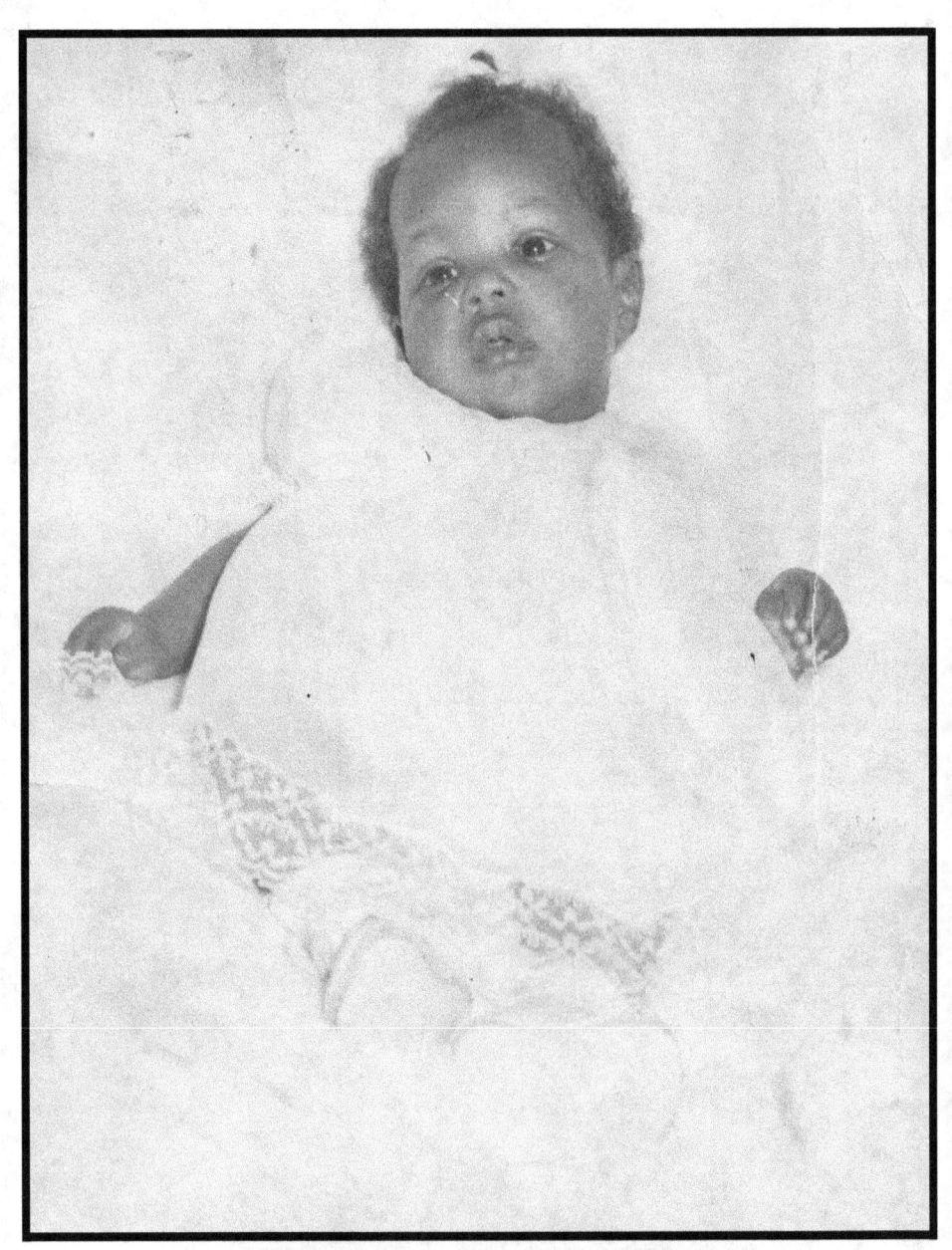

Riddy

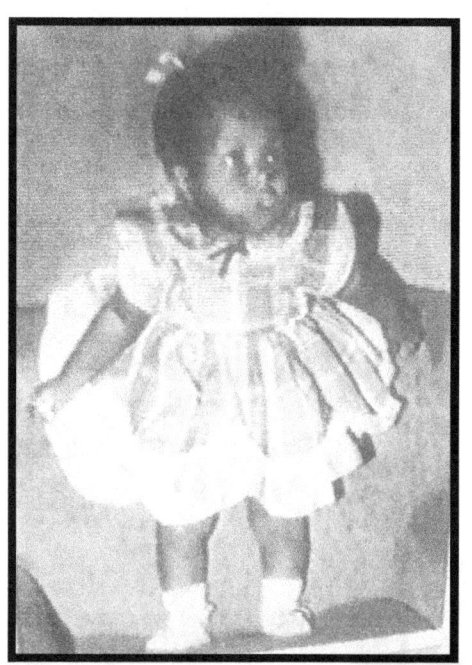

Riddy

Graduations

Big Mama

www.ingramcontent.com/pod-product-compliance
Lightning Source LLC
Chambersburg PA
CBHW070556300426
44113CB00010B/1282